MICROSOFT® WINDOWS SERVER® ADMINISTRATION

ESSENTIALS

MICROSOFT® WINDOWS SERVER® ADMINISTRATION

ESSENTIALS

Tom Carpenter

WILEY

John Wiley & Sons, Inc.

Senior Acquisitions Editor: Jeff Kellum
Development Editor: Tom Cirtin
Technical Editors: Naomi Alpern and Randy Muller
Production Editor: Christine O'Connor
Copy Editor: Kathy Grider Carlyle
Editorial Manager: Pete Gaughan
Production Manager: Tim Tate
Vice President and Executive Group Publisher: Richard Swadley
Vice President and Publisher: Neil Edde
Book Designer: Happenstance Type-O-Rama
Compositor: Craig Johnson, Happenstance Type O-Rama
Proofreader: James Saturino, Word One New York
Indexer: Robert Swanson
Project Coordinator, Cover: Katherine Crocker
Cover Designer: Ryan Sneed
Cover Image: © Suprijono Suharjoto / iStockPhoto

Dear Reader,

Thank you for choosing *Microsoft Windows Server Administration Essentials*. This book is part of a family of premium-quality Sybex books, all of which are written by outstanding authors who combine practical experience with a gift for teaching.

Sybex was founded in 1976. More than 30 years later, we're still committed to producing consistently exceptional books. With each of our titles, we're working hard to set a new standard for the industry. From the paper we print on, to the authors we work with, our goal is to bring you the best books available.

I hope you see all that reflected in these pages. I'd be very interested to hear your comments and get your feedback on how we're doing. Feel free to let me know what you think about this or any other Sybex book by sending me an email at nedde@wiley.com. If you think you've found a technical error in this book, please visit http://sybex.custhelp.com. Customer feedback is critical to our efforts at Sybex.

Best regards,

NEIL EDDE
Vice President and Publisher
Sybex, an Imprint of Wiley

I dedicate this book to my wife and children. You are the most important people in this world to me. I cherish every moment with you and love you more every day.

Acknowledgments

I would like to acknowledge the great staff at Wiley. You always make a good book great. Specific thanks go out to Thomas Cirtin and Jeff Kellum. Thomas, you did an exceptional job in the early editing of the manuscript. Jeff, you kept me on task. Thanks to both of you. Additionally, I would like to thank my family who tolerated me through yet one more book. You are all amazing. Finally, I want to thank God for giving me the strength to write this book and undertake every other endeavor in life. Thank you.

ABOUT THE AUTHOR

Tom Carpenter is a consultant and trainer based out of Marysville, OH. He is the founder and current Senior Consultant for The Systems Education and Consulting Company (SysEdCo). SysEdCo provides training on Microsoft technologies, wireless networking, security, and IT professional development. Tom is the author of several books on topics ranging from wireless network administration to SQL Server database administration and optimization. Tom holds several certifications, including MCITP: SQL Server 2008 Database Administrator, CWNA, CWSP, Project+, and several additional Microsoft certifications. He spends every spare moment he can with his amazing wife and children.

You can reach the author by writing to **carpenter@sysedco.com.**

CONTENTS AT A GLANCE

CONTENTS

CHAPTER 14   Performance Tuning   291

CHAPTER 15   Server Maintenance   321

APPENDIX A   Answers to Review Questions   349

APPENDIX B   Microsoft's Certification Program   361

INTRODUCTION

Servers are important tools used on modern networks. They provide email support, file and print services, application functionality, and so much more. Server administrators are in high demand, and modern technologies such as virtualization and cloud computing have only increased the importance of the server administrator's job.

The Microsoft Technology Associate (MTA) certification is a certification provided for entry-level professionals and those with long careers in the industry who have never acquired a certification credential. It includes three separate tracks: Information Technology (IT) Professional, Developer, and Database. The IT Professional track is for individuals pursuing work as administrators. The Developer track is for individuals pursuing work as programmers and software engineers. The Database track is for individuals pursuing work as database administrators and database developers.

The IT Professional series includes three certifications:

Windows Server Administration Fundamentals   This certification assumes no previous knowledge of Windows Server Administration and allows you to start from the beginning to learn how to administer Windows servers. The knowledge acquired through the Networking Fundamentals and Security Fundamentals certification programs will be helpful as you study Windows Server administration fundamentals, but it is important to remember that the MTA certification exams have no prerequisites. The Windows Server Administration Fundamentals exam and this book give you a solid foundation for working as a server administrator in a Microsoft technology environment. You earn this certification by taking and passing exam 98-365. This book covers the objectives for the 98-365 exam.

Networking Fundamentals   This is an important certification in the MTA IT Professional track. It provides the knowledge that lays a solid foundation of basic networking knowledge needed to administer modern networks and also helps you prepare for more advanced Microsoft Certified Technology Specialist (MCTS) and Microsoft Certified IT Professional (MCITP) tracks. You earn this certification by taking and passing exam 98-366.

Security Fundamentals   Security Fundamentals is the another important certification in the MTA IT Professional track. It complements the knowledge learned in the Networking Fundamentals certification process and adds fundamental security knowledge needed by administrators. IT administrators in any environment need to be aware of the risks with IT systems. You earn this certification by taking and passing exam 98-367.

Each of these certifications can serve as a stepping-stone to Microsoft's next levels of certifications: Microsoft Certified Technology Specialist (MCTS) and Microsoft Certified IT Professional (MCITP).

Who Should Read This Book

This book is for current or aspiring professionals seeking a quick grounding in the fundamentals of administration in a Microsoft Windows Server environment. The goal is to provide quick, focused coverage of fundamental skills.

If you want to start a career in server administration or are already working in the field and want to fill in some gaps on fundamental topics, this book is for you. You can use the knowledge gained from this book as a foundation for more advanced studies. Additionally, this book will act as an excellent reference for the day-to-day tasks you must perform as a Windows Server administrator.

This book is focused on the objectives of the Microsoft Technology Associates (MTA) Server Administration Fundamentals certification. This is the first numbered certification in the MTA IT Professional series (exam number 98-365), but you can take the three IT Professional series exams in any order you desire. You can read more about the MTA certifications and MTA exam certification paths at: www.microsoft.com/learning/en/us/certification/mta.aspx.

What You Will Learn

You will learn the essentials of server administration in a Microsoft environment. In addition, this book covers all the objectives of the Microsoft Technology Associates Windows Server Administration Fundamentals exam (exam 98-365).

What You Need

In order to perform the procedures provided throughout this book, you will need a Windows server. This server can be a virtual machine or a direct installation on computer hardware. The good news is that Windows Server 2008 R2 will run on practically any desktop computer that will run Windows 7. You can install the trial edition of Windows Server 2008 R2 and use it for up to 180 days. The trial edition can be downloaded from: http://www.microsoft.com/windowsserver2008/en/us/trial-software.aspx.

If you want to run Windows Server 2008 R2 in a virtual machine on top of Windows 7, you will need to have at least 4 GB of system memory in your Windows 7 computer, and you will need to download the free VMware Player virtualization software. This software can run 64-bit operating systems, unlike Windows Virtual PC that Microsoft provides for Windows 7. You can download the VMware Player from this location: http://www.vmware.com/go/downloadplayer. Chapter 2, "Installing Windows Servers," provides instructions for performing an installation of Windows Server 2008 R2.

What Is Covered in This Book?

Microsoft Windows Server Administration Essentials is organized to provide you with the information you need to master the basics of administration in a Microsoft server environment.

Chapter 1: Windows Server Overview   This chapter provides an overview of the Windows Server operating system and servers in general. It contrasts servers with clients and explains the benefits that servers provide. The concept of the server role is explained and the different server types are briefly discussed.

Chapter 2: Installing Windows Servers   Chapter 2 explains the options you have for Windows Server installation and discusses the important considerations that must be made when upgrading servers. Server Core is introduced as well, and the concept of working with device drivers is also explained.

Chapter 3: Managing Windows Server Storage   After installing Windows Server, you will need to configure the storage locations for file servers, application servers, and more. This chapter introduces data storage concepts and the technologies used for storage. You will also learn about fault tolerant storage through the use of RAID arrays and learn to identify storage technologies.

Chapter 4: Administering Services   Chapter 4 defines the concept of a service and the important roles services play on modern networks. You will explore service configuration and management procedures. The chapter concludes with an explanation of service problem troubleshooting procedures.

Chapter 5: Active Directory Infrastructure   Active Directory is Microsoft's directory service solution. This chapter introduces you to Active Directory concepts including the Domain Name System (DNS), sites, and replication. You will learn the information required to plan an Active Directory installation in this chapter.

Chapter 6: Configuring Active Directory   While Chapter 5 introduces the concepts of Active Directory, this chapter steps you through the process of installing Active Directory from start-to-finish.

Chapter 7: Managing Active Directory   Now that Active Directory is up and running, you will learn to manage it in this chapter. You will explore both the graphical user interface tools and the command-line tools available for Active Directory administration and management.

Chapter 8: Group Policy Management   Group Policy is used to centrally configure, manage, secure, and control your Windows computers that participate in an Active Directory domain. This chapter introduces the concepts of Group Policy and provides you with instructions for creating and managing policy settings.

Chapter 9: Application Servers   Application servers are implemented to support the applications that run on your network. This chapter introduces you to application servers in general and then explores specific server types, including database servers, mail servers, collaboration servers, monitoring servers, and threat-management servers.

Chapter 10: Internet Information Services (IIS)   Internet Information Servers (IIS) is the web server provided with Windows Server and even the Windows client operating systems. This chapter introduces you to the IIS components and management processes.

Chapter 11: File and Print Servers   File and print servers are among the oldest server types. This chapter covers file and share permissions and the proper implementation procedures for printer sharing.

Chapter 12: Remote Access Technologies   You cannot always go to a computer or server to manage it. This chapter introduces you to remote management tools that are available for administering Windows servers; it also addresses security through the use of virtual private networks (VPNs).

Chapter 13: Server Troubleshooting   Troubleshooting skills are important for a Windows server administrator, and this chapter provides an essential overview of these skills. You will learn about troubleshooting methodologies and specific tools you can use in the troubleshooting process.

Chapter 14: Performance Tuning   This chapter introduces you to performance analysis topics and then explores the different performance analysis tools in Windows Server. These tools include the Performance Monitor, the Resource Monitor, and the Task Manager.

Chapter 15: Server Maintenance   In this final chapter, you will learn about important tasks and tools that help you maintain a stable server implementation. You will learn how to maintain hardware, plan for server downtime, use Windows Update, automate using logs and alerts, and plan for business continuity.

Appendix A: Answers to Review Questions This appendix includes all of the answers to the review questions found in "The Essentials and Beyond" section at the end of every chapter.

Appendix B: Microsoft's Certification Program This appendix highlights the Microsoft certification program, and it lists the exam objectives for Exam 98-365 and how they map to this book's content.

In addition, we have created an online Glossary, the suggested or recommended answers to the additional exercises we have included at the end of each chapter, as well as additional exercises for instructors. You can download these at: www.sybex. com/go/winadminessentials.

Sybex strives to keep you supplied with the latest tools and information you need for your work. Please check their website at: www.sybex.com/go/winadminessentials, where we'll post additional content and updates that supplement this book if the need arises. Enter server administration essentials in the Search box (or type the book's ISBN: 978-1-118-01686-2), and click Go to get to the book's update page.

As the author, I would be glad to help you in your learning process. If you ever have questions along the way, feel free to email me at carpenter@sysedco.com. Thanks for reading.

CHAPTER 1

Windows Server Overview

Servers play a vital role on modern business computing networks. They provide such important services as e-mail, file storage, collaboration, and security. This chapter introduces you to servers in general and Microsoft Windows Server in specific. You will learn about the differences between servers and clients and the different designs of today's server hardware. Next, you will learn about the different roles servers play on modern computing networks and why these roles are important. Finally, you will explore the specifics of Windows Server. You will learn about the different interfaces it provides, networking features it offers, management features it supports, and the different editions of the product that are available. The following topics will provide coverage of this information:

▷ **Introducing Servers**

▷ **Understanding Server Roles**

▷ **Microsoft Windows Server Features**

Introducing Servers

If you want to understand Windows servers, you must begin by understanding servers in general. In this section, you will learn what servers are, how they differ from clients, and the various shapes and sizes in which they are manufactured. I will begin by defining what a server is so that you can keep this definition in mind as you read through the rest of this book.

Understanding Server Concepts

Computer networks are used to provide communications between computing devices. The computing devices include network infrastructure hardware devices, such as routers, switches, and firewalls. They also include clients and servers. Servers are used to provide services to the networked devices.

A *modem* is a modulator and demodulator that uses the telephone network to carry digital data as analog signals.

DNS names look like *mypc.domain .name* or *yourpc. domain.name*. The leftmost portion is the host name and the rest is the domain name. Together they form a *fully qualified domain name* (FQDN).

Because they provide more than one type of service, some services can be placed in multiple categories of service.

You will learn more about services in Chapter 4.

Servers must be connected to a network so that other devices (clients) can consume their services. These networks may include local area networks (LANs), wide area networks (WANs), and any other type of network on which the servers communicate. In the early days of computing, a server often sat on the other end of a telephone line allowing only one user to connect at a time. Even though this is not efficient, it still represents a network being used to access a server. The telephone line created the network connection between the client and the server.

The services provided by a server include three primary categories of service:

Network Services   Network services include any service that exists to provide network functionality. For example, the Dynamic Host Configuration Protocol (DHCP) is used to provide Internet Protocol (IP) configuration settings that allow client devices to communicate on the network. Another example is the Domain Name System (DNS) server service, which resolves Internet-like domain names to IP addresses. These Internet-like names are called *hostnames*.

Security Services   Security services include those services that provide authentication, authorization, confidentiality, or some form of protection to the network and networked devices. An example of a security service is the Active Directory Domain Service (AD DS), which could also be partially categorized as a network service. AD DS provides the user accounts that are used to log on to Windows Server-based networks. When these accounts are used for logon processes, authentication is performed and authentication is a security service. An additional security service is the IPSec Policy Service, which enforces security settings for Internet Protocol (IP)-based communications.

Information Services   Information services include any service that provides information access, information management, or information processing. For example, the Microsoft SQL Server service provides database access and database management. This functionality qualifies SQL Server as an information service. Microsoft SharePoint is another example of an information service. It provides for information storage and retrieval, as well as collaboration.

Understanding Client/Server Concepts

The term *client/server model* became very popular starting in the 1980s. The term simply indicates that an application is broken into two components: the *client* component—a computing device or application that consumes services— and the server component. Some of the processing is performed at the client and the rest is performed at the server. A modern example of this is a web-based application that depends on both the web server and the web browser (the client) to perform the required processing: The server retrieves and processes data that is then sent to the web browser. The browser reformats this data for the current screen resolution of the user's workstation. The point is that the two components work together.

It is not enough, however, to say that a server does part of the processing and the client does another part of the processing. In most client/server model systems, a single server can service many clients. You can define the relationship as a many-to-one relationship between the clients and the servers, as depicted in Figure 1.1: You can see that one file server provides file storage and retrieval services to multiple PC clients, a Mac client, and even a laptop computer. The clients are the many, and the server is the one in the many-to-one relationship.

The first multiuser computer sharing method was developed by Fernando Corbató at Massachusetts Institute of Technology (MIT) in 1961.

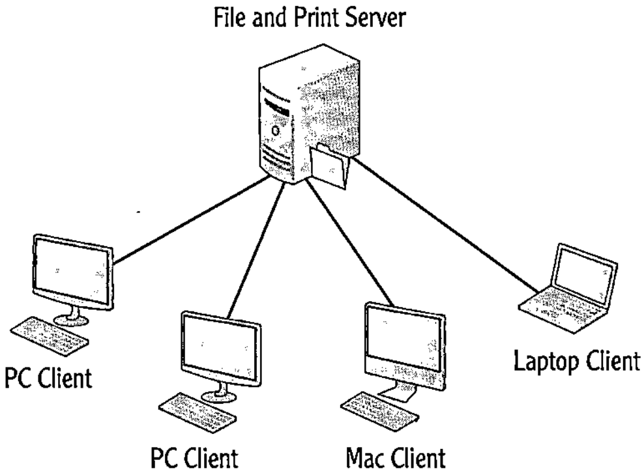

FIGURE 1.1 The many-to-one relationship of client/server computing

Additionally, the clients consume services from the network itself in that they utilize bandwidth made available by the network. *Bandwidth*, in this context, is defined as the maximum information that can be transmitted simultaneously across a communications channel. Each client consumes a portion of this bandwidth for network communications.

Table 1.1 provides a comparison of servers and clients.

TABLE 1.1 Comparing Servers and Clients

Typical Server Characteristics	Typical Client Characteristics
Used by many users	Used by one user at a time
Built from high-quality components	Built from average quality components
Optimized for background applications	Optimized for visual foreground applications
Provides services to the network	Consumes services from the network

In addition to the contrasting of servers and clients, you should understand the servers and clients available in the Microsoft product line. The following Microsoft server operating systems are still very popular today:

▶ Windows Server 2003

▶ Windows Server 2003 R2

▶ Windows Server 2008

▶ Windows Server 2008 R2

The following Microsoft client operating systems are very popular:

▶ Windows XP

▶ Windows Vista

▶ Windows 7

Historically, Microsoft has released a new version of their client and server operating systems every two to four years. For example, Windows Vista was released in 2006 for business customers, although it wasn't released until January, 2007 for consumers. Windows 7 was released in 2009. Similarly, Windows Server 2003 was released in 2003 and Windows Server 2003 R2 was released in 2005.

Furthermore, a greater period exists between major version number releases of the operating systems. For example, Windows Vista was considered a major version number release that changed the major version number of the operating system from 5 to 6, whereas Windows 7, released very shortly thereafter, was considered an interim minor version release. To see this, access a Command Prompt on a Windows 7 system by clicking Start ➢ All Programs ➢ Accessories ➢ Command Prompt and then execute the ver command. You will see that it is version 6.1, as shown in Figure 1.2. Windows Vista was version 6.0.

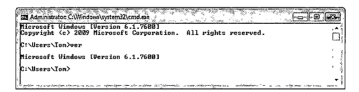

FIGURE 1.2 Viewing the version of Windows

The time between the release of Windows Vista and Windows 7 was approximately three years; however, the time between the release of Windows 2000 (a major version release at version 5.0) and Windows Vista (the next major version release) was six years. In most cases, the changes from a major version release to a minor version release are insignificant when compared to the changes made between major version releases, as is clearly seen when considering the minor differences between Windows 7 and Vista at the core operating system level and the major differences between Windows 2000 and Windows Vista. This is helpful to Information Technology (IT) professionals who must support these systems. In most cases, you will use the same or very similar operating system for a 4 to 6 year window of time. Every 4 to 6 years, you should be prepared to learn many new things and unlearn many old things in relation to the operating systems you support.

Clients can also be used to perform server functions. We often call these clients *peer servers* because they are not intended primarily as a server. They are also sometimes called *logical servers* because the services they provide are logical services that run on the machine (just like a dedicated server). The main difference between a server that runs server services and a client that runs server services is that the server is dedicated to running those services and the client is typically not.

> Many organizations plan upgrades for every other release. For example, they may have upgraded from Windows NT 4.0 to Windows XP, and their next upgrade will be to Windows 7, skipping Windows 2000 and Windows Vista.

UNDERSTANDING THE TERM "LOGICAL"

In this context, the word "logical" simply means that the device is intended as one thing but it performs the logic of another. For example, a client computer is intended to be a workstation for a user; however, if it shares a folder onto the network, it is providing the same service as a file server. The logic of sharing is included in both operating systems, but it is implemented more frequently in server operating systems. The server operating system is optimized to provide file sharing functions and overcomes connection limits in client operating systems. Additionally, the server operating system offers advanced share management tools for quota management and file filtering, which is used to limit the file types that may be placed in the shares.

An example of a server service that may run on a client machine is file and printer sharing. You may have a printer connected to your Windows 7 machine that you want to make available to other users in your work area. You can do this, assuming it is allowed by network policies, using the Windows printer sharing capabilities. Technically, this makes your Windows 7 machine a print server, but we would not call the machine a server because it is still primarily used as a user's workstation.

LOGICAL VERSUS DEDICATED SERVERS

If you browse around in the Services management tool on a Windows machine (accessed by clicking Start and typing **services.msc** into the Search field on a Windows Vista or later or Windows Server 2008 or later machine), you will notice that a service called Server exists. The existence of this service does not really classify the machine as a server in the traditional sense of the term. Technically, all network machines are servers in a logical sense, but they are not servers in a practical sense because they are not dedicated to server functions.

A Windows 7 machine may indeed respond to a network connection request and allow communications. Because the machine responded to a request and did not initiate the request, it is logically a server. However, we have traditionally considered a machine to be a server only when it is dedicated to server tasks. Therefore, a machine that sits in a special room and is rarely accessed at the console while being heavily accessed across the network is considered a server. But we would say it is impractical to consider a Windows 7 computer that is mostly used by a local user and rarely accessed as a logical server as a dedicated server.

While all of this might just seem like semantics, the reality is that we must clearly define servers versus clients so that we can plan our networks well. The placement of servers is very important because they are typically accessed by multiple users from multiple locations. The placement of desktop computing clients is typically fixed. We put them right in front of the users—at least, we do most of the time. This network location placement will impact security settings on routers and switches related to the devices. For example, you will allow certain communications to pass through a switch port to a server that you would not allow to pass through to a client. Keep this in mind as you're planning your servers, clients, and networks.

> The form factor of a server is a reference to the design of the server's physical case and mounting methods.

Choosing Server Hardware

The actual computing device we call a server comes in several form factors. The *form factor* simply defines the design of the server's case and internal component access methods. For example, the case may be slim and provide limited component access or it may be large and bulky with easy component access. The form factor also dictates how the server may be installed or mounted in the environment.

Today, three major form factors exist and are available from many different vendors:

► Desktop

► Rack Mount

► Blade

The Desktop form factor looks just like a regular user's client computer. It may be slightly larger, but it will look much the same. The Desktop form factor includes those that stand upright (also known as a tower case) and those that lay horizontal (the traditional Desktop form factor). Figure 1.3 shows the IBM Power 780 desktop server. While it may appear a little fancier than a regular user's desktop computer, it is essentially the same thing with extra monitoring features and higher quality components.

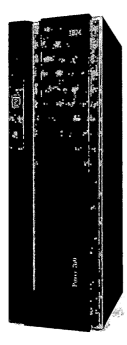

FIGURE 1.3 The IBM Power 780 Desktop form factor server

The rack mount servers are specially designed to mount in a rack cabinet. These cabinets typically have doors and are specially ventilated to provide cooling. Figure 1.4 shows the IBM Power 755 rack mount system. To make efficient use of space, you can mount more than one server in a single rack cabinet. In many scenarios, you can also use a shared uninterruptible power supply (UPS) for all of the servers in the cabinet.

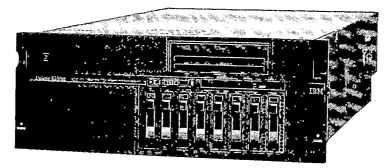

FIGURE 1.4 The IBM Power 755 Rack Mount form factor server

The final form factor is the server blade. In this case, the server is actually a removable blade that slides into a type of docking station used to house each blade. The docking station (called a BladeCenter by IBM, a Blade Enclosure by Dell, and by other names from other vendors) can house multiple blades. Because each blade is a server, you can store multiple servers in a single docking station. The blade docking station could be a desktop enclosure or it could mount in a rack cabinet, much like a rack server. Figure 1.5 shows the IBM BladeCenter PS701.

The form factor you choose will depend on the space in which it will be installed and the number of servers you require. For example, rack mount and blade servers are very popular when dozens or hundreds of servers are required. When only a few servers are required, the Desktop form factor is still quite common.

Understanding Server Roles

Now that you understand what a server is and how it differs from a client, it's important to grasp the concept of a *server role*. Much as you can play different roles in your life, the server can play different roles as well. In this section, you will first gain a clear understanding of what server roles are and then you will explore some common server roles.

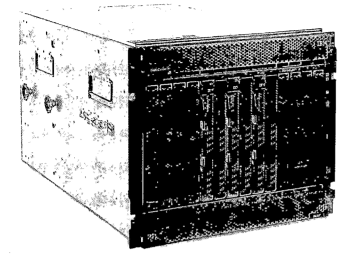

FIGURE 1.5 The IBM BladeCenter PS701 Blade form factor server enclosure

A server role is defined as a collection of responsibilities provided to the network or networked devices by a specific server. A more detailed definition is that a server role is a set of software programs (services) that enable a server to perform specific functions for users or computers on the network. Servers are typically dedicated to a role, but in smaller organizations a server may play several roles at the same time. Server roles are based on role services and one or more role services is used to implement a given server role. For example, the File Services role in Windows Server 2008 R2 includes the following role services:

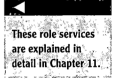

These role services are explained in detail in Chapter 11.

- ▶ Share and Storage Management

- ▶ Distributed File System (DFS)

- ▶ File Server Resource Manager (FSRM)

- ▶ Services for Network File System (NFS)

- ▶ Windows Search Service

- ▶ Windows Server 2003 File Services (for backward compatibility)

- ▶ BranchCache for network files

In addition to server roles, features may be added to a Windows server installation. A *feature* is much smaller than a role and may be defined as a software program that can support or add to the functionality of one or more server roles or the general functionality of the server. Features may require a server role be installed before they can be installed. As an example, the Windows Server Backup tools are installed as a feature on Windows Server 2008 R2. If you want to use the Windows Server Backup tools to schedule backups for your server's data, the feature must first be installed.

Deploying Applications on Your Network

The Application Server role, in Windows servers, provides an integrated environment for the deployment of custom business applications. The applications can be built using the Microsoft .NET Framework, which is a special software framework for application development. The Application Server role provides the ability to run services and applications that are built on COM+, Message Queuing, Web Services and Distributed Transactions:

> A software framework is a collection or prebuilt code and other functions that can be used to quickly develop complex business applications.

COM+ COM+ allows for the remote invocation of applications. You can execute application code that is stored on remote servers rather than require that the code be installed on the local machine.

Message Queuing Message Queuing allows for asymmetric network communications, which means that a request can come into an application and be processed when the application has the available resources rather than requiring instant processing.

Web Services The Web Services allow your application to communicate using the Hypertext Transfer Protocol (HTTP) that is common to web-based communications.

Distributed Transactions The Distributed Transactions component allows for applications to complete transactions against multiple databases stored on multiple computers that participate in the network.

> You will learn more about the Application Server role in Chapter 9.

The Application Server role can be installed using the Server Manager on Windows Server 2008 and later. When you add the Application Server role, the following role services may be installed:

- ▶ Web Server (IIS)
- ▶ COM+ Network Access
- ▶ TCP Port Sharing
- ▶ Windows Process Activation Services Support
- ▶ Distributed Transactions

Providing Internet Access and Collaboration on Your Network

Web servers are some of the most common types of servers used on modern networks. Web servers are used to provide content to client computers and applications using HTTP for communications. HTTPS, which is the encrypted and secured version of HTTP, may also be used. Windows servers provide web server role functionality using the Internet Information Services (IIS) application and several other supporting services for authentication, logging, and application development.

With a web server, you can provide many different services to your users, including:

► Provide information to Internet users through your public website

► Allow for uploading and downloading of files through HTTP or FTP

► Host servers that contain business logic for multi-tier applications.

► Implement collaboration servers such as Microsoft SharePoint Server

Like any other role in Windows servers, you can add the Web Server role in the Server Manager. When you add the role, it is called the Web Server (IIS) role. Once installed, you can add components to the web server as needed. For example, you can add support for PHP as a programming language or you can add PERL support. Like most web servers, Microsoft's IIS is modular and extensible, allowing you to add features and components as needed. Additionally, a management tool called the IIS Manager is provided; it allows you to easily manage the web server using a GUI interface. The IIS Manager for IIS 7.5 running on Windows Server 2008 R2 is shown in Figure 1.6.

Multi-tier applications are applications that reside on more than one machine and perform different processes or functions, such as display, data access, and data retrieval, on each machine.

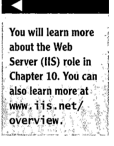

You will learn more about the Web Server (IIS) role in Chapter 10. You can also learn more at www.iis.net/overview.

FIGURE 1.6 The IIS Manager used to manage the web server on Windows Server 2008 R2

Managing Files and Printers on Your Network

In the past, File and Print Services were referenced as a single role. In Windows Server 2008 R2 installations, the File Services role and the Print and Document Services role are now separate.

The File Services role provides features such as share management, storage management, file replication, and search services. Additionally, a collection of tools called the File Server Resource Manager (FSRM) provide simplified management of quotas, file screening (restricting the file types allowed on the server), storage reports generation, file management tasks (such as searching for files on the server), and management of remote storage resources.

The Print and Document Services role allows you to share printers and scanners on the network. You can centralize both printer and scanner management through this role. Management tools called the Print Management console and Scan Management console are provided for centralized management. Additionally, you can install the management tools on Windows 7 clients so that administrators can run them remotely from the client computers.

> You will learn more about the File Services role and the Print and Document Services role in Chapter 11.

Providing Network Access for Remote Users

In earlier versions of Windows servers, the remote access capabilities are easier to locate because they were simpler. You installed Routing and Remote Access Services (RRAS), and you had a remote access server. In Windows Server 2008 and later, RRAS is part of the Network Policy and Access Services role. This role provides several functions to your network:

Network Access Protection (NAP) NAP provides a client health policy service to your network. NAP ensures that a connecting client meets a minimum set of requirements before allowing the client to communicate on the network. For example, it may require that the client have antivirus software installed and updated or that specific security updates have been applied to the operating system.

> The IEEE is the Institute of Electrical and Electronics Engineers, and they are responsible for many of the standards used on modern computer networks.

When a client is not incompliance with the NAP requirements, the client may be denied access to the network or granted restricted access. The restricted access option is typically used to allow the client to download antivirus updates or other updates that will allow it to come into compliance with the NAP policies.

IEEE 802.1X Authentication The IEEE developed an authentication mechanism that is used to ensure that devices are authenticated before they are allowed to communicate on a network. This mechanism is known as 802.1X authentication. When a device first connects to the network, it is allowed to communicate only with an authentication server. Once authenticated, it is permitted to communicate with the rest of the network.

RADIUS Server   The Remote Authentication Dial-In User Service (RADIUS) was originally developed to authenticate users dialing in on modem lines. Today, it is used for authentication of Virtual Private Network (VPN) traffic and wireless clients, as well as wired clients that authenticate using 802.1X authentication. The Microsoft RADIUS server component is included in the Network Policy and Access Services role.

Routing and Remote Access Services (RRAS)   RRAS provides for both VPN server functionality and dial-up access to your network. As a VPN server, it allows client computers to connect across the Internet, or another network, and establish secured and encrypted communications. As a dial-up server, it allows client computers to connect using a modem, which is a communications device that allows network connections to be established across traditional telephone lines.

A VPN is a secured and encrypted link between two computers. It allows for secure communications across public networks.

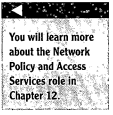

You will learn more about the Network Policy and Access Services role in Chapter 12.

Adding More Roles as Needed

Windows servers can support several additional roles. In addition to the roles mentioned in the preceding sections, the following roles are also supported:

Active Directory Certificate Services   This role provides certificates for users and computers to use in authentication and encryption processes.

Active Directory Domain Services   This role provides the Active Directory services to the network, which include user and group provisioning as well as computer and server management.

Active Directory Federation Services   This role allows for two different authentication realms to share credentials so that users can use single sign-on procedures and not be required to sign on individually to each network.

Active Directory Lightweight Directory Services   This role enables a minimal version of the Active Directory services for application use. It is used when Active Directory is not your primary network directory service.

You will learn more about the Active Directory role in Chapters 5, 6, and 7.

Active Directory Rights Management Services   This role is used to control access to and distribution of digital assets, such as documents and media. The assets are signed and secured so that only authorized users can access them.

DHCP Server   The Dynamic Host Configuration Protocol (DHCP) Server role provides the dynamic configuration of the IP protocol for devices on the network.

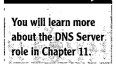

You will learn more about the DNS Server role in Chapter 11.

DNS Server   The Domain Name System (DNS) Server role is used to resolve domain names to IP addresses.

Fax Server   This role can be used to allow sending and receiving of faxes through the server.

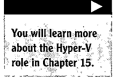

You will learn more about the Hyper-V role in Chapter 15.

Hyper-V   Hyper-V is Microsoft's server virtualization solution starting with the Windows Server 2008 operating system.

Remote Desktop Services   This role allows for remote access to the Desktop of the Windows server through the use of a special client application. Once enabled, a user can control the Desktop from a remote machine.

Windows Deployment Services   This role provides operating system deployment services so that networked computers may install their operating system from the server.

Windows Server Update Services   This role checks with the Microsoft Update or Windows Update sites and downloads updates to the server. Clients can then receive their updates from the server rather than being required to access the Internet.

All of the roles are installed using Server Manager, as follows:

1. Click Start ➤ Administrative Tools ➤ Server Manager.

   When it loads you will see a screen similar to the one in Figure 1.7.

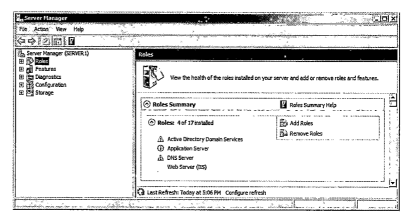

FIGURE 1.7 The Server Manager is used to view installed roles, add new roles, and manage existing roles.

2. Select the Roles node in the left pane.

3. Right-click Roles and select Add Roles to add a new role to the server.

4. Use the Add Roles Wizard, shown in Figure 1.8, to add the various roles.

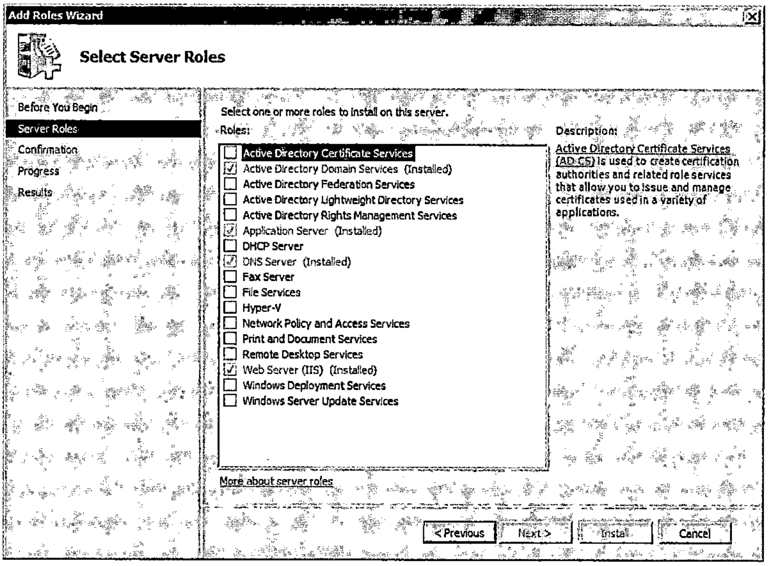

FIGURE 1.8 The Add Roles Wizard is used to add roles to a Windows server installation.

Microsoft Windows Server Features

Now that you understand the basics of what a server is and how servers can play different roles, it's time to explore the specifics of Windows Server as an operating system. In this section, you will learn about the Windows Server user interfaces, which include both a graphical interface and a command-line text-mode interface. Next, you will learn about the basic networking features offered by the operating system. You'll then learn about the management features, which include Server Manager, Microsoft Management Consoles, PowerShell, and the traditional Command Prompt. Finally, you will compare and contrast the different editions of the Windows Server operating system, which will prepare you for the next chapter where you will learn to install Windows servers.

Windows Server User Interfaces

Microsoft Windows has provided a graphical user interface (GUI) for more than two decades. Starting in the early 1980s, Windows has evolved into a rich and useful GUI. However, the Windows operating system offers more than just a GUI interface; command-line interfaces are provided as well.

The Windows GUI interface is the same on the server and the client versions of the operating system. By default, Windows Server 2008 and Windows Server 2008 R2 have the fancy animations and special features disabled, but they are there just as they are in Windows Vista and Windows 7.

Figure 1.9 shows the Windows Server 2008 R2 Desktop. Like the Windows 7 Desktop, it includes a Start menu, taskbar, notification tray, and Desktop for icon placement. The Start menu is used to launch application and access special features like the Control Panel and your personal folders. The taskbar displays icons for the running applications so that you can switch between tasks. The notification tray is used to display icons for running services and applications that may need to notify the user of state changes. The Desktop is your personal space for the placement of icons and folders so that you can have quick access to frequently used items.

> To enable the Windows 7 Desktop features, you must add the Desktop Experience feature in Server Manager and then enable an Aero theme.

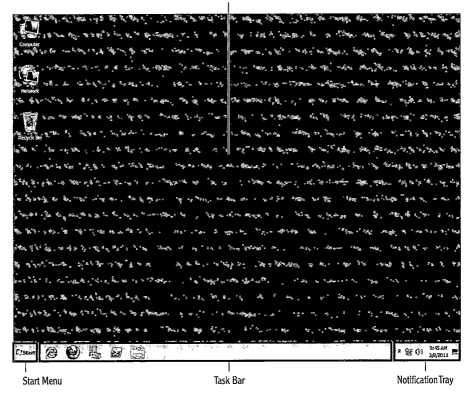

FIGURE 1.9 The Windows Server 2008 R2 Desktop

The oldest command-line interface in Windows operating systems is the Command Prompt, which is based on the older operating system named DOS. The Command Prompt is not DOS, but it supports commands similar to those in DOS. The Command Prompt is loaded using one of two common methods:

> **The Command Prompt is CMD.EXE in Windows server and client operating systems.**

▶ Use the Start menu shortcuts: Click Start ➤ All Programs ➤ Accessories ➤ Command Prompt.

▶ . Use the Start menu Search field:

    a. Click Start.

    b. Type cmd into the Search field.

    c. Press Enter.

While the second option may seem longer, in practice you will find that it is the faster method. I recommend that you develop the habit of executing the Command Prompt using the Search field method. Figure 1.10 shows the process of entering the cmd command into the Search field.

In addition to the Command Prompt, Microsoft introduced Windows PowerShell, or simply PowerShell, in 2006. PowerShell is very new in the history of Windows interfaces, but it offers several benefits that will be discussed in the later section titled "Management Features." Both the Command Prompt and Windows PowerShell provide a text-mode interface to the operating system.

FIGURE 1.10 Launching the Command Prompt from the Start menu's Search field

Networking Features

Windows servers support the popular protocols in use on modern networks. Thanks to the Internet's rapid growth in the 1990s and the fact that it uses the TCP/IP protocol suite, the most popular protocols used today are part of this protocol suite. Windows servers support both the older Internet Protocol (IP) version 4 (IPv4) and the newer IP version 6 (IPv6). The primary difference between the two versions is in their addressing requirements. IPv4 uses a 32-bit (32 ones and zeros) address, and IPv6 uses a 128-bit address for each node on the network. Additional differences exist, but the change in address sizes has the greatest initial impact on organizations moving from IPv4 to IPv6.

Windows servers use the TCP/IP protocol suite, as well as other protocols, in order to provide network services. Built right into the Windows Server operating system is the ability to provide several network services including:

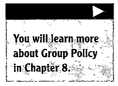

For more information on the specifics of the TCP/IP protocol suite, see Darril Gibson's book titled *Microsoft Windows Networking Essentials* (Sybex, 2011).

▶ File sharing

▶ Printer sharing

▶ Network authentication

▶ Web serving

▶ Media streaming

▶ Network-based operating system deployments

▶ Network-based operating system update deployments

▶ Network configuration and resolution services (DHCP and DNS)

▶ Centralized fax services

▶ Data caching services

▶ Remote command-line services (Telnet)

When using Telnet, remember that your username and password are sent across the network as cleartext.

In addition to these network services, Windows servers can also be used to centrally manage and configure Windows clients across the network. A feature known as Group Policy is used to accomplish centralized administration. Using Group Policies on the network, you can deploy software to machines, configure operating system settings, and restrict which applications the users can run and much more.

You will learn more about Group Policy in Chapter 8.

Management Features

When it comes to managing your servers, you have several options. You can use the Server Manager and Control Panel in the GUI interface as well as several graphical administration interfaces found on the Start menu in Administrative Tools. Additionally, you can use Windows PowerShell to administer the server and you can use the traditional Command Prompt.

The Server Manager is the primary GUI tool for managing your Windows servers. Figure 1.11 shows the Server Manager with the available nodes expanded in the left pane. Server Manager is used to manage roles and features. It is also used for diagnostics and troubleshooting with tools such as the Event Viewer, Performance, and the Device Manager. You can configure Task Scheduler events, the settings for the built-in firewall, services, and WMI Control options. Finally, you can manage storage using both Windows Server Backup and Disk Management.

You will learn more about Server Manager in Chapters 3, 4, and 16.

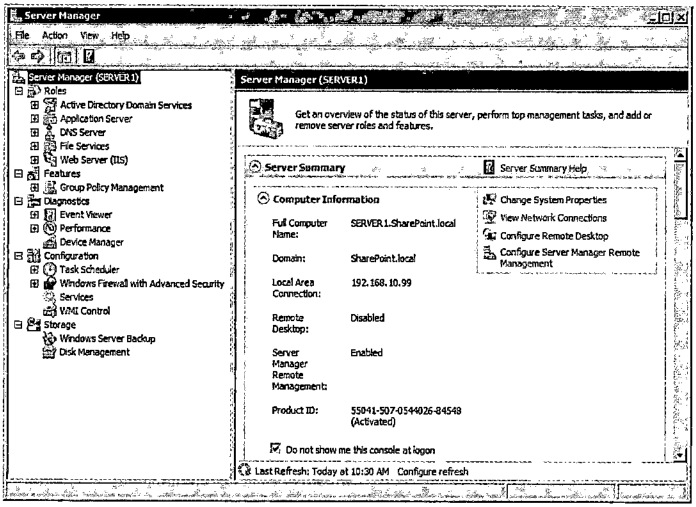

FIGURE 1.11 The Server Manager with all nodes expanded

Windows PowerShell provides a modern text-mode interface to the Windows operating system. It offers several features beyond the traditional Command Prompt, including:

► Improved scripting capabilities

► Object-based commands (all system information is considered in object and object property terminology)

▶ Cmdlets (the new name for a command in PowerShell) are available for administration of many Microsoft technologies

▶ Consistency for commands (all commands use a verb-noun or verb-object construct, such as Get-Process or Set-Item)

The Windows PowerShell interface is shown in Figure 1.12. In this image, the Get-Process command was executed to show several selected processes and the properties of those processes.

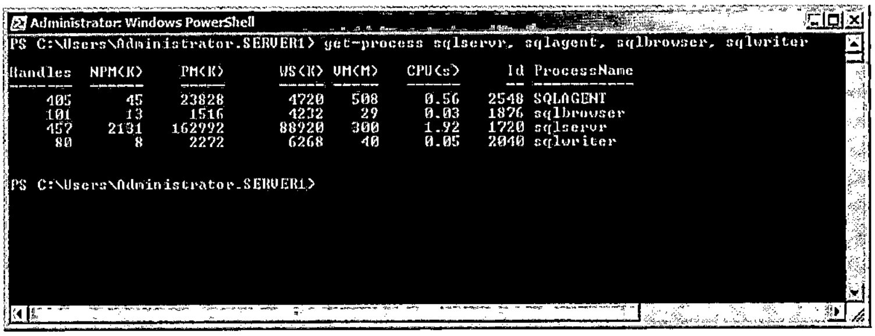

FIGURE 1.12 The Windows PowerShell interface

The Command Prompt is the oldest Microsoft interface still used today. In fact, the Command Prompt is one of the most commonly used administration interfaces by Windows Server professional administrators. Microsoft continues to release new Command Prompt features. For example, the new PowerCfg command introduced with Windows 7 allows you to manage power management profiles from the Command Prompt. Microsoft continues to support the Command Prompt with each new version of Windows on the clients and the servers. They add new commands and enhance existing commands to add new capabilities. You can be sure that an investment in learning to use the Command Prompt will be useful for years to come.

Windows Server Editions

In this final section, you will learn about the different editions of Windows Server and the various features they offer. Like many software applications, Microsoft Windows comes in different editions. Windows Server 2008 R2 comes in seven different editions:

Windows Server 2008 R2 Foundation   The Foundation Edition is a low cost, entry-level version of Windows Server. Microsoft recommends it for small business use only. The Foundation Edition supports the basic server roles such as Active Directory Domain Services, Application Server, DHCP Server, DNS Server,

Print and Document Services, and Web Services. It includes partial support for File Services in that only one Distributed File System (DFS) root can be created.

Windows Server 2008 R2 Standard   The Standard Edition is the most common edition used in both small and medium-sized businesses simply because it offers the majority of features that an organization requires. A key difference between Foundation and Standard is that Standard supports Hpyer-V for virtualization and Foundation does not. The Standard Edition has the same limits on the File Services role as the Foundation Edition.

Windows Server 2008 R2 Enterprise   The Enterprise Edition of Windows Server 2008 R2 is the first level at which all server roles are completely supported. For this reason, medium-sized and large organizations usually choose the Enterprise Edition of Windows Server 2008 R2. Additionally, the Enterprise Edition allows you to run four virtualized installations of Windows Server 2008 R2 within Hyper-V without requiring additional licenses.

Windows Server 2008 R2 Datacenter   The Datacenter Edition is a special edition of Windows Server 2008 R2 that comes only on pretested hardware. It is not supported on just any computer that you might choose to use. Instead, you buy tested hardware with a preconfigured installation of Datacenter Edition and in exchange you receive high availability guarantees. In most cases, the Datacenter Edition is an Original Equipment Manufacturer (OEM) install. This simply means that it comes preinstalled on tested and authorized equipment and is not supported on just any old machine. The Datacenter Edition provides unlimited virtual machine licenses, which far exceeds the Enterprise Edition allowances. However, the cost of Datacenter is much higher because it is licensed on a per-processor basis only. The licensing fees can quickly exceed $20,000.

Windows Web Server 2008 R2   The Web Server Edition is intended to be just what its name implies: a web server. It supports only the DNS Server and Web Server roles and is a streamlined installation of Windows Server 2008 R2 aimed at providing efficient delivery of web hosting services.

Windows HPC Server 2008 R2 Suite   The Higher Performance Computing (HPC) Edition of Windows Server is focused on performance. It supports significantly fewer roles than Standard Edition, but it is intended to run in a clustered configuration. A head node is the single point of management and job scheduling for the cluster and compute nodes receive computational task requests from the head node. The point of the HPC Edition is to provide rapid computations through the uses of multiple compute nodes in a cluster.

Windows Server 2008 R2 for Itanium-Based Systems   While the Itanium-Based Edition is still available, it is very limited in functionality. You can install the

> A *cluster* is a group of computers working together as one to improve performance or availability.

Application Server role and the Web Services role, but no other roles are available. For this reason, Itanium-Based systems are mostly used as web servers when they run Windows Server 2008 R2.

With an understanding of the different editions of Windows Server, you are prepared to make educated decisions as you select the right operating system for your needs. You can learn more about these editions at:

```
http://www.microsoft.com/windowsserver2008/en/us/
r2-editions-overview.aspx
```

THE ESSENTIALS AND BEYOND

It is important to know that a server is used to provide services to multiple devices on a network. Servers are different from clients because they are dedicated to service provisioning, while clients are not dedicated to this task. Servers can play many different roles, and Windows servers even use the phrase "server role" to define the roles they play. For example, Windows servers can play the role of a file server, a print server, a DNS server, an Active Directory server, and many other roles. Windows servers have many features that make them easy to deploy, manage, and troubleshoot. These features include a familiar graphical interface in the Windows Desktop and a familiar text-mode interface in the Command Prompt. Newer versions of Windows Server also include a new text-mode interface called Windows PowerShell, which enhances the capabilities of the old Command Prompt while still supporting many of its features.

ADDITIONAL EXERCISES

▶ Research the different editions of Windows Server online. Select the best edition for use as a dedicated web server in a small business with a limited budget.

▶ Add the File Services role to a Windows Server 2008 R2 installation and work with the FSRM tool.

▶ Browse a vendor's website and explore the different types of servers they sell. Pay special attention to the form factor of each server.

▶ Review the history of Microsoft Windows to learn how it has evolved to become the operating system it is today.

To compare your answers to the author's, please visit:

www.sybex.com/go/serveradminessentals

THE ESSENTIALS AND BEYOND (Continued)

REVIEW QUESTIONS

1. Which one of the following is the best definition of a server?

   A. A network-connected device that provides IP routing to the network

   B. A network-connected device that provides services to the network and the devices on that network

   C. A stand-alone device that is used by a user to perform mathematical analysis

   D. A network-connected device that is used to access websites using a web browser

2. True or false. SQL Server may be categorized as an information service.

3. What kind of computing device consumes services on a network?

   A. Web Server

   B. DNS Server

   C. Client

   D. Ethernet cable

4. What Command Prompt command can be used to determine the version of Windows running on a machine?

5. Which server form factor allows multiple services to be placed in an enclosure much as add-on cards are installed in individual computers?

   A. Blade

   B. Desktop

   C. Rack Mount

   D. Convertible

6. Define a server role.

7. Define a feature.

8. What server role, in Windows Server 2008 R2, supports centralized scanner management?

   A. File Services

   B. Application Server

   C. Web Server

   D. Print and Document Services

9. What command is used to launch the Windows Command Prompt in Windows Server 2008 R2?

   A. Command.com

   B. PowerShell

   C. CMD

   D. Prompt

10. True or false. Windows Server 2008 R2 supports only IPv4.

CHAPTER 2

Installing Windows Servers

The Windows operating systems become easier to install as each new version is released. With the release of Windows Server 2008 and Windows Server 2008 R2, Windows Server is easier to install than ever before. However, just because the installation process is easy, you must not forego planning and assume the installation engine will make all of the right decisions for you. Instead, you must plan the installation well, which includes choosing the right hardware and installation method.

While the manual installation methods are much easier than they were in the past, Microsoft also provides many different automated and custom installation methods. These methods are much more complex and require careful consideration and extensive knowledge to use them.

In this chapter, you will learn about the different installation options and even see how to install Windows Server onto a virtual machine. In fact, you'll learn about all of these topics:

▷ **Installation Options**

▷ **Upgrading Servers**

▷ **Using Server Core**

▷ **Working with Device Drivers**

Installation Options

Several items must be considered when a new installation of Windows Server 2008 or Windows Server 2008 R2 is planned. First, you must define the target of the installation or the installation destination. You can install to physical machines or virtual machines, so you must understand each of these destination types. Second, you should understand the process of an interactive installation. An interactive installation is the typical install performed when you insert the Window Server DVD and boot the machine from it to start the process. Third, unattended installations must be considered. In large organizations, it's often helpful to automate installations as much as possible to minimize the time investment requirements for the administrator. Fourth, you should be aware of a technology that helps you provide images of operating systems for deployment across the network. This technology is called Windows Deployment Services. Finally, I'll walk you through the process of an interactive installation of Windows Server 2008 R2.

Choosing an Installation Destination

In modern computer networks, it is not uncommon to have several dozen or even hundreds of servers on a large network. In the first decade of the twenty-first century, a new technology called virtualization saw rapid growth. With *virtualization,* one physical server can host multiple virtual servers and each virtual server can have full network access. As a Windows Server administrator, you need to make good decisions when choosing between physical servers and virtual servers.

Several virtualization solutions are available today. Microsoft provides Hyper-V on the servers and Windows Virtual PC on the clients. Other virtualization solutions include VMware and VirtualBox.

Virtualization is simply the process of creating a PC or server through software so that operating systems can be installed onto the virtual machine that is created. Table 2.1 provides a comparison of physical and virtual server types.

TABLE 2.1   Virtual Servers Compared to Physical Servers

Virtual Server	Physical Server
Lower cost per server	Higher cost per server
Lower input/output speeds	Higher input/output speeds
Faster recovery from failure	Slower recovery from failure (when used as a single server and not in a cluster)
Less power consumption	More power consumption

As Table 2.1 makes clear, virtualization has significant benefits. The primary problem area for virtual servers is input/output (I/O). While you can use storage area networks (SANs) and even direct disk access to speed up I/O operations, virtual servers are not yet as fast as traditional physical servers at storage operations. For this reason, you are less likely to use a virtual server for I/O intensive servers such as database servers and file processing service servers (for example, search indexing).

Several vendors compete in the virtualization market space, and even open source solutions are available. The two most commonly used virtualization solutions today are VMware and Microsoft Hyper-V. Other solutions include Qemu, VirtualBox, and Parallels.

In addition to choosing between physical and virtual machines, you must ensure that the machine meets the requirements for your installation. The following are Microsoft's minimum system requirements for Windows Server 2008:

- ► 1 GHz processor (32-bit) or 1.4 GHz processor (64-bit)
- ► 512 MB RAM
- ► 10 to 20 GB or more disk space (32-bit) or 32 GB or more disk space (64-bit)
- ► Super VGA (800 × 600) or higher display resolution

The following are Microsoft's minimum requirements for Windows Server 2008 R2, which only comes in a 64-bit edition:

- ► 1.4 GHz (single core processor) or 1.3 GHz (dual-core processor)
- ► 512 MB RAM
- ► 32 GB or more disk space
- ► Super VGA (800 × 600) or higher display resolution

It is important to remember that the minimum requirements are just that—minimum. You are not likely to be satisfied with the performance of a Windows Server installation running on the specifications listed as minimum requirements. Consider at least doubling the RAM and processor speeds to achieve acceptable performance. Some server types, such as a database server, will need even more resources.

The final thing you must do before launching into an installation is determine the appropriate operating system version and edition. Windows Server 2008 R2 comes in seven different editions. You will have to know the intended use of the server to choose the right edition. The intended use is defined by the applications that run on the server. If it is to be a database server, it will require more RAM than if it is to be a file server. If the intended user determines that you need more than 32 GB of RAM, you will have to use the Enterprise or Datacenter editions of Windows Server. You can view the differences in technical specifications of the Windows Server editions at:

```
http://www.microsoft.com/windowsserver2008/en/us/
r2-compare-specs.aspx
```

When defining the hardware required for a specific implementation, remember that the requirements should be defined by the applications running on the server and not by minimum requirements specified by the operating system vendor.

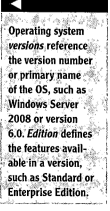

Operating system *versions* reference the version number or primary name of the OS, such as Windows Server 2008 or version 6.0. *Edition* defines the features available in a version, such as Standard or Enterprise Edition.

Additionally, you must use the right version of Windows Server. Windows Server 2003 and later are still frequently used in organizations. You must inspect the documentation for your server-based software to determine the operating system versions on which it will operate. You may have software that works only on Windows Server 2003 R2. In such a case, you will have to use that version of Windows Server. You may choose to run Windows Server 2008 R2 as the primary operating system and then run a Windows Server 2003 R2 virtual server on top of it. This will allow you to use newer software on the Windows Server 2008 R2 installation and still use the older software in the virtual server. On Windows Server 2008 R2, virtual servers are implemented using Hyper-V.

> You will learn about Hyper-V specifically and virtualization technologies in Chapter 15.

Performing an Interactive Installation

Installing Windows Server is a fairly simple process once you get to the actual installation stage. However, several planning and preparation tasks should be performed before you begin the actual installation. You have already learned about several of these in the previous section, but the following list will act as a reminder of these preparation tasks so that you can get the installation right the first time:

> You may need to adjust the boot sequence within the BIOS to allow the system to boot to the DVD drive.

> In some cases, you may have to press a special key sequence to boot from the DVD. You can find this information in your server hardware documentation.

▶ Determine the appropriate operating system version and edition.

▶ Verify that the target server meets the requirements.

▶ Perform firmware and BIOS updates on any required hardware.

The last item, performing firmware and BIOS updates, requires a bit more attention. Hardware devices often have firmware installed on them. The *firmware* is software that determines how the chips on the device function in the particular implementation of that device. The Basic Input/Output System (BIOS) is the software typically stored on a chip on the system's motherboard within the server that determines hardware configuration such as hard drive controllers, memory settings, and more. It is important to use a stable firmware and BIOS for all hardware in your server. You will not always want to use the latest version because it may not be the most stable.

With the planning complete, you are ready to begin the installation. The most common installation method is an *interactive installation*, which is performed as follows:

1. Insert the DVD into the server and power it on.

    When the Windows Server 2008 R2 installation starts, the first screen you will see is the language selection screen, as shown in Figure 2.1.

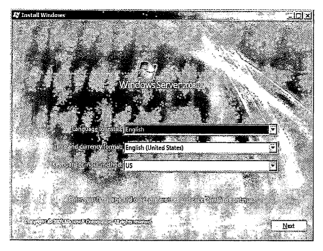

FIGURE 2.1 The language and input selection screen

2. Select the language you want to install, the format for time and currency, and the keyboard input method, and then click Next. On the next screen, you can choose to:

- ► Repair your computer.

- ► Learn more about installing Windows with the What To Know Before Installing Windows option.

- ► Click Install Now to begin the installation, as shown in Figure 2.2.

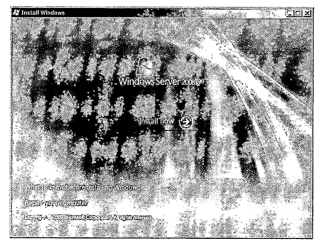

FIGURE 2.2 The installation launch screen

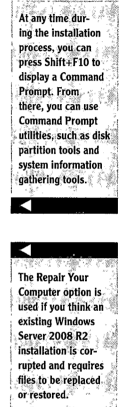

At any time during the installation process, you can press Shift+F10 to display a Command Prompt. From there, you can use Command Prompt utilities, such as disk partition tools and system information gathering tools.

The Repair Your Computer option is used if you think an existing Windows Server 2008 R2 installation is corrupted and requires files to be replaced or restored.

3. Click Install Now to begin the installation.

   You will be presented with a screen that allows you to select the operating system edition you want to install. The Windows Server 2008 R2 DVD includes all of the available editions, so you must be careful to select the edition for which you possess a valid license.

4. Determine the appropriate edition by referring to your pre-installation planning.

   You will have to choose between a Full Installation and a Server Core installation as well. The full installation includes the complete GUI interface and all features for that edition of Windows Server. The Server Core is a streamlined installation without the complete GUI interface or a complete set of features. Figure 2.3 shows the selection of the Windows Server 2008 R2 Enterprise (Full Installation) option.

For more information about Server Core, see the section later in this chapter titled "Using Server Core."

FIGURE 2.3 Choosing the server operating system edition and installation type

   After you choose the operating system edition and type to install, you will be presented with the license agreement. You must accept the terms of the agreement before you can continue with the installation.

5. Accept the license terms, and click Next.

You will be asked whether you want to perform an Upgrade or a Custom (advanced) installation, as shown in Figure 2.4. You cannot perform an upgrade on a server without an existing operating system.

For more information on upgrade options, see the later section of this chapter titled "Upgrading Servers."

Which type of installation do you want?

Upgrade
Upgrade to a newer version of Windows and keep your files, settings, and programs. The option to upgrade is only available when an existing version of Windows is running. We recommend backing up your files before you proceed.

Custom (advanced)
Install a new copy of Windows. This option does not keep your files, settings, and programs. The option to make changes to disks and partitions is available when you start your computer using the installation disc. We recommend backing up your files before you proceed.

Help me decide

FIGURE 2.4 Choosing an upgrade or custom installation

6. Click Custom (Advanced), as this is a new installation.

Disk partitioning is the next task you must perform to install Windows Server 2008 R2 on a new server. On the disk partitioning screen of the installation, you can either:

► Click Next to use all free space on the selected drive.

► Click Drive Options (Advanced) to manually partition the drive according to your needs.

Figure 2.5 shows the options available. If you click the Drive Options (Advanced) link, you can do the following:

► Create a new partition.

► Format an existing one.

► Delete an existing one.

► Extend a partition to include space on another physical drive.

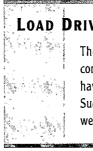

FIGURE 2.5 Partitioning the storage space for the installation

7. Click Next to use the free space on Disk 0.

LOAD DRIVER OPTION

The Load Driver option allows you to load custom drivers for a storage controller. If your storage device does not show up in this screen, you may have to load a driver from the vendor to continue with the installation. Such drivers are typically available for download from the server vendor's website.

The partitioning task is the last required task before the actual installation begins. Figure 2.6 shows the Installing Windows screen, which breaks the installation into five high-level stages:

- ► Copying Windows Files
- ► Expanding Windows Files
- ► Installing Features
- ► Installing Updates
- ► Completing Installation

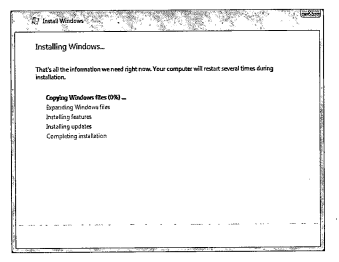

FIGURE 2.6 The five-stage Windows installation process

All Windows Server 2008 and Windows Server 2008 R2 installations are image-based. This statement simply means that images are used to install the operating system. An image is a file-based capture of an installed operating system stored in one big file called an *image*. The one big file actually contains the thousands of files that make up the operating system installation. During the Copying Windows Files stage of the installation, this big image file is copied to the server's hard disk.

During the Expanding Windows Files phase, the image file is extracted to the hard disk. Default permissions are automatically set for the files that are extracted to the hard disk. These permissions, for example, do not allow standard users to delete files from the Windows installation directory.

The next two stages, Installing Features and Installing Updates, install and configure a default set of features within the operating system. They also install any updates that are included on the DVD installation media. The Completing Installation stage is used to perform final cleanup and configuration tasks on the server.

When the installation completes, it will automatically reboot the server. You will be presented with a screen that says "The user's password must be changed before logging on the first time."

1. Click OK to change the password.

    This is the password for the local Administrator account on the server, so it is important that you assign a strong password.

2. Enter a valid password and confirm it, and then click the button to apply the changed password

After changing the password, you will be logged onto the server automatically.

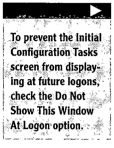

To prevent the Initial Configuration Tasks screen from displaying at future logons, check the Do Not Show This Window At Logon option.

At the first logon, you will be presented with a screen titled "Initial Configuration Tasks," which is shown in Figure 2.7. The tasks are broken into groups labeled Provide Computer Information, Update This Server, and Customize This Server. The most important initial tasks are in the Provide Computer Information and Update This Server sections.

FIGURE 2.7 The Initial Configuration Tasks screen

The first task you should perform on a production server is activating Windows. This process ensures that you have a valid license for the Windows operating system. You have 30 days after installation to activate the operating system. You may be required to reactivate Windows if significant hardware changes are made to the system.

You can extend the trial period for up to 120 days using the SLMGR command. The command gives you another 30 days and you can use it three times.

Next, you will need to set the time zone for your server. This will ensure that the time is set appropriately and that the time changes according to Daylight Savings Time, if it is applicable in your area.

A Word about Windows Activation

The Windows activation process includes an inventory of your hardware. The process assumes that significant changes in hardware indicate that the operating system is now running on a different computer. Adding RAM, swapping non-operating system hard drives, and adding USB devices will not require reactivation. However, if you replace the system board, it is very likely that activation will be required.

Networking settings must also be configured. A server is only a server if it is providing a service and if it is accessible to users in the environment. That statement may sound odd, but the reality is that you must place the server on some network in order for clients to consume services offered by the server. As a part of configuring networking, you will configure IP addressing and other network-related settings.

The computer name identifies the system on the network in a memorable way. For example, you may name a server SRV-MKT01 to indicate that it is the server for the Marketing department in your organization and it is the first server for that department. The second server could be named SRV-MKT02 and so forth. The benefit of placing the SRV prefix (or some other prefix you define) in the name is that it will clearly differentiate between the servers and the clients on your network.

Additionally, the computer name is easier for users and administrators to use than the IP address. For example, if SRV-MKT01 had the IP address of 192.168.57.43, it will be easier to remember SRV-MKT01 than 192.168.57.43. This is especially true if you have dozens or hundreds of servers.

Finally, you should update the server with drivers, system patches, and potentially new features through the online update service. You can configure automatic updates to either retrieve updates from the Microsoft Update website or from an internal update server. You can also manually check for updates. If you installed the operating system from the Microsoft factory DVD, you will have many updates that should be installed. Microsoft releases security updates on the second Tuesday of every month, and these updates are essential for maintaining a secure server installation. If you install the server several months or years after the DVD was originally created, you will have many "Patch Tuesday" updates to install.

Because Microsoft releases security updates each month on the second Tuesday, it has become known as *Patch Tuesday*.

WINDOWS SERVER F8 BOOT OPTIONS

After installation is complete, Windows Server should boot up each time for you without problems; however, during installation you may install a device driver or another system component that prevents you from booting the machine normally. This is where the F8 boot options come into play.

Using the F8 hotkey, you can boot a Windows server with various boot-time options. When you power on the server, after the Power On Self-Test (POST) is completed, press F8 to access a special boot menu that allows you to boot the system for troubleshooting purposes. The most common reason for using the F8 menu is to boot into safe mode. Safe mode is a special boot mode that allows you to start a system with a minimal set of device drivers. If you can boot the system in safe mode, you may be able to reinstall drivers or perform other repair tasks in order to get the system up and running again in normal mode.

Automating an Installation

The preceding section provided you with the information you need to perform an interactive installation of Windows Server. You may have noticed that you really cannot select many options during the installation. Microsoft has made the installation process as effortless as possible by reducing the options you have during the installation.

If you want more control over what is installed during the installation, or you want to automate the installation so that system interaction is not required, then you should use an unattended installation. Windows Server 2008 and Windows Server 2008 R2 support unattended installation using files that specify how the installation should proceed. The file is normally named unattend.xml and can be created with the Windows System Image Manager (WinSIM), which is part of the Windows Automated Installation Kit (WAIK). WAIK is a free download from the Microsoft website.

> An unattended installation is an installation that is automated through the use of an unattend.xml file.

Because Setup.exe is no longer used to install the newer versions of Windows Server, you will need to capture a custom image to deploy with an unattend.xml file. This task is performed as follows:

1. Boot an existing installation of Windows Server using a special boot disk called a Windows PE boot disk.

You create this boot disk with the WAIK that is downloaded from Microsoft, or simply use the one that comes with the WAIK.

2. After booting with the disk, use the SYSPREP command to specify that an image should be captured and an unattend.xml file should be used.

This task is accomplished with the sysprep /unattend:{path} unattend.xml file command, where {path} is replaced with the actual path to the unattend.xml file.

As an alternative, you can download the Microsoft Deployment Toolkit in addition to WAIK and use a GUI interface to import the factory Windows Server image and then apply a custom unattend.xml file to the factory image. For more information on WAIK and the Microsoft Deployment Toolkit, which work for both Windows clients and Windows Server, visit:

http://technet.microsoft.com/en-us/library/dd744270(WS.10).aspx

Understanding Windows Deployment Services

The final choice for Windows Server installation is to use Windows Deployment Services (WDS). WDS runs on Windows Server 2008 and Windows Server 2008 R2 servers and is used to deploy operating systems across the network. Both client and server operating systems may be deployed.

WDS is an implementation of a Preboot Execution Environment (PXE) server. Many NICs are designed to support the PXE standard. PXE allows a computer to boot, obtain an IP address from a DHCP server, and then connect to the network with a minimal operating system so that a full operating system may be selected for installation from the boot servers, in this case a WDS server.

The basic PXE boot process is shown in Figure 2.8. The Dynamic Host Configuration Protocol (DHCP) is used to provide network settings to the PXE client; however, an extended DHCP activity is performed. Beyond the normal IP configuration settings provided by the DHCP server, it also provides the following extended information:

> ▶ A PXE control field that specifies the access method (multicast, broadcast, or unicast) for use when contacting the PXE server

> ▶ The list of IP addresses for available PXE servers

> ▶ A PXE prompt to inform the user how to access the boot menu

> ▶ A timeout value for launching the first boot menu entry should the user fail to select one manually

WDS is the new version of Remote Installation Services (RIS), which shipped with earlier versions of Windows Server.

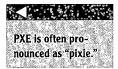

PXE is often pronounced as "pixie."

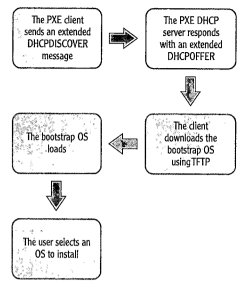

FIGURE 2.8 The PXE boot process

The Trivial File Transfer Protocol (TFTP) is used to download the initial boot-strap OS from the PXE server. In the case of a Windows Server, this is the WDS server. After the bootstrap OS is loaded, it reads the list of available operating systems for install from the WDS server and displays them to the user. The user selects an OS to install and the normal installation process continues from here. The installation process may be either interactive or unattended, depending on how the administrators set up the images on the WDS server.

Upgrading Servers

Upgrades are beneficial because they maintain existing settings while a new operating system is installed on the server. However, upgrades also come at a cost—they may be less stable than clean installations. To help you understand the important issues related to server upgrades, this section provides informa-tion on supported upgrade paths, comparing upgrades to clean installations, and understanding the actual upgrade process.

Supported Upgrade Paths

As Microsoft releases new operating systems, they usually allow you to upgrade from the previous version. It may even be possible to upgrade from versions that preceded the previous version. Windows Server 2008 R2 is not different. You can upgrade to Windows Server 2008 R2 from any of the following operating systems:

▶ Windows Server 2003 with SP2 (64-bit)

▶ Windows Server 2003 R2 (64-bit)

▶ Windows Server 2008 (64-bit)

You cannot upgrade from a 32-bit edition of Windows Server to Windows Server 2008 R2. The installed operating system must already be running a 64-bit edition. Additionally, you cannot perform a downgrade to a lower edition's level during the upgrade process. In other words, you cannot upgrade an Enterprise Edition installation of Windows Server 2003 (64-bit) to a Standard Edition installation of Windows Server 2008 R2. You must upgrade to the same edition or a higher edition. You can upgrade, for example, from Windows Server 2003 R2 Enterprise Edition to Windows Server 2008 R2 Datacenter Edition.

Upgrades Versus Clean Installations

A clean installation is simply an installation of Windows Server on a system that does not maintain the settings and applications from an existing installation. In most cases, a clean installation is placed on an empty hard drive; however, it can also be performed as a dual-boot configuration or onto a hard drive with another operating system that will no longer be bootable.

You must choose between a clean installation and an upgrade when you have an existing operating system on the server. If the existing operating system is not supported for upgrades, your decision is easy—you must do a clean install. If the operating system is supported for upgrades, you have to make the decision based on other factors. In most cases, it is best to perform a clean install. Even Microsoft recommends that you perform a clean installation whenever possible. The reasons for choosing a clean installation over an upgrade include:

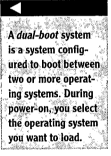

A *dual-boot* system is a system configured to boot between two or more operating systems. During power-on, you select the operating system you want to load.

▶ Clean installations do not keep files around that are no longer needed.

▶ Clean installations do not bring existing problems to the new installation.

▶ Clean installations provide a solid foundation for building a stable server.

The second point is the most important: A clean installation starts from scratch and any existing corrupted files or improper configurations will not have an impact on the new installation.

Understanding the Upgrade Process

Like an interactive clean installation, upgrades should begin with planning. Microsoft provides a list of steps you should take to prepare for an upgrade here:

`http://technet.microsoft.com/en-us/library/ff972408(WS.10).aspx`

The basic tasks they suggest include:

▶ Ensure that your server hardware is supported.

▶ Perform a clean installation whenever possible.

▶ Ensure that your applications are compatible with the new version of the operating system.

▶ Test your applications against the new version of the operating system.

▶ Ensure that all kernel-mode software is signed.

▶ Back up your existing server installation.

▶ Understand that you cannot uninstall the new OS.

▶ Review the known issues at:

`http://technet.microsoft.com/en-us/library/ff972310(WS.10).aspx`

After you finish the planning process, you can begin the upgrade by inserting the Windows Server 2008 R2 disc in the DVD drive on the target server. If the server is running and AutoRun is enabled, a screen will appear allowing you to begin the upgrade process. If the AutoRun feature is not enabled, simply launch the setup program manually from the DVD and follow the instructions through the screens to complete the upgrade.

When the upgrade is complete, you should fully test your new operating system. Make sure all services, applications, and operating system features are working as expected. If you have problems with any components, try troubleshooting them first to resolve the problem. If you cannot resolve the problem, you may have to reload the old operating system and restore your data from a backup. Before you try upgrading again, make sure you locate a different service or application that will work on Windows Server 2008 R2 for your needs.

For more information on troubleshooting Windows servers, see Chapter 13.

Using Server Core

With the release of Windows Server 2008, Microsoft introduced a new installation option called Server Core. It's included with Windows Server 2008 R2, as well. A Server Core installation of Windows Server provides many benefits, but it also has limitations. In this section, you will learn about Server Core with all its features and drawbacks.

Server Core Features and Limitations

The Server Core installation provides a reduced footprint installation of the server. The benefits of the reduced footprint include improved performance and a reduced attack surface.

Server core is managed primarily through the command line. You can use the Command Prompt or the Windows PowerShell cmdlets to administer it. Therefore, extensive knowledge of the Windows command-line interface is useful if you plan to manage a Server Core installation. For details listings of Windows Command Prompt commands, see the A-Z command reference at:

```
http://technet.microsoft.com/en-us/library/cc772390(WS.10).aspx
```

While the Server Core installation is faster and potentially more secure than the full installation, it does have limitations. Windows Server 2008 Server Core installations can run only the following server roles:

You can also manage a Server Core installation from a GUI on a remote computer.

- ▶ Active Directory Domain Services (AD DS)
- ▶ Active Directory Lightweight Directory Services (AD LDS)
- ▶ DHCP Server
- ▶ DNS Server
- ▶ File Services
- ▶ Hyper-V
- ▶ Print Services
- ▶ Streaming Media Services
- ▶ Web Server (IIS)

Windows Server 2008 R2 can run the following server roles on a Server Core installation:

- ▶ Active Directory Certificate Services
- ▶ Active Directory Domain Services
- ▶ Active Directory Lightweight Directory Services (AD LDS)
- ▶ DHCP Server
- ▶ DNS Server

► File Services (including File Server Resource Manager)

► Hyper-V

► Print and Document Services

► Streaming Media Services

► Web Server (including a subset of ASP.NET)

It is important that you verify you can run the required roles on the server before you select the Server Core installation. If you are planning to take the MTA: Windows Server Administration exam, be sure to know what roles are available with Windows Server core installations.

Performing a Server Core Installation

See the section *"Installation Options"* earlier in this chapter for installation procedures.

A Server Core installation of Windows Server 2008 or Windows Server 2008 R2 is performed just like a full installation. The only difference is that you select the Server Core option when you choose the operating system to install, as shown in Figure 2.9.

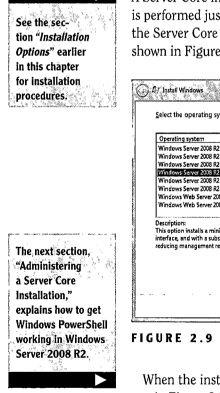

The next section, "Administering a Server Core Installation," explains how to get Windows PowerShell working in Windows Server 2008 R2.

FIGURE 2.9 Selecting the Server Core installation option

When the installation is complete, you will log on and see a screen like the one in Figure 2.10. Notice that the Start menu and Desktop are no longer available to you. You have a colored backdrop (typically, a teal/blue backdrop by default) and a Command Prompt window in the foreground.

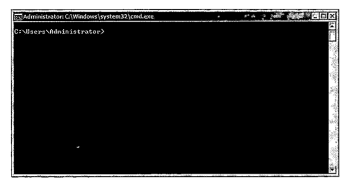

FIGURE 2.10 The default look of the Server Core installation
after the first logon

Administering a Server Core Installation

One of the most important tools you can use to manage a Windows Server 2008
R2 Server Core installation is Windows PowerShell. As you learned in Chapter 1,
"Windows Server Overview," Windows PowerShell is an enhanced command-line
interface to the Windows operating system. Windows PowerShell is not enabled
on a Server Core installation by default. To enable Windows PowerShell, follow
these steps:

1. At the Command Prompt, type sconfig and press Enter.

2. Select option 4: Configure Remote Management (see Figure 2.11).

FIGURE 2.11 The initial sconfig administration screen

3. Select option 2: Enable Windows PowerShell (see Figure 2.12).

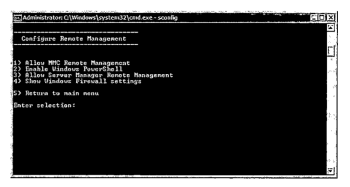

FIGURE 2.12 The Configure Remote Management administration screen of sconfig

4. Click Yes in the Restart dialog that appears.

It will take a few minutes for the PowerShell installation process to complete. When it does, you will be prompted to restart your server.

5. Click Yes to restart.

MORE ABOUT SCONFIG

In addition to installing Windows PowerShell, you can use the `sconfig` program to configure the same initial configuration settings that the Initial Configuration Settings application provides in a full installation. These settings include the computer name, Windows Update settings, network settings, and data and time settings. Interestingly, `sconfig` is simply a batch file (a collection of Command Prompt commands in a text file) that calls a VBScript script file. It is not an actual compiled command, but it definitely makes the initial configuration of Windows Server 2008 R2 Server Core much easier.

The `sconfig` utility also lets you shut down or restart the server.

While the `sconfig` utility allows you to initially configure the Server Core installation, you'll need other commands to perform more advanced administration procedures. The most important commands to be aware of are:

NET: Used to perform many functions related to user and group administration.

SHUTDOWN: Used to shut down the server or restart the server.

LOGOFF: Used to log off the current user.

NETSH: Used to configure IP settings, Windows Firewall, and many other network-related settings.

WUSA: Used to install updates on the server.

TASKLIST: Used to view a list of running tasks.

TASKMGR: Used to launch the Task Manager and manage processes.

DISKPART: Used to create and mage disk partitions.

DEFRAG: Used to defragment hard disks.

PNPUTIL: Used to install and manage device drivers.

OCLIST: Used to view available server roles for installation.

OCSETUP: Used to install server roles.

Working with Device Drivers

In this last section of the chapter, you will learn about device drivers. First, it's important to understand what a device driver is and what it does so that you can better grasp the problems that can be caused by poorly coded devices drivers and the reasons why the same hardware with different devices drivers can perform very differently. Next, you'll discover how to locate device drivers and install them. You'll also learn about the different driver maintenance options and, though it's not an issue you face as often today as in the past, you'll learn about hardware resources and how resource conflicts can cause problems when your device drivers attempt to communicate with the hardware.

Understanding Device Drivers

Many people become confused when they attempt to discover what a driver actually is. Don't be confused by them. A *device driver* is simply a software module or application that knows how to perform two functions:

A device driver is a software module that talks to the device and the operating system.

- ▶ Communicate with the hardware device

- ▶ Communicate with the operating system and applications

Understanding device drivers is much easier if you remember that a device driver is a software application that runs on your computer. The device driver must communicate with the hardware and potentially provide logic to the hardware, but this thing we call a driver is really just a software application.

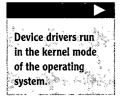

Device drivers run in the kernel mode of the operating system.

However, it is important to know that device drivers run in what is called *kernel mode*. This is where the operating system itself runs. In other words, the device drivers run at the operating system level; and this means that when they have problems, they often crash the entire operating system. Only device drivers retrieved from a trusted source should be used on Windows servers. A *trusted source* is a website or driver installation media source that you know you can trust. This typically means the vendor website or the media that came with the device.

Device drivers are needed for all hardware in the system. Many administrators do not realize this simply because Windows operating systems usually come with many device drivers out of the box. The following list describes just a few of the devices that will require device drivers in your Windows servers:

▶ Video cards

▶ Audio cards

▶ Motherboard chipsets

▶ Network interface cards (NICs)

▶ Storage controllers, such as SATA and SCSI controllers

▶ SAN adapters, such as Fibre Channel or iSCSI adapters

▶ Hardware that attaches through USB ports, such as printers and scanners and the USB ports themselves

Obtaining and Installing Drivers

Device drivers should always be acquired from trusted sources. In most cases, this means getting drivers from one of the following three sources:

▶ The device vendor

▶ The operating system vendor

▶ The computer or server vendor

If you purchase an aftermarket hardware item, such as an improved NIC or a different storage controller, you will usually have to acquire the drivers from the device vendor. The operating system vendor and the server vendor will sometimes have the device drivers you need in such cases. The process of acquiring device drivers from the device vendor follows these basic steps:

1. Visit the vendor's website.

2. Click the support link.

3. Find the link that suggests you can download software or drivers and click it.

4. Locate your specific device and download the drivers for it.

Thankfully, the vast majority of vendors have implemented their websites in a manner that allows the process to be similar to this sequence each time. Figure 2.13 shows the driver download section of the Intel website.

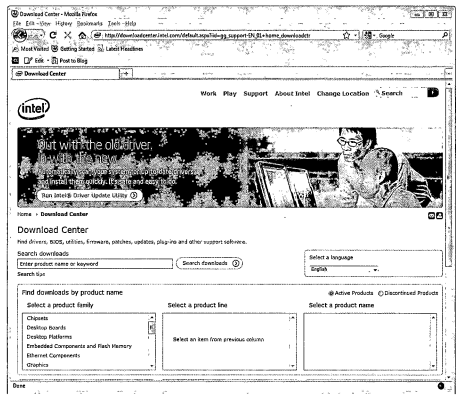

FIGURE 2.13 Using the driver download page at Intel.com

When the server is shipped with specific hardware from the vendor, they will usually provide the drivers for download at their website. For example, if you purchase a Dell server, you can download drivers for all of the hardware included in the purchased server from the Dell website.

When you are installing the Windows Server operating system on an older server, there is a good chance that the operating system installation DVD will come with the needed drivers for your server. Additionally, drivers may be available through Microsoft Update. Always be cautious when installing device driver updates through Microsoft Update (or any other automated update system for that matter). While the drivers are typically tested well, you want to know when drivers are updated on your servers. If you begin having problems, but you were not aware that a new video driver, for example, was recently installed automatically, you may miss the fact that the driver could be the cause of the problem.

Consider installing device drivers only through manual update processes to increase stability for your servers.

After downloading the required device drivers, you can install them in several ways, depending on the drivers file format. Some drivers are provided in executable containers that perform the installation for you. In such cases, simply launch the installation and follow the prompts to install the driver. For USB devices, it is common to install the driver before connecting the USB device. Read your device documentation to find out whether you should install the driver first or connect the hardware first.

Sometimes drivers are provided in a compressed archive, such as a ZIP file. In this case, you will need to extract the files to a folder and then use the Device Manager to install the driver. In the extracted folder, you will find an INF file that provides the details of the driver to the operating system. The process for installing a driver on Windows Server 2008 or Windows Server 2008 R2 for a newly added device through Device Manager is as follows:

1. Click on the Start menu and then right-click on Computer and select Manage.

2. Expand the Diagnostics node in the left pane and click on Device Manager.

3. Find the device in the Other Devices node in the Device Manager pane and then right-click on it and select Install Driver.

4. Follow the prompts in the Driver Installation Wizard to locate the driver in the extracted folder and perform the installation.

Driver Maintenance

As time passes, the device drivers for your hardware will likely become outdated. Vendors often release 5 to 10 device drivers for a single device in its lifetime. The new device drivers may not be relevant to your installation, as their new features or fixes may not impact you. When evaluating device driver updates, consider the following questions:

▶ *Is the update a security update?* If it is, you will likely need to plan for the driver update in the near future.

▶ *Are you having stability or performance problems with the current driver?* If you are not and the update is not security related, you may be able to skip the driver update.

▶ *Do support contracts depend on updating the driver?* While it is not common, some support contracts will require that you update device drivers periodically.

If you review these questions and determine that you must update the device driver, you will need to perform the installation of the new driver. Like new driver installations, an update or upgrade of a driver may come as a self-installing executable or as a compressed archive containing the driver. To update an INF-based device driver (one that comes from the compressed archive), follow these steps:

1. Launch the Device Manager.

2. Locate the target device in the Device Manager pane.

3. Right-click the device and select Update Driver Software.

4. Choose Browse My Computer For Driver Software (see Figure 2.14).

5. Direct the wizard to the extracted driver location to perform the update.

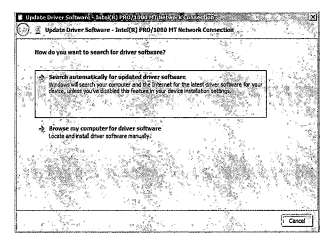

FIGURE 2.14 Performing a device driver update

At times, after upgrading a device driver, your system may begin to experience problems. In such scenarios, you have the capability to roll back the device driver. This action simply means that you are reverting the system to the previously installed device driver. It is like taking a new car for a test drive and then deciding to go home in your old car. The new car didn't quite work out (because of costs, features, or some other source of discontent). In the same way, you can upgrade a device driver and then later discover that it is not working properly. At that point you would roll back to the previous version of the device driver. If a driver update has not occurred, the option to roll back the driver will not be available. You can roll back a driver to a previous version with the following steps:

> You can only roll back a device driver when a new version has been installed on the server.

1. Launch the Device Manager.

2. Locate the target device in the Device Manager pane.

3. Right-click the device and select Properties.

4. On the Driver tab, if the button is available, choose Roll Back Driver (see Figure 2.15 and notice that the button is not available).

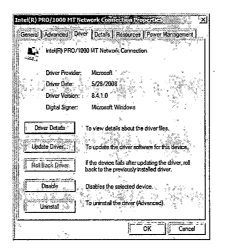

FIGURE 2.15 Checking to see if a device driver can be rolled back

In some scenarios, if you think that a device driver is causing problems on your server, you may need to troubleshoot further to be sure. If the driver is not essential to all operations (like the PCI bridge driver or storage controller driver), you can temporarily disable the driver and device to see if the problem is resolved. To disable a driver, follow these steps:

1. Launch the Device Manager.

2. Locate the target device in the Device Manager pane.

3. Right-click the device and select Properties.

4. On the Driver tab, click the Disable button.

If the issue is resolved by disabling the driver, you may need to remove it from your system all together. You also may need to remove a driver if you are no longer using the device for which the driver is intended. In either case, to remove a device driver, right-click on the device in the Device Manager and select Uninstall.

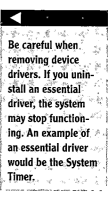

Be careful when removing device drivers. If you uninstall an essential driver, the system may stop functioning. An example of an essential driver would be the System Timer.

DRIVER SIGNING

In newer versions of Microsoft Windows, including both the client and server versions, device drivers may be signed. A signed device driver simply comes with a digital signature. To digitally sign a driver, the vendor must acquire a certificate from a trusted third-party (such as Verisign or Thawte). This certificate is then used to digitally sign the driver. You can verify the signature to ensure that the device driver you are using really came from the vendor.

When a device driver is signed from the vendor, it will install with no notifications. When a device driver is unsigned or is signed with an untrusted certificate, you will see a notification indicating such. If you see this notification, it does not mean that you cannot use the driver. It simply means that you must ensure the driver is safe and then force the operating system to install the driver even though it is not properly signed.

One major advantage of driver signing is that it allows nonadministrators to install drivers as long as they are signed. By default, unsigned device drivers can be installed only by an administrator.

Understanding Hardware Resources

Add-on components must have some method for communicating with the CPU in a server. Like desktop computers, servers use interrupt requests (IRQs) and I/O addresses for these communications. You can think of an I/O address much like your street address for your home. Just as the mail carrier requires the street address to get mail (messages) to your house, the CPU requires I/O addresses to get messages to a device.

The IRQ is used to get the attention of the CPU. When a device needs the attention of the CPU, it places voltage on the interrupt wire or connection to the

The IOAPIC receives interrupt requests from devices and sends them to the CPU. The CPU gets the IRQ from the IOAPIC so it can contact the appropriate device.

CPU. The interrupt wire connects the CPU to an I/O advanced programmable interrupt controller (IOAPIC), which is the proxy between the add-on devices and the CPU. All devices must have an IRQ associated with them so that the CPU knows which device is seeking attention based on the IRQ. For example, it is not uncommon for a network interface card to work on IRQ 19 and COM port 1 to work on IRQ 4. Table 2.2 lists common IRQ assignments in desktops and servers.

TABLE 2.2　Common IRQ Assignments

IRQ	Device
0	System Timer
1	Keyboard
2	A hook into IRQs 8–15 to allow more devices
3	COM 2
4	COM 1
5	LPT 2 or Audio
6	Floppy Disk
7	LPT 1
8	Real Time Clock
14	Primary Hard Disk Controller
15	Secondary Hard Disk Controller

IRQs provide the communications from the device to the CPU, but the CPU still requires a method for communicating with the devices. For this, the system uses I/O addresses. The I/O addresses are 32-bit addresses and look like those shown in Figure 2.16. To see that information, open Device Manager and click View ➢ Resources By Type.

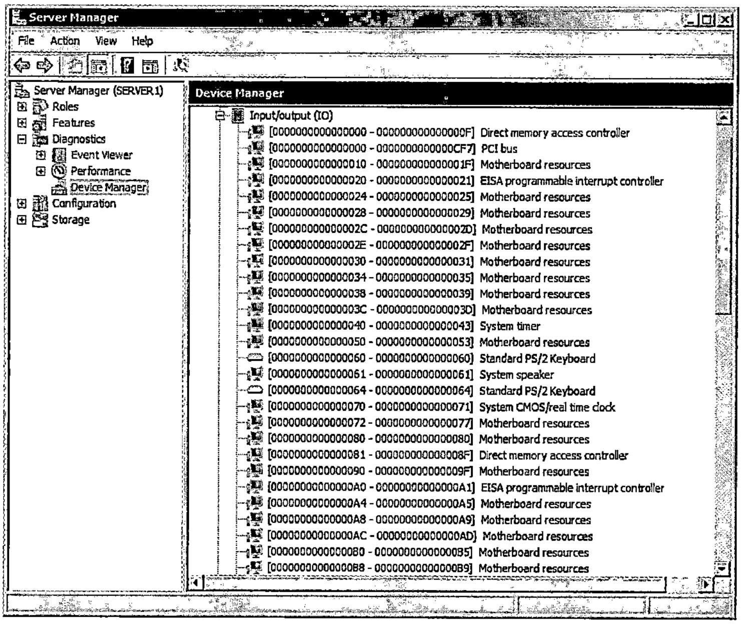

FIGURE 2.16 Viewing I/O addresses in the Device Manager

PLUG-AND-PLAY SAVES THE DAY

Plug-and-play technology was introduced in the 1990s. This technology allows automatic configuration of hardware resources. In the past, you often defined the IRQ and I/O addresses for devices using jumpers or dip switches on the physical adapter cards. Today, you simply plug it in and let the operating system do all the work for you.

Thanks to plug-and-play technology, we rarely have to configure IRQs today. The operating system configures these during startup so that the many devices in a system can work together in harmony. It is still possible that you could install more devices than the system can automatically configure. In such cases, you will need to use the Device Manager to determine which devices are in conflict. Thankfully, this problem is rare and systems usually work without resource conflicts.

THE ESSENTIALS AND BEYOND

Windows servers may be installed using interactive installations, unattended installations, or from Windows Deployment Servers (WDS). Interactive installations are common because many organizations have fewer than a dozen servers. In organizations with dozens or hundreds of servers, unattended installations are very useful because they save time during the installation process. You can also upgrade a server to Windows Server 2008 R2 as long as it is running Windows Server 2003 with SP2 or later and is a 64-bit edition of the server product. Windows Server Core installations, which provide a Command Prompt interface as the primary administrative method, provide streamlined operations, but also have limited support for server roles. Finally, one of the most troublesome aspects of operating system installation is acquiring the proper devices drivers. Windows servers have several benefits in this area, including the ability to install, upgrade, disable, and remove device drivers.

ADDITIONAL EXERCISES

▶ Install Windows Server 2008 R2 on a machine and go through the Initial Configuration Wizard.

▶ Perform a Server Core installation and use the `sconfig` command to perform initial configuration.

▶ Browse a vendor's website to see where you can retrieve device drivers for their server equipment.

▶ Review Microsoft's documentation on upgrading to Windows Server 2008 R2.

To compare your answers to the author's, please visit:

`www.sybex.com/go/networkingessentials`

REVIEW QUESTIONS

1. What kind of server is less likely to perform well in a virtual installation?

    A. Print servers   **C.** Domain Controllers

    B. Database servers   **D.** Web server

2. True or false: Virtualization helps to reduce power consumption in server rooms.

3. What is the minimum processor requirement for a Windows Server 2008 R2 installation when the processor is a dual-core processor?

    A. 1.4 GHz   **C.** 1 GHz

    B. 1.3 GHz   **D.** 2 GHz

THE ESSENTIALS AND BEYOND *(Continued)*

4. What is the minimum requirement for RAM for either Windows Server 2008 or Windows Server 2008 R2?

5. What keystroke sequence will display a Command Prompt window during the early stages of Windows Server installation?

   A. Ctrl+Shift+Esc   **C.** Shift+F10

   B. Ctrl+C   **D.** Shift+C

6. Define a device driver?

7. What does PXE stand for?

8. Which one of the following is not an initial configuration task?

   A. Configuring networking   **C.** Setting a computer name

   B. Configuring the date and time   **D.** Adding the Active Directory Domain Services role

9. What tool is used to create the unattend.xml answer file?

   A. Initial Configuration Wizard   **C.** Windows System Image Manager

   B. Microsoft Deployment Toolkit   **D.** Application Compatibility Toolkit

10. True or false: An unsigned driver is always just as safe as a signed driver.

CHAPTER 3

Managing Windows Server Storage

One of the primary reasons for using a server is the provisioning of centralized storage. Centralized storage can be used to provide file storage, data storage, and configuration storage for network connected devices. In addition to providing centralized storage for your networked computers, Windows servers must use storage for the operating system, applications, and services that they run.

In this chapter, you will learn about data storage concepts and the specific storage management features and tools available in Windows Server 2008 and Windows Server 2008 R2, including:

▷ **Data Storage Concepts**

▷ **Understanding RAID**

▷ **Identifying Storage Technologies**

▷ **Understanding Disk Types**

Data Storage Concepts

You need to understand several different technologies so that you can plan and implement storage solutions for Windows servers. First, you must understand the physical devices used for storage, primarily hard drives. Second, you should understand the way in which data is stored on these hard drives, which means you need to understand file systems. Finally, you should understand the technologies, such as Distributed File System and network storage mechanisms, that utilize hard drives and file systems. The primary focus of this section is on defining these concepts. A later section, titled "Identifying Storage Technologies," will provide more detail on specific hard drive types and network storage types.

Selecting Hard Drives for Your Network

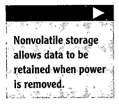

Hard drives (or hard disks) provide nonvolatile storage of data. *Volatile* storage loses all data when power is removed. *Nonvolatile* storage retains data even if power is removed. Volatile storage includes:

System RAM   The internal memory of a computer

Video RAM   The memory used for video processing

Nonvolatile storage includes:

Hard Drives   The internal and external disks with large storage capacity

Flash Drives   An external drive that is typically a USB drive with small to medium storage capacity

NVRAM   The internal storage chips used for system BIOS settings

Traditional hard drives use moving platters for data storage. These platters are simply spinning disks used to store the actual data. Such a device consists of a motor, spindle, platters, read/write heads, and electronics. The motor spins the spindle so that the read/write heads can read and write data from and to the platters. The electronics include a printed circuit board (PCB) and various chips for drive operations. Some drives have all of the electronics integrated and others rely on controllers to send commands to the drive for normal operations.

SOLID STATE DRIVES

Newer technology, called *solid state drive* (SSD) technology, uses nonmoving storage. SSD is far more expensive than traditional storage hard drives and is not currently used for typical server storage solutions. SSD may be used for the operating system drive, but it is rarely used for data storage due to high costs per gigabyte of storage. Modern servers must store thousands of gigabytes of data, and cost is a significant factor when you're deciding whether to use SSD technology or traditional storage.

The best hard drive for your needs depends on the answers to the following questions:

▶ What storage capacity is required?

▶ What read and write speeds are required?

► What hard drive types are supported by the drive system?

► How many drive bays or drive connections are provided?

The first step is to clearly define the required storage capacity. When selecting the drive for operating system installation, you can define this requirement based on the operating system vendor's recommendations. When selecting a drive for data storage, you must estimate the amount of data that will be stored on the drive.

Once you've determined the capacity requirements, you must define the drive speed requirements, measured as *revolutions per minute* (RPM). Within each type of hard drive are variable speeds. For example, the *serial advanced technology attachment* (SATA) hard drives commonly come in 4,200 RPM, 5,400 RPM, 7,200 RPM, and 10,000 RPM speeds. The newer SATA drives can even support 15,000 RPM rates. The RPM rate has a direct correlation to the speed of the drive. During each revolution, only so much data can be read. The higher RPM drives will read data faster because they read the same amount of data per revolution as the lower RPM drives, but many more times per minute. Drives with a higher RPM are typically more expensive, so your budget may also help define the speed you select.

Several different hard drive types have been developed over the years. The following sections describe the newer standards that are still supported today:

Integrated Drive Electronics (IDE) IDE was the first version of a hard drive technology that later become known as AT attachment. It was very popular in the mid-90s and is still supported by many production servers. It is often used for optical drive connections, but the newest servers no longer support it for hard drive connections.

ATA The advanced technology attachment (ATA) technology was later renamed to Parallel ATA (PATA) to differentiate it from SATA technologies. Like IDE, ATA drives are falling out of popularity, but may still be seen in some older servers that remain in production.

SATA Serial advanced technology attachment (SATA) is still widely supported in servers. It has speeds that are comparable to SCSI drives with speeds ranging from 1.5 Gbps (SATA 1.0) to 6 Gbps (SATA 3.0). SATA drives are supported in both server and desktop computers, and many SATA RAID controllers are available for RAID implementation. External SATA (eSATA) drives may be connected using external connectors on the computer. SATA has replaced PATA in both clients and servers today.

◄

All else being equal, a drive with higher RPM ratings will provide faster data access.

SCSI   Small computer system interface (SCSI) is a peripheral connection technology. It is not used for storage drives alone, but can also be used for scanners and other devices. SCSI drives come in many versions, but the Ultra-640 SCSI version can support speeds up to approximately 5 Gbps. SCSI commands are used across TCP/IP connections when iSCSI is used.

Removable Storage   In addition to SATA and SCSI drives, many removable drive form factors are supported. The most common removable drive form factors are USB and FireWire. eSATA is also growing in popularity. For lower storage capacity drives, flash-based media is very popular. Flash-based media includes USB flash drives, CompactFlash (CF), and Secure Digital (SD) storage.

Of course, you can only use drive types that are supported by the target system. The target system may be the actual server (when selecting internal storage) or a dedicated storage system (when selecting external storage). In either case, you must use the supported drive types. If the storage system supports only *small computer system interface* (SCSI, pronounced "skuzzy") drives, you must select SCSI drives of the size and speed you require.

The final factor is the number of drives the target system supports. Most servers have at least two hard drive bays, and some will have six or more. When the server does not have sufficient internal drive bays, you can select external storage solutions that connect to the server through *universal serial bus* (USB), *external SATA* (eSATA), SCSI, or *FireWire* connections. In many cases, external storage solutions are preferable to internal storage solutions because the external system can be accessed by more than one server.

Choosing a File System

A file system defines the way in which data is placed on a storage medium and the file access methods used. For example, the file system defines the minimum data size that must be written to the drive and the method used to index the data on the drive. The minimum data size used for storage is known as the cluster size or the allocation unit size. The index of the data is the file table, which tracks the files on the drive and the storage locations used for those files.

Windows servers support two primary file systems: FAT and NTFS. The file allocation table (FAT) file system is the older of the two, and the NT file system (with the NT characters coming from the Windows NT operating system for which it was originally created) is the newer. FAT is a simple file system, and NTFS is a more complex file system offering advanced features, including security. Table 3.1 compares the features of the FAT and NTFS file systems.

The FAT file system has been with us since the 1980s. The NTFS file system has existed since the release of Windows NT 3.1 in 1993.

TABLE 3.1   FAT and NTFS File Systems Comparison

FAT (File Allocation Table)	NTFS (NT File System)
Maximum volume size of 2 terabytes with FAT32 or 4 gigabytes with FAT16	Maximum volume size of 256 terabytes with a 64 KB cluster size (when using the master boot record partition table, this is limited to 2 terabytes)
Maximum file size of 4 GB	Maximum file size of approximately 16 terabytes
Up to 4.2 million files per volume	Up to 4.3 billion files per volume
File attributes provide limited security	NTFS permissions provide advanced security
No sparse file support	Sparse files are supported
Best performance on smaller drives	Best performance on larger drives
No inherent support for encryption	Built-in data encryption support, using the Encrypting File System (EFS)

Although Microsoft's new *extended FAT* (exFAT) file system is sometimes referred to as *FAT64*, this isn't a Microsoft-supported name. exFAT overcomes the 4 GB limit of FAT volumes, but it is intended for removable storage devices.

A mount point is an additional feature of NTFS, which was introduced with the release of Windows 2000 Professional and Windows 2000 Server. A *mount point* is a directory or folder on an existing volume that actually points to another volume on the same physical drive or a separate physical drive. Mount points allow you to add storage to an existing drive letter through the use of a folder on that drive. Applications are unaware that the folder is actually a reference to a completely separate storage volume.

When selecting a file system, be sure to check the software vendor's literature. To perform properly, some applications may require either FAT or NTFS. In some cases, you may have to create a special FAT16 or FAT32 volume on a drive just to support a specific application, although this has become less common today.

Understanding Networked Storage

Modern networks demand more storage space than ever before. You may be required to support storage for thousands of users and hundreds of applications.

In such environments, using the built-in server storage may be insufficient. Networked storage provides a viable solution.

Networked storage systems come in two basic implementations:

▶ Network attached storage (NAS)

▶ Storage area network (SAN)

These two technologies are very different, and you must understand them so you can choose the right technology for a given scenario.

NAS solutions are really nothing more than dedicated file servers. You can purchase NAS devices at consumer electronics stores, and you can purchase more advanced NAS devices directly from vendors such as HP and IBM. Advanced NAS devices support internal drive redundancy and special communications protocols; however, they are accessed using communications protocols that run across your existing network. In other words, NAS devices are accessed using standard network communications—in most cases, on the same network as all other network communications. Although NAS devices could be implemented on a dedicated Ethernet network separate from the user access network through the use of multiple network adapters in a server, the performance will still not equal that of a SAN.

A SAN uses block-level access across the network, which means that it reads and writes blocks of data instead of entire files. NAS devices typically read and write entire files. This is a key difference between the two. Special protocols are implemented to provide far better performance than that which can be provided by a NAS device. Two major SAN solutions are common today:

▶ Fibre Channel

▶ iSCSI

> The Fibre Channel and iSCSI solutions are discussed in more detail later in this chapter in the section titled "Identifying Storage Technologies."

Using the Distributed File System

In addition to storage hardware, such as internal hard drives and networked storage, you need to consider storage-related software when planning your storage solutions. Microsoft provides a storage solution called the *Distributed File System* (DFS), which is used to distribute files across multiple servers or to aggregate files that exist on multiple servers.

DFS can distribute files across multiple servers using the File Replication Service (FRS). Users place files into a share, and the FRS automatically copies those files to multiple locations as defined by DFS. This allows files to be

> The Distributed Files System (DFS) can be used to replicate files to multiple locations and to aggregate files from multiple locations into one virtual share.

distributed to locations that are closer to the users who need the files, as shown in Figure 3.1.

FIGURE 3.1 DFS used to distribute files to multiple locations

DFS can also aggregate files that exist on multiple servers into a single virtual location. For example, notice that Figure 3.2 shows multiple file shares on multiple physical servers. After DFS replication, all of these shares appear as subfolders in the DFS root share on Server1. This DFS-provided aggregation makes file access simpler for the network users.

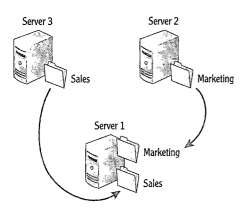

FIGURE 3.2 DFS used to aggregate files from multiple shares into a single virtual location

When DFS is used to aggregate multiple shares into a single virtual location, the files still exist in the individual shares but they appear to be in a single location to the users. This single location is the DFS root. The access to the actual shares is made transparent to the users. This functionality simplifies access for users and provides simpler administration for applications as well. For example, an application may require access to multiple files. For performance reasons, you may want to place some files on one server and other files on another server. DFS can be used to make those files appear to be in a single location for the application.

Understanding RAID

Redundant array of independent disks (RAID) is an internal or external storage technology that uses an array of hard disks and may be hardware or software based. Hardware-based RAID uses hardware drive controllers that have built-in RAID processing software. Software-based RAID uses standard hard drive controllers and handles the RAID processing as a software layer that is either built into the operating system or is installed as an extra feature.

RAID is often said to stand for either Redundant Array of Independent Disks or Redundant Array of Inexpensive Disks. Regardless of the acronym's meaning, RAID always involves an array of disks.

The phrase *RAID level* is used to define the different implementations of RAID. Many different RAID levels exist, but the most commonly used RAID levels are listed here:

- ▶ RAID 0
- ▶ RAID 1
- ▶ RAID 5
- ▶ RAID 0+1
- ▶ RAID 1+0 or RAID 10

Figure 3.3 shows the various RAID levels in a graphical representation. RAID 0 is depicted as three physical drives acting as one logical drive. Under the hood, data is *striped* (written) evenly across the three drives. For example, if 99 KB of data is being written to drive D using RAID 0, one third would be written to Drive 1, one third to Drive 2, and the final third to Drive 3. No fault tolerance is provided by RAID 0 alone. RAID 0 is used only to improve read and write performance, and it is typically referred to as a *striped set*.

Parity is a mathematically calculated value used to regenerate missing data. Fault tolerant RAID uses parity bits for recoverability.

Most controllers require a minimum of two drives to create a stripe set without parity or a RAID 0 array. Some will require three drives in the array. The drawbacks of RAID 0 include the fact that one drive failure makes the entire array unavailable and that the large amount of storage represented by the individual physical drives aggregates into one very large, possibly difficult to manage, storage location. The positives include faster data reads and writes because the data is spread across multiple drives that can be simultaneously accessed, as well as complete availability of the drive space from the hard drives included in the array.

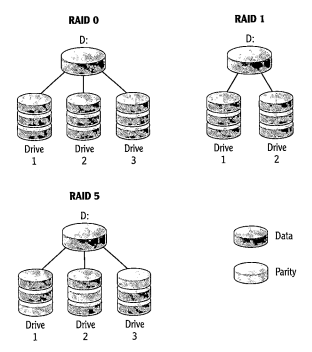

FIGURE 3.3 RAID levels 0, 1, and 5

The next level of RAID represented in Figure 3.3 is RAID level 1. At level 1, data is mirrored across two physical drives. If the RAID is implemented through hardware as opposed to software, users and applications see only a single logical drive at the operating system level. When RAID is implemented through software, the operating system sees the separate drives (in tools like Disk Management). RAID 1 provides fault tolerance through the fact that all data is written twice:

▶ The data is written to the "visible" drive, called the *primary drive* in the mirror set.

▶ The data is also written to the "invisible" drive, called the *mirror drive* in the set.

There is no striping of data during writes, but some RAID controllers (hardware drive controllers that support RAID configurations) will read the data from both drives. RAID 1 is used to provide fault tolerance and quick failover. The negatives of RAID 1 include the loss of half of your storage space and the reduced performance of writes. The positive is that RAID 1 provides the highest level of data availability because all the data is completely written to two separate physical devices.

Fault-tolerance is the ability to handle a failure or a fault and continue operations. Failover occurs when a secondary device is enabled automatically to continue operations when a primary device fails.

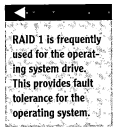

RAID 1 is frequently used for the operating system drive. This provides fault tolerance for the operating system.

RAID 5 attempts to balance RAID 0 and 1. RAID 5 arrays stripe data across the drives in the array. However, unlike RAID 0, RAID 5 arrays also provide fault tolerance. This is done through the generation of *parity bits*. For example, assume there are three physical drives that make up the logical drive array. When data is written to the array, half the data will be written to one drive, half the data to another, and then parity bits will be written to the third drive. In most implementations, the parity bits are stored evenly across the drives in the array. Now, if any single physical drive fails, the controller or software can regenerate the data that was stored on the failed drive from the parity stored on the remaining drives. This regeneration generally occurs on-the-fly with no administrative intervention. Of course, should another drive fail at this time, the entire array will be lost.

Because parity bits are used with RAID 5, it requires a minimum of three drives: Two drives store the data and one drive stores the parity bits. Most implementations rotate the parity bits across the drives for each write operation. If a drive fails, it should be replaced as soon as possible and then the RAID solution can rebuild the data that was lost onto the new drive.

To understand how RAID 5 functions, consider a simple analogy. Imagine you have the numbers 5 and 7 that you want to store. If you store 5 in one notebook and 7 in another, when either notebook is lost, you've lost the ability to recover all of your meaningful data. However, imagine you have a third notebook. In this third notebook, you store the number 12 (5+7). Now, if you lose one of the three notebooks, you will always be able to get your data back. For example, if you lose notebook two, you can subtract 5 (the number in notebook 1) from 12 and recover the number 7 that was in the second notebook. While RAID 5 striping and parity algorithms are more complex than this analogy, it should help you conceptualize how the RAID level functions. It is also important to keep in mind that when you add more drives to your system, you increase the likelihood that one of those drives will fail on any given day and actually increase the need for fault tolerance.

RAID 0+1 combines the stripe sets with mirroring. First, you would configure two stripe sets first and then configure those two stripe sets to appear as one drive that is a RAID 1 implementation. For example, you might have three drives in each stripe set and in the end, all six drives will appear as one virtual drive. This gives you a balance between the performance of RAID 0 and the complete fault tolerance of RAID 1.

RAID 1+0, also known as RAID 10, is just the opposite of RAID 0+1. In this case, you will actually implement two or three mirror sets and then stripe data across those mirror sets. This provides fault tolerance as the foundation and performance as an added layer.

RAID 0 is a stripe set without parity. RAID 1 is mirroring. RAID 5 is a stripe set with parity.

When using drive arrays, the likelihood of one of the drives failing is increased due to the simple reality that you are running multiple drives. Increased heat can also increase the likelihood of failure.

Understanding the various levels of RAID is important. As you make decisions related to the server hardware that you purchase, this knowledge and understanding will prove useful. If you determine that you need fault tolerance at the drive level, you will want to purchase a server that provides this feature through hardware. Although you can implement RAID through software, the performance is not generally as high and it will take away processing power from the server itself.

HARDWARE RAID VERSUS SOFTWARE RAID

Software-based RAID levels 0, 1, and 5 are supported through the Disk Management snap-in in Windows Server. When you implement RAID in this way, you are implementing software-based RAID, which means that the RAID operations are handled through an operating system driver and not through hardware processes. Hardware-based RAID is handled within the RAID controller and is typically configured through a special application provided by the hardware vendor.

Hardware-based RAID is preferred over software-based RAID for performance reasons. When a hardware RAID controller is used, it has a processor that performs the RAID operations. In other words, the computer's CPU is not used to separate the data for striping or to generate the parity bits for RAID calculations, and the computer's CPU is not required to regenerate data in a RAID 5 array when a single drive fails.

Software-based RAID is useful for stripe sets or mirror sets because they are not as CPU intensive as RAID 5 arrays; however, hardware-based arrays are still preferred even in these scenarios. I typically use software-based RAID for educational purposes and the implementation of lab environments. I use hardware-based RAID for production implementations whenever possible.

Identifying Storage Technologies

At this point, the storage concepts have been addressed and you understand hard drives, file systems, networked storage, and specialized storage solutions such as the Distributed File System and RAID. Now, it's time to explore the different networked storage solutions that you may choose to implement in greater detail.

Networked Storage Solutions

Earlier in this chapter, NAS and SAN storage solutions were briefly defined. In this section, I will address NAS and SAN storage in more detail. First, you will learn about the Network File System (NFS), which is often supported by NAS devices. Then you will learn about the hardware required to implement SAN solutions such as Fibre Channel and iSCSI.

NFS is the file system most often used with NAS devices. While many NAS devices support operating as *server message block* (SMB) share servers, they also typically support NFS. NFS was originally developed by Sun Microsystems and is an open standard defined in RFCs today. RFC 1090 defines the NFS version 2 standard, RFC 1813 defines the NFS version 3 standard, and RFC 3010 defines the NFS version 4 standard.

NFS runs across TCP and UDP (Used Datagram Protocol), meaning that it is an OSI Model Layer 5 and upward technology that relies on the IP infrastructure for communications. This is a key area of difference between NAS and SAN solutions. Most SAN solutions use specialized adapter cards to communicate with the SAN. NAS typically uses the same network adapter to communicate with the NFS server as is used to communicate with all other network services. The result is typically inferior performance to SANs. However, NFS does allow remote directories to be mounted to local directories and appear as if they are part of the local file system on a machine. This is similar to the way SMB works for Windows shares, with the exception of data writing granularity. NFS supports granular data writes at the block level, while SMB only supports complete file writes to the server.

Fibre Channel is a SAN technology that uses special adapters known as *host bus adapters* (HBAs). HBAs are basically network adapters that are specially designed to communicate with the Fibre Channel SAN. Fibre Channel offers very high-speed communications with the SAN and true block-level access so that drives can be written to and read from as if they were internal drives. In fact, Windows servers use special drivers for Fibre Channel SAN access that make the SAN appear to be normal local storage in applications and file management software.

In larger implementations, Fibre Channel switches are used to build a more complex SAN infrastructure. The switches provide access to the storage so that the clients (the servers accessing the SAN) do not have to be aware of the actual drives that are being accessed.

> ▶
>
> SMB is the protocol used for Microsoft servers to provide and access shared folders on the network.

iSCSI is an implementation of the SCSI storage system across the internetwork. iSCSI uses TCP/IP protocols, including TCP and UDP, to access the SAN. In the best performing implementations, special iSCSI network adapters are installed in the servers so that the iSCSI communications are offloaded from the system CPU and memory. This allows for high-speed iSCSI communications. In most cases, a dedicated TCP/IP network is created for iSCSI communications between the servers and the iSCSI SAN.

Understanding Disk Types

The Windows operating systems, including both servers and clients, support three disk types for hard drive access. The first two types define the way in which a standard internal hard drive is used. The third type defines a file that is mounted as a hard drive. In addition to the three hard drive types, Windows operating systems can use optical media, which you also need to understand.

Basic and Dynamic Disks

When you initialize a new hard drive in a Windows operating system, the disk type for the hard drive needs to be specified before logical partitions or volumes can be created and formatted for use. Windows operating systems support either basic or dynamic disk types. Depending on the features you require, you can choose how to configure your disks within the Disk Management utility.

Basic disks provide the basic features and functions required for typical storage tasks. For this reason, they are the most common disk type used. A basic disk contains partitions, which may include up to four primary partitions or three primary partitions and one extended partition. An extended partition can be divided into additional logical disk drives. When the partitions or logical drives are formatted with a file system, such as FAT or NTFS, they are called *volumes*. When formatted with NTFS, volumes on basic disks can be expanded to include space from other partitions or logical disks on the same physical disk.

◄

Basic disks support the most commonly used features of Windows servers when software-based RAID is not required.

Some tasks can be performed on a basic disk that cannot be performed on a dynamic disk:

- ► Creating and deleting primary or extended partitions
- ► Creating and deleting logical drives

- ▶ Formatting partitions

- ▶ Marking partitions as active

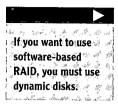

If you want to use software-based RAID, you must use dynamic disks.

Dynamic disks, which were a new feature in Windows 2000, provide several features not available in basic disks. The most important feature that dynamic disks support is software-based RAID. If you want to implement RAID arrays using software, the disks used in the array must be dynamic disks.

The following tasks can be performed only on dynamic disks:

- ▶ Creating RAID volumes

- ▶ Creating spanned volumes (non-RAID arrays that use space from multiple disks)

- ▶ Extending spanned volumes

- ▶ Repairing RAID 1 and RAID 5 arrays

- ▶ Breaking a mirror array

- ▶ Reactivating missing or offline disks in arrays

Regardless of the disk-level management features you want to implement, the Disk Management utility is used to perform the tasks. To access Disk Management, click Start, right-click Computer, select Manage, and then expand the Storage node. Figure 3.4 shows the Disk Management tool.

FIGURE 3.4 The Disk Management utility with a basic disk

Virtual Hard Disks

Virtual Hard Disk (VHD) files have been used with virtualization systems such as VMware and Hyper-V for several years. VHD files are data files on a physical hard disk that are used as hard drives within virtual machines. Windows 7 and Windows Server 2008 R2 introduced the ability to mount a VHD file as a hard drive within the operating system as if it were a physical drive. You can even boot an operating system, such as Windows Server 2008 R2 or Windows 7, from a VHD file that is stored on the local disk. Additionally, the Disk Management tool can now be used to create a VHD file using the following steps:

1. Launch the Disk Management utility:

   a. Click Start.

   b. Right-click Computer and select Manage.

   c. Expand the Storage node.

2. Right-click the Disk Management node and select Create VHD.

3. In the Create And Attach Virtual Hard Disk windows, choose the location for the VHD file and the size of the drive.

4. Choose whether the drive should immediately consume the required space (Fixed) or consume space only as data is placed into the VHD file (Dynamically expanding), as shown in Figure 3.5.

5. Click OK when completed.

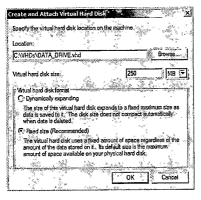

FIGURE 3.5 Creating a new VHD file in Disk Management

When the system finishes creating the VHD file, it will be mounted automatically. You can then initialize the disk and create a volume on it for data storage. Because the drive is really a VHD file, you can easily dismount it (right-click the disk and select Detach VHD). One huge benefit in using VHD files to store data content is that once they are dismounted, they can be copied to another server and then mounted for use on the new server.

Optical Media

In addition to the hard drive storage technologies discussed throughout this chapter, Windows servers support the same optical media as Windows clients. If you can use a particular optical drive in a Windows Vista or Windows 7 client, it can most likely be used in a Windows Server 2008 or Windows Server 2008 R2 server as well. Of course, the server must provide the drive bay space for the optical drive, but the server operating system has always supported the same optical drive types that the client operating system has supported. Today, you can use CD-ROM, DVD, and Blu-Ray drives in Windows servers. In fact, Blue-Ray writers are becoming more and more popular as backup devices for servers. With 50 GB of storage available on dual-layer Blu-Ray discs, they are very useful as a backup solution. A newer Blu-Ray specification (Blu-Ray Disk XL) provides up to 128 GB of storage.

THE ESSENTIALS AND BEYOND

Windows servers support the same storage solutions as Windows clients with additional support for enhanced network storage features, such as the Distributed File System. Storage may be implemented as internal, external, and networked storage. Internal storage is usually implemented with hard drives. Hard drives come in many different sizes and form factors, and they should be selected based on storage requirements and performance requirements. Networked storage includes both network attached storage (NAS) and storage area networks (SANs). The FAT file system does not offer the security enhancements offered by the NTFS file system. When implementing internal storage, you must choose between basic and dynamic disks. In most cases, basic disks are used unless software-based RAID is required.

RAID provides fault tolerance or improved performance, and it can be implemented in several different levels. RAID level 0 provides improved performance using at least two drives as a stripe set. RAID level 1 provides fault tolerance using two drives as a mirror set. RAID level 5 provides improved performance and fault tolerance using at least three drives in a stripe set with parity.

THE ESSENTIALS AND BEYOND *(Continued)*

ADDITIONAL EXERCISES

▶ Research the different speeds available in SATA storage solutions.

▶ Browse the features of a vendor's SAN solutions.

▶ View the file system used for a drive on Windows Server 2008 R2.

▶ Create and mount a VHD file in Windows Server 2008 R2.

To compare your answers to the author's, please visit www.sybex.com/go/serveradminessentials.

REVIEW QUESTIONS

1. What file system supports the use of EFS?

    A. FAT   **C.** exFAT

    B. FAT32   **D.** NTFS

2. True or false: exFAT is primarily used for removable media.

3. What kind of storage solution provides block-level access across the network in every implementation?

    A. NAS   **C.** SATA

    B. SAN   **D.** SCSI

4. What level of RAID provides mirroring on the drives?

5. Why is software-based RAID inferior to hardware-based RAID?

    A. Because software-based RAID does not support the same RAID levels

    C. Because software-based RAID has a dedicated hardware CPU for RAID processing

    B. Because software-based RAID requires the computer's CPU for RAID processing

    D. Because hardware-based RAID is less expensive

6. What type of disk must be used in order to implement software-based RAID in a Windows operating system?

7. What Microsoft services can be used to aggregate multiple server shares into one virtual location for user access?

8. What is the maximum file size on FAT file system drives?

    A. 4 terabytes   **C.** 4 kilobytes

    B. 4 megabytes   **D.** 4 gigabytes

(Continues)

THE ESSENTIALS AND BEYOND *(Continued)*

9. What is the adapter called that provides access to a Fibre Channel SAN?

    A. NIC   **C.** SCSI

    B. HBA   **D.** NAS

10. True or false: You can create a primary partition on a dynamic disk.

CHAPTER 4

Administering Services

If a server does not offer services, it provides no value. The entire purpose for a server's existence is to offer services. While these statements may seem excessively philosophical and insufficiently technical, they are important none-theless. If you hope to have a career in computing technology or a career that depends on computing proficiency, you must remember to keep these truths in mind. They will help you implement technology with reduced costs and greater efficiency because you will only implement technologies that provide value to the organization. The concept of the *service* is internal to the very name of the entity: *server.* A service serves. For this reason, I've chosen to cover services in this chapter—very early in the book.

This chapter is all about the services that servers provide. You will learn what a service really is in the context of a Windows server, and you will learn how to manage these services. To help you understand these concepts, the following topics will be addressed:

▷ **Services Defined**

▷ **Service Configuration**

▷ **Service Management**

▷ **Troubleshooting Service Problems**

Understanding Services

If you want to understand services, you must have a clear definition of what a service is in the forefront of your mind. Additionally, you can understand services better by reviewing examples of services and the functions they provide to the system or network they serve. You will learn what services are in the section "Applications as Services." Then you will explore important Windows services as well as add-on services available for the Windows Server operating system.

Applications as Services

A *service* is an application or innate operating-system component that runs on a computer and provides services to the local machine, the networked devices, or both. In most cases, services run in the background, meaning that they do not have a visual interface that you can see on the server's Desktop. Although a few services may be exceptions to this rule, they are also exceptions to the common practice of service development. The service itself should not be confused with the service management tools or interfaces that allow administrators to configure the service.

Windows servers come with many services built-in and others that can be installed as needed. You can install these extra services so that they may provide functions or capabilities to networked computers or the local server. In many cases, you will not even have to install the service. Dozens of services are installed on the server (built-in) by default, and they require only that you enable them to use them. This is true for both Windows servers and Windows clients. In fact, many services are shared between the Windows servers and clients and perform the same functions for each.

Additional services may be added to Windows. In the later section titled "Add-On Services," you will read about commercial services that must be purchased to run on the network and free services that can be downloaded and installed without cost-based licensing.

> Windows 7 clients and Windows Server 2008 servers run many of the same services. A Windows server runs the same base operating system code as a Windows client and shares many features and services.

SERVICE INSTALLATION PROCESSES

Services can be installed in several different ways on a Windows server. They may require installation procedures similar to applications on client computers, or they may be installed through specialized interfaces.

Services that are installed as supporting components for server roles and server features are installed through the Server Manager application. These services are installed automatically when you use the Add Role or Add Feature wizards. After adding the role or feature, you may be required to configure the service before it actually begins running on the server.

Services that come pre-installed with the operating system only need to be enabled. You can configure these services to start automatically when the operating system loads, or you can start them manually every time you want to use them. In most cases, pre-installed services cannot be removed from the operating system.

(Continues)

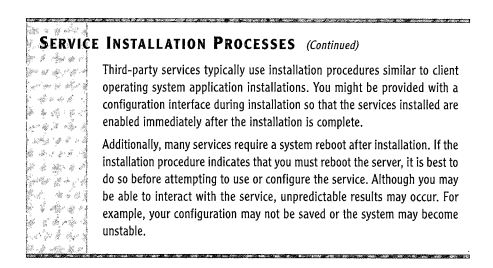

SERVICE INSTALLATION PROCESSES *(Continued)*

Third-party services typically use installation procedures similar to client operating system application installations. You might be provided with a configuration interface during installation so that the services installed are enabled immediately after the installation is complete.

Additionally, many services require a system reboot after installation. If the installation procedure indicates that you must reboot the server, it is best to do so before attempting to use or configure the service. Although you may be able to interact with the service, unpredictable results may occur. For example, your configuration may not be saved or the system may become unstable.

Important Windows Services

Windows servers have many services pre-installed. Covering each service in great detail is beyond the scope of this book, but it is important that you understand the purpose of several services. The following services are covered in detail because of their fundamentals importance to the operations of a Windows server. They are listed in alphabetical order so that no unintended level of importance can be placed on any single service.

Application Identity   The Application Identity service is required for AppLocker policies to be processed. AppLocker is a new software control solution first made available in Windows 7 and Windows Server 2008 R2. It can be used to disallow the execution of specified applications through rules configured within Group Policies.

Background Intelligent Transfer Service (BITS)   BITS is a service that allows data to be transferred across the network in the background. The data is transferred during idle times so that the transfers do not interfere with user-requested network operations. One of the primary uses of BITS is for Windows updates. The Windows Update process uses BITS for file transfer.

Cryptographic Services   The Cryptographic Services service provides for the management of certificates. Certificates are used to provide authentication and encryption in secure systems. The service is used frequently in Windows operating systems because it is needed to validate the digital signatures of signed device drivers and application software.

Dynamic Host Configuration Protocol (DHCP) Client   The DHCP Client service is used to acquire an IP configuration from a DHCP server. The client is needed on Windows Server 2003 R2 and earlier servers even if static IP addresses are used because the DHCP Client service is also responsible for registering the server's hostname with the dynamic DNS servers used by Active Directory Domain Services on these older versions.

> The Active Directory Domain Services (AD DS) server role is covered in detail in Chapters 5 through 7. Dynamic DNS plays an important role in AD DS implementations.

Disk Defragmenter   The Disk Defragmenter service is new to Windows 7 and Windows Server 2008 R2, and it provides disk defragmentation functions as a scheduled process. When a third-party defragmentation solution is used, this service should be disabled.

DNS Client   The DNS Client service is responsible for Domain Name System (DNS) name resolution. It resolves domain names to IP addresses and stores the results in the DNS cache on the local machine. If this service is disabled, DNS name resolution will still occur, but the cache will not be updated. This service does not register the local server's hostname with a dynamic DNS server on Windows Server 2003 R2 and earlier versions of Windows Server. It does perform the hostname registration task on Windows Server 2008 and later versions.

Encrypting File System (EFS)   The EFS service provides the functionality required to implement encryption on the NTFS files system. If the service is not running, users will be unable to access data encrypted with EFS.

Extensible Authentication Protocol (EAP)   First added in Windows Vista and Windows Server 2008, the EAP service provides port-based 802.1X authentication for wired and wireless networks, Virtual Private Networks (VPNs), and Network Access Protection (NAP).

> Network Access Protection (NAP) is used to test the health of a computer before allowing it to access the network. For example, NAP may verify antivirus software is installed with updated virus definitions.

Group Policy Client   Group Policy is used to centrally manage computers by applying policies to them that configure or control their capabilities. Windows Vista and Windows Server 2008 introduced new Group Policy capabilities called Group Policy Preferences. The newly introduced Group Policy Client service provides support for these enhancements and other new features that are not supported in earlier versions of the Windows client and server operating systems.

IKE and AuthIP IPsec Keying Modules   The IKE and AuthIP IPSec Keying Modules (IAIKM) service provides modules for Internet Key Exchange (IKE) and the Authenticated Internet Protocol (AuthIP). The modules are used for key exchange and authentication when the IP Security (IPSec) protocol is used for network communications security. This service is required for proper IPSec operations.

IP Helper   The IP Helper service was first introduced in Windows Vista and Windows Server 2008 and provides tunnel connectivity using IP version 6 (IPv6) transition solutions. These transition solutions include 6-to-4, ISATAP, and Teredo. Tunneling solutions simply allow IPv6 communications to be transmitted across IPv4 networks.

IPSec Policy Agent   Windows Server operating systems include a Microsoft Management Console (MMC) snap-in called the IP Security Policies snap-in. With this tool, you can create IPSec policies for network-level authentication, data integrity, data source authentication, encryption, and protection from replay attacks. The policies are then processed and enforced by this service.

Link-Layer Topology Discovery Mapper   In the Network and Sharing Center, you may view a map of your network. The feature is disabled by default (it is set to Manual, but the service itself is off or disabled) on AD DS member computers, but it may be enabled by the administrator through Group Policies. The Link-Layer Topology Discovery Mapper service is responsible for building this map. It collects PC and device topology (infrastructure devices such as switches and routers) information and descriptive data related to each PC and infrastructure device.

Netlogon   The Netlogon service is used to log on to an AD DS domain. Without this service, you cannot join a machine to a domain. Servers installed as part of a workgroup or home network do not require this service.

A replay attack occurs when an attacker sniffs (reads) a network packet off of the network and then plays the packet back onto the network with possible alterations to the packet contents.

Print Spooler   The Print Spooler service is used to provide local and network printing queue so that a single printer can handle more print jobs than its internal memory would allow. When used on a server to share a printer, the server spools the print job on behalf of the clients. On servers that do not provide printing services and from which you rarely print locally, this service can be safely stopped. You can later start the service, if you need to print, and all installed printers will still be available.

Remote Desktop Services   The Remote Desktop Services service must be running to allow a user to control the Windows Server Desktop across the network. Through this service, a user can log on to the Windows Server Desktop using the Remote Desktop Connection client. The user can control the Desktop using her keyboard and mouse as if she is sitting at the server locally.

Remote Registry   The Remote Registry service has been available since Windows 95 and Windows NT 4.0 were released in the mid-1990s. The service allows remote access to the Windows Registry, which is the central configuration database for the operating system and applications. Using the Registry

Editor, you can connect to other remote computers running the Remote Registry service, if you have the appropriate permissions.

Server   The Server service allows for sharing of printers, files, and named-pipes across the network. The Server service implements the Server Message Block (SMB) protocol. The Server service is the peer to the Workstation service. Both the Server service and the Workstation servers are typically enabled on all Windows clients and servers.

Task Scheduler   The Task Scheduler service monitors for scheduled tasks and executes them at the defined time. Many scheduled tasks are built into the Windows operating system. For example, by default, every Wednesday at 1:00 A.M., the disks are defragmented. Additionally, every 14 days, a power efficiency analysis is executed to discovery potential conditions causing overconsumption of power. Figure 4.1 shows the Task Scheduler tasks on a Windows Server installation.

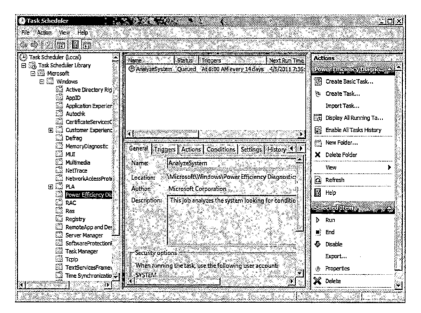

FIGURE 4.1   Viewing the Task Scheduler tasks on Windows Server 2008 R2

Volume Shadow Copy   The Volume Shadow Copy service provides the background backup processes used by shadow copies and other backup services. Shadow copies of files allow for recovery of previous file versions. Volume Shadow Copy was first introduced in Windows XP and Windows Server 2003.

Windows Event Log The Windows Event Log service is used to log events that are viewed with the Event Viewer application; however, it does much more than this. The Windows Event Log service is also responsible for querying events, subscribing to events on remote machines, archiving event logs based on archive settings, and managing event metadata.

The Event Viewer and event logging are covered in more detail in Chapter 13.

Windows Firewall The Windows Firewall service is a client firewall that runs on Windows servers and client operating systems. The Windows Firewall supports using IPSec rules for security, as well as basic application and protocol filtering. The Windows Firewall functions will not be active if this service is disabled.

Windows Management Instrumentation Windows Management Instrumentation (WMI) is to Windows operating systems what the Simple Network Management Protocol (SNMP) is to networked devices. SNMP allows administrators to monitor settings and states on network devices like switches and routers. WMI allows for the same with Windows operating systems. WMI was first introduced with Windows XP and Windows Server 2003. The WMI service provides access to the management information exposed by the WMI model.

Windows Remote Management One of the most important new features in Windows Vista and Windows Server 2008 was Windows Remote Management (WinRM). The service that provides WinRM is the Windows Remote Management service. WinRM provides access to remote computers, including the WMI data, and allows for event collection with Event Viewer. The WinRM service may be configured locally or through Group Policies.

Windows Update The Windows Update service uses either the Windows Update or Microsoft Update Internet services to download and install updates on the local system. The service must be running to check for, download, and install updates even if automatic updates are disabled.

Workstation The Workstation service is responsible for network connections to Server Message Block (SMB) servers. Without this service, you cannot connect to shares on other Windows machines.

Add-On Services

Add-on services are provided by Microsoft and third-party providers. These services often require complex planning and installation procedures. For example, Microsoft's SharePoint product is a multi-service application used for Internet or intranet collaboration services. It depends on the Internet Information Services

(IIS) service, which is included in Windows Server operating systems, but it also depends on several unique services for searching, indexing, displaying, and manipulating information. In addition, SharePoint uses Microsoft's SQL Server service as the backend database. To add to this complexity, SharePoint may be installed as a distributed application, which means that some of its services are on one server, while other services are installed on other servers.

Add-on and third-party services are often installed just like standard applications on a client operating system computer. You will launch the installation routine (typically SETUP.EXE) and then step through the installation process. More complex services may require configuration during and after the installation. In some cases, you will have to start the services manually after installation is complete. In other scenarios, the services will start automatically. In still other scenarios, you may be required to reboot the server after service installation.

As an example of an add-on service provided by Microsoft, consider the SQL Server service. SQL Server is a database management system server. It provides support for database storage, access, backup, recovery, and management. When you install SQL Server, it installs several services including the database engine service (which provides access to databases), the SQL Server Agent service (which manages scheduled jobs), and the SQL Monitor service (which allows for multiple instances of SQL Server on a single machine). The point of this example is simple. SQL Server is a single application, but it is made up of several services. As you manage services on Windows servers, it is important that you understand how the services work together and the roles that the services play on the network. SQL Server comes in a free edition (SQL Server Express Edition), but most companies implement the licensed versions that require purchase.

Additional add-on services from Microsoft include:

> ► Microsoft Exchange Server for email

> ► Microsoft SharePoint Server for collaboration and intranet implementation

> ► Microsoft Threat Management Gateway server for Internet proxy services

> ► Microsoft System Center Data Protection Manager for centralized backups

> ► Microsoft Dynamics for Enterprise Resource Planning (ERP) and Customer Relationship Management (CRM) services

You will not be required to know about SharePoint or SQL Server specifically for the MTA exam. This information is provided to help you further understand services in the context of real-world installations.

In addition to Microsoft add-on services, you can find services from third-parties. These services include both free and paid services. An example of a free add-on service is the Apache web server for Windows. This open source web server is an alternative to IIS and may run on Windows servers. An example of a paid third-party service is a Trivial File Transfer Protocol (TFTP) server like the one from WinAgents Software Group available at http://www.winagents.com. The WinAgents TFTP Server software is a perfect example of a solution that is available both in free and paid solutions. Vendors attempt to differentiate the features and support offerings to make their product appealing as a purchase.

Configuring Services

Services can be configured with many different settings. The settings impact the way the services start and recover. They impact the privileges the services will have. In this section, you will learn about the configuration settings available for all services running on Windows servers.

Service Startup Types

Services may be configured to start automatically or manually. They may also be configured as disabled. Table 4.1 lists the service startup types and the meaning of each type. Use this table as a reference to determine the proper startup type for a specific service.

TABLE 4.1 Service Startup Types

Startup Type	Description
Automatic	Services configured to start automatically will start when the operating system starts.
Automatic (Delayed Start)	Services configured to Automatic (Delayed Start) will start after all services configured for Automatic start.
Manual	A manual startup type indicates that the services will not start automatically; however, it may be started when needed by a user or by an application that requires its use.
Disabled	A disabled service is one that will not be started automatically and cannot be started manually.

◀ In many cases, the only difference between a paid product and a free product from a different vendor is the included support. Many organizations choose paid products in order to have support for their implementations.

◀ Services may only be configured by users who are members of the Account Operators, Domain Admins, Enterprise Admins, or the local Administrators group.

Service Recovery Options

Like all applications, services may fail. If a service fails, the Windows Server operating system supports recovery actions. These actions include restarting the service, running a program, such as a script or batch file that you create to perform maintenance on the service and attempt to prevent future failures, restarting the computer, and doing nothing. In some cases, you may choose to do nothing because no automatic action would be sufficient. In these scenarios, manual interaction must be taken by the administrator. Figure 4.2 shows the Recovery tab for a service.

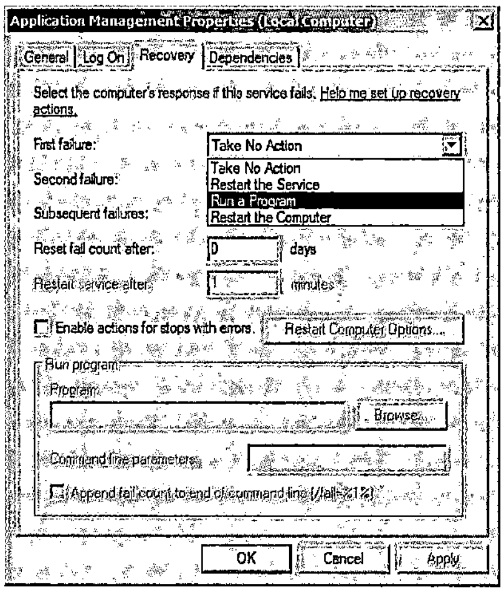

FIGURE 4.2 Managing the Recovery
tab settings for a service

Services can be in one of several statuses at any given time. These include stopped, started, and paused.

In addition to the four optional responses to a failure, you can determine what happens on the first, second, and subsequent failures. On the first failure, for example, you may simply restart the service. On the second failure, you may choose to run a maintenance program. On the subsequent failures, you may choose to restart the entire server. You can set a reset fail counter so that the first and second failure must be within a given time frame in order to escalate through the first, second, and subsequent failure actions.

Service Privileges

Most services run as the operating system by default. This default is acceptable for most built-in services. However, it's important to understand that you can configure a service to run as a user by configuring the user account on the Log On tab of the service Properties dialog. The privileges of the service are derived from the context in which it runs. If it runs in the operating system context, it can do anything the local system itself can do. If it runs in a user account context, it can do whatever that account can do. The importance of service accounts is covered in more detail in the later section of this chapter titled "Understanding Service Accounts." Figure 4.3 shows the Log On tab with an account configured for use.

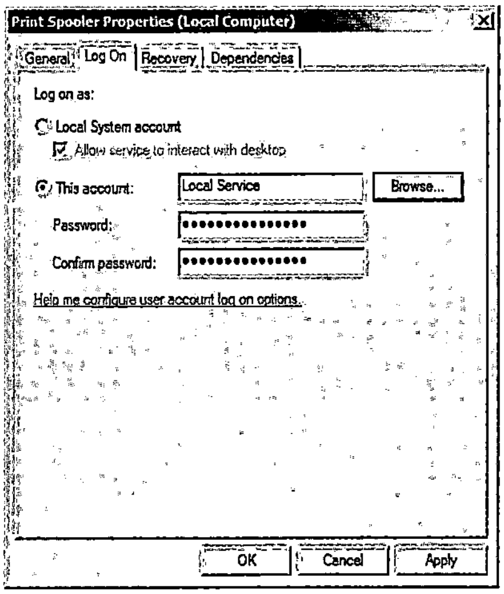

FIGURE 4.3 Viewing the Log On tab of a service

Managing Services

The primary tasks related to service management are starting, stopping, and restarting services. In addition to these tasks, you must configure the services, as addressed in the preceding section.

Starting Services

Services can be started using the same three methods you learned in the preceding section for stopping them.

To start a service in the Services GUI, use the following procedure:

1. Click Start and search for Services.msc and press the Enter key.

2. Select the service you want to start and click the Start button on the toolbar.

3. Right-click the service and select Start.

4. Click the Start option on the Action menu, or double-click on the service and click the Start button on the General tab.

To start a service at the CMD Command Prompt, use the following procedure:

1. Click Start ➤ All Programs ➤ Accessories ➤ Command Prompt.

2. Execute the following command: net start spooler.

3. When the command processing completes, execute the exit command to exit the Command Prompt.

To start a service in the Windows PowerShell command-line interface, use the following procedure:

1. Click Start ➤ All Programs ➤ Accessories ➤ Windows PowerShell ➤ Windows PowerShell.

2. Execute the following command: start-service spooler.

3. When the command processing completes, execute the exit command to exit the Command Prompt.

Stopping Services

Services can be stopped using one of three methods:

▶ The Services GUI interface

▶ The Windows CMD command-line interface

▶ The Windows PowerShell command-line interface

To stop a service using the GUI interface, you must do the following:

1. Launch the Services management GUI. You can do this easily on Windows servers as follows:

   a. Click Start.

   b. Type services.msc into the Search field.

   c. Press the Enter key.

   You will see a screen similar to the one in Figure 4.4.

2. Select the service you want to stop.

3. Stop the service by one of the following methods:

   ▶ Click the Stop button on the toolbar.

   ▶ Select Stop from the Action menu.

▶ Right-click the service and select Stop.

▶ Double-click on the service and then click the Stop button on the General tab of the service Properties dialog.

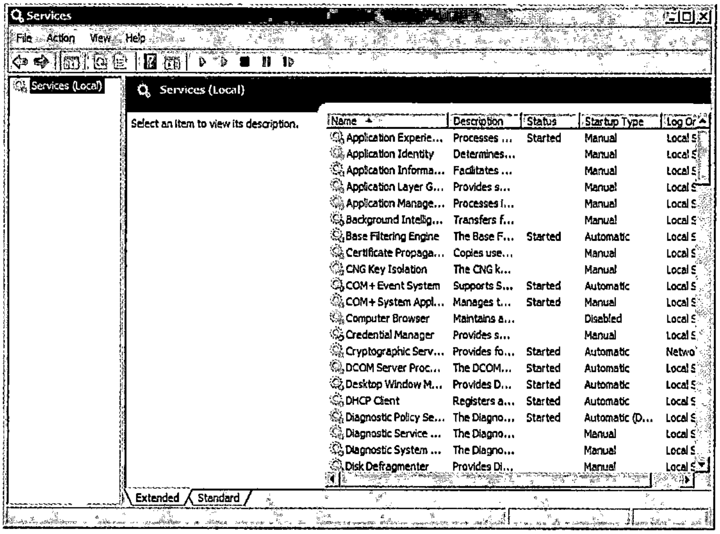

FIGURE 4.4 Viewing the Services.msc application

If you want to stop a service at the CMD command-line interface, you must know the service name. The service name is displayed in the Service Name field of the General tab in the service's Properties dialog, as shown in Figure 4.5 for the Print Spooler service.

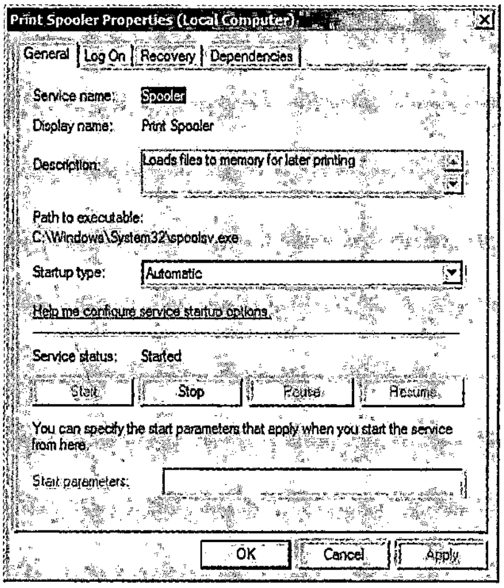

FIGURE 4.5 Discovering a service name using the Service Name field

After you have determined the name of the service, you can stop it at the CMD command-line interface using the following procedure:

1. Click Start ➤ All Programs ➤ Accessories ➤ Command Prompt.

2. Execute the following command: net stop spooler (see Figure 4.6).

3. When the command processing completes, execute the exit command to exit the Command Prompt.

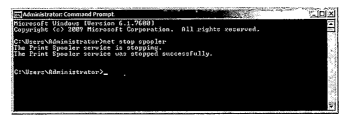

FIGURE 4.6 Stopping the Print Spooler service at the CMD Command Prompt interface

You can also stop services at the Windows PowerShell command-line interface using the following procedure:

1. Click Start ➤ All Programs ➤ Accessories ➤ Windows PowerShell ➤ Windows PowerShell.

2. Execute the following command: Stop-Service Spooler (see Figure 4.7).

3. When the command processing completes, execute the exit command to exit the Command Prompt.

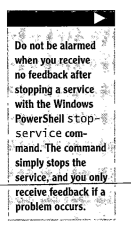

Do not be alarmed when you receive no feedback after stopping a service with the Windows PowerShell stop-service command. The command simply stops the service, and you only receive feedback if a problem occurs.

FIGURE 4.7 Stopping the Print Spooler service in Windows PowerShell

Restarting Services

Sometimes a service will stop responding. When you look at the service status in the Services.msc application, it may show Started as the status even though it is no longer responding. In such cases, you should try restarting the service to get it running properly again. An additional reason for restarting a service manually is to apply configuration changes. In some cases, configuration changes will not be applied until the service is restarted. You can restart a service in the GUI interface by simply taking one of the following actions:

▶ Click on the service and then click the Restart Service button.

▶ Select the Action menu and choose the Restart option.

To restart a service at the CMD Command Prompt, you will need to perform a stop and start procedure:

1. Use the net stop command to stop the service.

2. Use the net start command to start it again.

You may alternatively use the Command Prompt sc command, but it also requires one command to stop the service and another to start it.

In Windows PowerShell, you can use the restart-service command to restart a service. It works just like the start-service and stop-service commands. Use the following procedure to restart a service in Windows PowerShell:

1. Click Start ➤ All Programs ➤ Accessories ➤ Windows PowerShell ➤ Windows PowerShell.

2. Execute the following command: restart-service spooler.

3. When the command processing completes, execute the exit command to exit the Command Prompt.

There is no actual restart option with the net command.

Troubleshooting Services

Server service problems tend to fall into three categories. The first is service dependencies. Services may depend on other services, so it is important to understand the relationships between different services. The second is configuration problems. It is important to understand how to properly configure services. The third and final problem is improper permissions. Services must interact with the operating system, storage, and network. To perform these interactions, the service must have the appropriate permissions. Because permissions provide services through the service account, you must understand its importance.

Service Dependencies

If you have used Microsoft Office, you know that you can use the different applications in the suite together. For example, you can take a graph generated in Excel and load it into PowerPoint. Even though the graph is in PowerPoint, you can double-click it and edit it as if it were still in Excel. In order to perform these actions, both Excel and PowerPoint must be installed on the same computer. They depend on each other to provide this functionality.

In a similar way, services may depend on other services. If a dependency service is not running, the dependent service may fail to start or simply not function correctly. If you suspect a service dependency problem, you can use the following procedure to view service dependencies:

1. Click Start and search for Services.msc and press the Enter key.

2. Double-click on the service for which you want to view dependencies.

3. View the service dependencies in the upper pane labeled This Service Depends On The Following System Components (see Figure 4.8).

> Dependencies may be considered from two perspectives. From the depending service's perspective, the dependencies are the services on which it depends. From the providing services perspective, the dependencies are the services that depend on it.

> You can also see other services that depend on the selected service on the Dependencies tab of a service's Properties dialog.

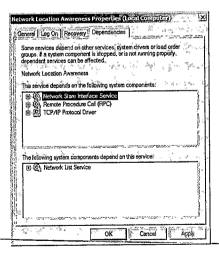

FIGURE 4.8 Viewing service dependencies for a service on Windows Server

Service Configuration

The second common cause of service problems has to do with service configuration. In the simplest scenarios, the service may be configured to start manually when it should be configured to start automatically. Such changes are simple and can be made through the Services.msc application. When the service requires a more complicated configuration, you must use a special utility or software application to configure the service.

   As an example of a service configuration utility used to perform complicated configuration tasks, consider the Windows Firewall service. This service cannot be fully configured from within the Services.msc application. You must use either the Windows Firewall application or the Windows Firewall with Advanced Security application. These two applications actually do the work of configuring the service itself. Services.msc is used only to determine how the service runs and the privileges with which it runs. This statement leads us to the next common problem with services—service accounts.

Understanding Service Accounts

As you learned earlier in this chapter, service accounts can be used to run services in the context of a user account. In most cases, accounts are created specifically for the services that use them and real users never log on with those accounts. From a service troubleshooting perspective, it's important to remember that a service must be able to do what it is designed to do. Services may attempt to perform any of the following operations:

- ► Read and write from or to the file system
- ► Read and write Registry data
- ► Access remote servers
- ► Access internal system hardware

   Although services can do more than the preceding list indicates, I chose this list to show the capabilities that a service may require. For example, if a service required access to remote servers, you must run the service in the context of a user account with access to those remote servers. If the service must read and write file system data, you must run the service as a user with those capabilities.

   At the same time, it is important that you do not give the service more capabilities than it requires. As explained in the sidebar titled "When You Want the Least and Not the Most," it is always best to abide by the principle of least privilege.

WHEN YOU WANT THE LEAST AND NOT THE MOST

The *principle of least privilege* states that users and systems should have no greater access than is required to perform their intended duties. This definition means that systems can do what they need to do and nothing more. Other systems can access the secured system to perform their intended operations and can do nothing more. Least privilege is essential to secure network operations.

If a service is configured with privileges beyond what it requires and that service receives requests from the network, an attacker could take advantage of a vulnerability (a security flaw) in the service and force it to execute commands. If the service is running with privileges greater than those required to perform its duties, the service is unnecessarily exposing your system and network. If it is running with least privilege, in the worst case scenario, the attacker could do whatever the service could do and nothing more.

Least privilege is achieved through a four-step process:

1. Determine the actions the service will need to take.

2. Define the permissions required to take those actions.

3. Create an account with those permissions.

4. Configure the service to run in the context of that account.

By doing this, you will increase the security of your network and systems.

THE ESSENTIALS AND BEYOND

Services are applications or innate operating system components that run on a Windows server and provide services to the local machine, the network, or both. Services may be configured to start up automatically, or they may be configured to be started manually. Services can also be disabled. You can start, stop, and restart services in the GUI with the Services.msc application, at the Command Prompt with the net commands, and in Windows PowerShell with the start-service, stop-service, and restart-service commands. When troubleshooting service problems, be sure to consider service dependencies, check for appropriate configuration settings, and verify that the service is running with the proper privileges.

THE ESSENTIALS AND BEYOND *(Continued)*

ADDITIONAL EXERCISES

▶ Research the Software Protection service online to discover its purpose and functions.

▶ Configure the Print Spooler service to start using the Automatic (Delayed Start) startup type.

▶ Discover the service name for the DNS Client service and then restart the service using the Command Prompt.

▶ Configure the options for the Disk Defragmenter service so that it starts automatically (without a delay) and so that it restarts should a failure occur.

To compare your answers to the author's, please visit www.sybex.com/go/ networkingessentials.

REVIEW QUESTIONS

1. What service must be running so that a user can check for updates at the Microsoft Update website?

   A. Microsoft Update   **C.** Workstation

   B. Windows Update   **D.** Server

2. True or false: Only Microsoft provides services that run on Windows Server operating systems?

3. What service startup type will require a change in the startup type value before you can manually start the service?

   A. Disabled   **C.** Automatic (Delayed Start)

   B. Manual   **D.** Automatic

4. What security principle states that a system should have no more capabilities that it requires to perform its intended purpose?

5. What Windows service must be running in order to encrypt and decrypt individual folders on the C: drive of the server?

   A. Encrypting File System   **C.** Server

   B. Group Policy Client   **D.** Workstation

6. Define a service.

7. Define service dependencies.

(Continues)

THE ESSENTIALS AND BEYOND *(Continued)*

8. Which one of the following is not a common cause for service problems?

   A. Service dependencies   **C.** Excessive available memory

   B. Improper service configuration   **D.** Insufficient privileges

9. Which of the following services provide some level of remote access to servers? (Choose two.)

   A. Windows Remote Management   **C.** Remote Desktop Services

   B. Volume Shadow Copy   **D.** Print Spooler

10. True or false: Only Windows Server operating systems include the Server service.

CHAPTER 5

Active Directory Infrastructure

Active Directory was first introduced with the release of Windows 2000, and it has evolved to meet changing business needs since that time. Active Directory is based on technologies developed by groups ranging from the Internet community to the Massachusetts Institute of Technology (MIT). Before you can implement and manage Active Directory, you must understand the foundational technologies on which it is built.

In this chapter, you will learn about Active Directory and its supporting components. You will move on to plan the required Active Directory servers based on the different functions they provide. Next, you will explore the important topic of planning a Domain Name System (DNS) namespace for your environment. Finally, you will uncover the purpose for sites and the replication processes in an Active Directory installation. These topics will be addressed in the following sections:

▷ **Understanding Active Directory**

▷ **Planning for Active Directory servers**

▷ **Planning a DNS namespace**

▷ **Exploring sites and replication**

Understanding Active Directory

In the Microsoft networking world, two approaches to networking have been used for nearly 20 years:

Workgroup   The workgroup has been used since the 1980s. A workgroup is a network of Windows machines utilizing the same workgroup name and sharing their resources with each other. Workgroups provide no real means of centralized management or control.

Domain   Domains were first introduced with the release of Windows NT 3.1 in 1993. Domains provide a central method of control through the use of domain controllers. Early domains supported basic system policies, and modern domains support enhanced Group Policies. The domain is the Microsoft implementation of a centralized directory service.

Group Policies are covered in detail in Chapter 8.

Active Directory (AD) is Microsoft's network directory service and is the method used to create a domain. A *network directory service* contains the objects tracked and managed by the network. It includes objects such as users, groups, computers, servers, and printers. The network directory service is used as a central repository of networked device information for querying, updating, and authenticating against the data. When users log on to the network, the directory service is used to retrieve user information for authentication purposes. When users search for printers or contacts, the directory service can be used to retrieve that information as well.

In order to understand AD, you must understand several components that make up the AD infrastructure. These components include:

- ▶ Domains

- ▶ Domain trees

- ▶ Forests

AD Domains

A Windows network domain was a security boundary in the Windows NT 4.0 and earlier server operating systems. With the release of Windows 2000 Server, this changed. Now, the forest is the security boundary. Forests are explained later in the section "AD Forests." Now that AD domains can exist in a hierarchy, they are more of a logical administrative container than they are a security boundary. That is to say that you can assign administrative capabilities to an individual in one domain, while not giving him administrative capabilities in another domain that exists in the same forest.

A *security boundary* is the boundary within which users can operate. For example, a user logging on to a domain in a forest may be granted access to objects within the security boundary—the forest.

Domains contain objects, including the following:

User accounts   The users are account objects stored in the AD database. These account objects are used to allow users to log on to the network. When a user logs on to a domain, the user has access to resources within that domain based on the permissions assigned to those resources. Users may also be given access to resources in other domains within the forest. This will all become clearer as the AD logical architecture unfolds.

Groups   Groups are created so that users and other groups may be managed as a collective instead of as individuals.

Computers   Computers represent individual computing machines on the network. The computers may be physical machines or they may be virtual machines running in Windows Virtual PC, Microsoft Hyper-V, or some other virtualization solution. For the most part, AD knows no difference between a physical and virtual machine.

Servers   Servers are really just computer objects, but AD detects that they are running the server version of the OS and places them in the Servers container.

Organizational Units   Organization units (OUs) provide for a logical hierarchy within the domain. This logical hierarchy allows for simpler administration and management of user accounts, groups, computers, and servers.

Built-in containers   Several built-in containers exist. These containers hold the user accounts and groups by default (the Users container), the computer accounts (the Computers container), and the server accounts (the Servers container).

The domain is the primary building block of the AD logical architecture. These domains have names like company.com, organization.local, or acmepetco.local. The names may look familiar to you because they are the same kind of names you see on the Internet. They are called DNS domains or DNS domain names. Figure 5.1 shows the concept of the domain and the objects it may contain.

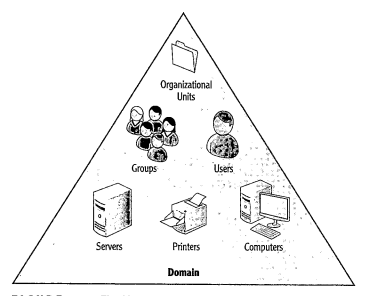

FIGURE 5.1 The AD domain and the objects it may contain

There are several reasons to have more than one domain. For example, you might want to improve domain performance for the users in those domains. By creating separate domains, you partition the pool of users into smaller groups, which results in smaller domain database sizes. While some properties and objects are replicated to all domain controllers (DCs) in the forest that run the Global Catalog functions, the majority of a domain's objects are stored only within that domain.

The next reason to have multiple domains is to decentralize administration. You can create separate domains and then delegate administrative capabilities to individuals within that domain. This allows for administration of subsets of your network without allowing each domain administrator to have control over the entire forest. Indeed, administrators can be assigned forest-level administrative capabilities, but you can limit the number of administrators with such power. By assigning administrators to specific domains, you distribute the administrative workload so that a single administrator is not overburdened.

Another reason to create separate domains is more political than technical. You may simply need to divide the users along organizational lines. This is often the case when organizations merge and desire to maintain their own identities. You can provide a separate domain for each division of the organization.

> The Global Catalog, as its name implies, is the central reference for all objects in the forest. Servers running the Global Catalog role contain a partial replica of all the data in all the domains in a forest.

THE TALE OF TWO COMPANIES

In the 1990s, I worked for a large multinational organization that employed thousands of people around the world. The organization owned several companies that operated under different brands. The two largest companies were involved in similar markets and had very different ideas about how they should run their internal systems.

I worked in one of these two larger companies. Our company used Banyan Vines (at the time), and the other company used Novel Netware. As the two companies began to implement Windows NT (version 3.5 at the time), they had very different ideas about how it should be configured and utilized. Most of these differences were simply based on experiences with differing technologies and not based on any real technical or business requirement. This is very common and must be dealt with carefully.

Concessions were made from both sides so that each organization felt their needs were met. Along the way, many intense debates occurred, but the implementation projects were ultimately successful for both companies in the end. Looking back, I can now see that both companies were better off because of the opinions of the other company. Although we often look at

(Continues)

A final and very important reason for separate domains is regulatory compliance. Some divisions within your organization may have governmental or organizational policies that specify how their computer operations must function. If these regulations or policies result in more intensive CPU processing (such as encryption) or increased storage space requirements (such as data retention policies), you may choose to implement separate domains. One domain can implement and support the required regulations and policies, and the other domains may be more lax in their implementation.

> **Regulatory compliance is the state an organization achieves when it conforms to government or industry regulations that require specific procedures for computing operations. These regulations include Sarbanes-Oxley and HIPAA regulations in the United States.**

AD Domain Trees

An AD domain tree is a group of domains that share the same root namespace. For example, Figure 5.2 shows a group of domains sharing the root namespace of company.com. By default, all domains in a domain tree trust each other because they are in the same forest. (This will be covered in the next section titled "AD Forests.")

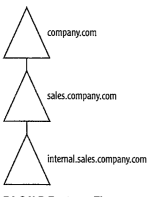

company.com

sales.company.com

internal.sales.company.com

FIGURE 5.2 The company.com domain tree

A domain tree is mostly organizational. Stated differently, when multiple domains are required within a single forest, domain trees are created and used to organize the domains into a logical hierarchy. For example, you may require different domains at each location on your wide area network (WAN). This allows a separate domain database to exist at each WAN site, and the only data that will require replication between locations will be forest-level data, such as the Global Catalog and Universal Groups.

AD Forests

An AD *forest* is a collection of one or more domain trees sharing the same Global Catalog and schema. In many cases, they also share the same root namespace; however, a shared root namespace is not required for the domains to exist in the same forest. In AD, the forest acts as the default trust boundary.

Figure 5.3 shows a forest with the root namespace company.com. Notice that marketing.company.com and sales.company.com are in the same root namespace called company.com. If the three domains that can exist in this namespace (company.com, marketing.company.com, and sales.company.com) are to be in the same forest, they must be installed so that they exist in the same forest.

▶

Replication is the process used to ensure that all copies of the AD database are synchronized across AD servers.

▶

A forest can contain domain trees from different root namespaces or a single domain tree. A single domain is a forest even though only one domain exists.

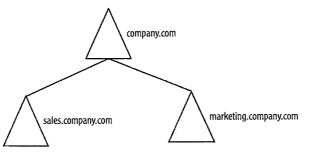

FIGURE 5.3 The company.com root namespace with the marketing.company.com and sales.company.com domains

In Chapter 6, "Configuring Active Directory," you will see the installation process used to install and configure AD. One of the screens will ask you if you want to configure the server to function in an existing domain and forest or in a new forest. If you create a domain with the name marketing.company.com and another with the name sales.company.com, but you do not select to place them in an existing forest, you will end up with three separate forests that share a root DNS namespace.

By default, a group exists within the first domain in the forest called the Enterprise Admins group. Anyone who is a member of this group is automatically an administrator in all domains in the forest. The Enterprise Admins group is very powerful and should be used with great caution. In most environments, very few administrators require membership in the Enterprise Admins group.

Planning for Active Directory Servers

Chapter 7 provides more information about groups and group management.

With all this information about domains, domain trees, and forests, you may be feeling a bit overwhelmed. The good news is that everything becomes clearer' when you see the components that actually make the *logical architecture* work. The logical architecture has to do with the domains, domain trees, and forests. It is called the logical architecture because a domain can be implemented with one physical server or with dozens of physical servers. The servers may be in a single data center or they may be distributed across the world using WAN links. However, the reality is that no domain, domain tree, or forest exists until a physical server is installed on the network. This server is part of the physical architecture of AD.

The physical architecture includes the servers that make up the AD implementation and the sites used to define replication procedures. This section discusses the servers, and the later section titled "Exploring Sites and Replication" addresses the sites. Two service types are required to implement AD:

► Domain controllers

► Supporting servers

Domain Controllers

A domain controller (DC) is a Windows server that stores and manages a copy of the AD database. Domain controllers are responsible for several important tasks related to AD, including:

User Account Provisioning The DCs store the AD database, which contains the user accounts. These accounts are used to allow logons. The user accounts include dozens of properties that define the users and the network resources they use, such as profile storage locations and home directories for data storage.

Logon Processing When a user attempts to log on to the domain, a DC is contacted to process the logon request. This process is known as *authentication,* and the primary authentication protocol in Windows domains is Kerberos. When the user logs on to the network, the Kerberos authentication process

The AD database is stored on disk just as any other database would be. It is stored in a file named NTDS.DIT.

User profiles store configuration settings for the operating system and applications that are specific to the individual users.

provides the user with a ticket called the User Ticket or the Ticket Granting Ticket (TGT). This User Ticket is used to request a Session Ticket (ST) whenever access to other network resources is required.

Resource Access Processing   As stated under "Logon Processing," the DC is also responsible for granting the STs so that users may access network resources. This only applies to clients using the Kerberos authentication protocol; however, the vast majority of clients do use this protocol today. Kerberos is used when any client from Windows 2000 or later accesses a DC running Windows 2000 or later. This covers the great majority of all connections on Windows networks today.

Database Replication   When a change is made to the AD database on a DC, that DC becomes the master replicator for that change. This simply means that the DC is responsible for replicating the change out to other DCs in the domain or forest. AD uses a multi-master replication model. All DCs are master replicators—meaning they are in charge of objects to be replicated—but only for the objects they create or modify.

A DC is created by installing the Windows Server operating system on a server and then installing the Active Directory Domain Services (AD DS) server role. After the server role is added, you can use the DCPROMO command to configure the server as a DC. The very first time you run the DCPROMO command, you will have to create a new domain in a new forest. If you want all remaining domains to exist as part of the same forest, you must choose to create a new domain in an existing forest when running DCPROMO on those DCs.

DCs can play different roles with the forest and domain environment. These roles are called Operations Master (OM) roles. There are five OM roles in all, including:

Domain Naming Master   The Domain Naming Master role is used to ensure that no two domains are created with the same name in the same forest. A single DC plays this role for the entire forest.

Infrastructure Master   The Infrastructure Master ensures that group changes are updated properly across DCs. A single DC plays this role in each domain.

Schema Master   The Schema Master is the only DC that can make changes to the schema. All other DCs learn of the schema structure from the Schema Master. A single DC in the entire forest plays this role.

> You will learn to use the DCPROMO command in Chapter 6 when you install the AD DS role and configure the first domain in a forest.
>
> ▶

> The *schema* defines the objects that can be created in the AD database. Think of the schema as the blueprint for what can be created. It defines attributes and classes. The classes are collections of attributes for objects such as users and groups.
>
> ▶

PDC Emulator   The Primary Domain Controller (PDC) Emulator performs two primary roles. First, it acts as the PDC for any Windows NT Backup DCs (BDCs), which is a rare need today. Second, and more important, it acts as the primary password change server. When a password is changed, it is changed first on the PDC role DC, and then it is replicated out to other DCs. One DC in each domain plays this role.

RID Master   The Relative ID (RID) Master assigns pools of RIDs to other DCs so that they can create security principals. When a security principal, such as a user account, group, or computer account, is created, it is assigned a globally unique ID (GUID), which is a combination of the domain security ID (SID) and the next available RID. One DC in each domain plays this role.

DCs can be used to change the functional level of the domains and forests as well. The *functional level* defines the support for older AD versions and newer AD features, as follows:

> ► Lower functional levels support older AD versions and DCs.

> ► Higher functional levels support newer AD features.

With Windows Server 2008 R2, domains can be in one of four functional levels:

Windows 2000 Native   When the domain is in Windows 2000 Native functional level, DCs may run Windows 2000, Windows Server 2003, Windows Server 2003 R2, Windows Server 2008, and Windows Server 2008 R2. New features introduced in Windows Server 2003 AD and later may not be used.

Windows Server 2003   When the domain is in the Windows Server 2003 functional level, DCs may run Windows Server 2003 and later server operating systems. New features introduced in Windows Sever 2008 and later may not be used.

Windows Server 2008   When the domain is in the Windows Server 2008 functional level, DCs may run Windows 2008 and later server operating systems. New features introduced in Windows Server 2008 R2 may not be used.

Windows Server 2008 R2   When the domain is in the Windows Server 2008 R2 functional level, only Windows Server 2008 R2 DCs may be used. All of the newest AD features may be used as long as the forest is also at the Windows Server 2008 R2 functional level.

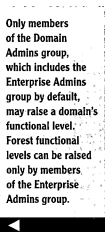

Windows Server 2008 and Windows Server 2008 R2 domains no longer support Windows NT 4.0 BDCs. This restriction may require the maintenance of Windows Server 2003 domains until the Windows NT 4.0 BDCs can be removed.

Only members of the Domain Admins group, which includes the Enterprise Admins group by default, may raise a domain's functional level. Forest functional levels can be raised only by members of the Enterprise Admins group.

The AD forest may also be in one of four functional levels:

Windows 2000 Native   This forest functional level supports domains running at any supported functional level. It supports DCs running any operating system from Windows 2000 through Windows Server 2008 R2.

Windows Server 2003   This forest functional level supports only domains running at the Windows Server 2003 functional level or later. It supports DCs running any operating system from Windows Server 2003 through Windows Server 2008 R2.

Windows Server 2008   This forest functional level supports only domains running at the Windows Server 2008 functional level or later. It supports DCs running any operating system from Windows Server 2008 through Windows Server 2008 R2.

Windows Server 2008 R2   The Windows Server 2008 R2 forest functional level supports only Windows Server 2008 R2 domain controllers and domains, but it enables newer features. For example, you can use the AD Recycle Bin only when the forest is at the Windows Server 2008 R2 forest functional level.

> Before a forest can be set to a specific functional level, the domains in the forest must be set to that level.

When implementing AD, you should consider installing more than one DC, regardless of the size of the domain. If you have only one DC and it goes down (becomes unavailable to the network), users cannot log on to the network. They may be able to log on with cached information, but they will be prevented from accessing many network resources. If you implement at least two DCs, the odds are increased that a DC will be available when it is needed. Having additional DCs will also increase the performance of logon processes as the logons can be distributed across the available DCs.

Supporting Servers

> Most network administrators use static IP addresses on servers and dynamically assigned IP addresses on clients. This makes for simpler configuration of the clients but consistent configuration of the servers.

Additional servers are required to make AD work. These servers are used to provide the name resolution for the network and the IP configuration for the clients on the network. The DNS servers provide the name resolution for the network, which is discussed in detail in the next section titled "Planning a DNS Namespace." The Dynamic Host Configuration Protocol (DHCP) service provides the dynamic configuration of the IP protocol for the computers on your network.

Although DHCP is not technically required to make AD work, it can make your life much simpler. Without it, you would have to track the IP addresses assigned to clients through static (manual) configuration. In the old days, we used a spreadsheet or a simple text file to track them; however, when you have hundreds or thousands of clients on the network, this type of tracking system becomes difficult to manage. DHCP allows for the dynamic configuration of the clients, and, if you need to view the IP configuration settings for a given computer, you can utilize the DHCP administration tools. Figure 5.4 show a typical network infrastructure for a small AD DS deployment.

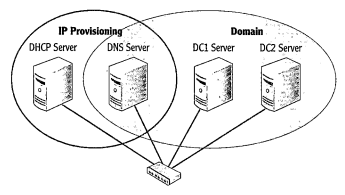

FIGURE 5.4 A small-scale Active Directory deployment

Planning a DNS Namespace

AD domain names are based on the Domain Name System (DNS). DNS is used on the Internet and has existed since the late 1980s. To implement and understand AD, you should have a working knowledge of what functions DNS provides to the network and you should understand the concept of namespace hierarchies.

DNS Overview

DNS is an essential service in an AD environment. You should understand the basic terminology related to DNS and the process used to resolve hostnames.
Here is a basic list of DNS terms you should know:

Hostname A hostname is an alias or character-based name assigned to a machine that may be mapped to an IP address. Hostnames are used to simplify access to network resources through the use of easier-to-remember names, as opposed to easily forgotten IP addresses. Using hostnames for communications also allows the IP address to be changed and the device to still be located.

Fully Qualified Domain Name (FQDN) The FQDN is the combination of the hostname and the DNS domain name. For example, the hostname of computer03 in the domain name of company.local would result in the FQDN of computer03.company.local.

Name server The name server is the DNS server that resolves hostnames to IP addresses. Windows Server has the capability to function as a DNS server

In Chapter 6, you will learn how to install and configure the DNS Server role on your Windows Server 2008 R2 installation.

service, and this service can communicate with other standards-based DNS servers on the Internet.

Hosts file   The hosts file is a text file located on the local drive of the Windows machines (both servers and clients). It contains hostname-to-IP address mappings for name resolution. By default, the hosts file overrides DNS. Stated differently, it is used before DNS queries are attempted. The file is located in the c:\windows\system32\drivers\etc folder of a standard installation.

DNS servers can resolve hostnames queries in one of two basic methods: with the aid of forwarding servers and by recursion.

Forwarding server   A forwarding server is a server that can perform lookups when the local DNS server cannot resolve the request.

Recursion   Recursion simply means that the DNS server starts at the root and contacts the top-level domain server (for example, the .com server).

When a forwarding server is used, the process works as depicted in Figure 5.5. Notice that the first DNS server to receive the request does not perform recursion. Instead, it submits a client request to the forwarding DNS server and relies on it to perform the recursion. Recursion is still performed either way, but with forwarding, the initial DNS server does not execute the recursion.

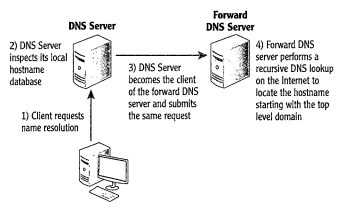

FIGURE 5.5 The DNS name resolution process with forwarding

Figure 5.6 shows the operations when recursion is used. In this case, the first DNS server contacted by the client performs the recursion. This server tells the DNS server which server manages the second-level domain zone. The DNS server then contacts this second-level server. That server may respond with other servers or with the hostname mapping information if it has the hostname in its database.

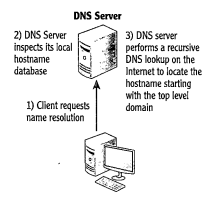

DNS Server

2) DNS Server inspects its local hostname database

3) DNS server performs a recursive DNS lookup on the Internet to locate the hostname starting with the top level domain

1) Client requests name resolution

FIGURE 5.6 The DNS name resolution process with recursion operations

This DNS name resolution system is used in AD environments. The servers have hostnames and the clients have hostnames; however, the system is used for more than just hostname resolution. DNS also has the ability to resolve service requests. Service records indicate the hosts that are providing specific services. For example, in an AD environment, service records are used to locate DCs so that a user can log on to the network.

In addition to the way in which DNS servers resolve hostnames, you'll find it useful to understand how Windows clients resolve hostnames in entirety. The process involves hosts files, DNS, and even NetBIOS name resolution. When you attempt to connect to a computer by using its hostname (for example, computer03), the process represented in Figure 5.7 is used to determine the IP address of the specified hostname.

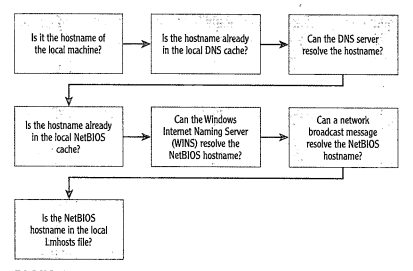

FIGURE 5.7 The Windows hostname-to-IP address resolution process

◄

Understanding the way Windows machines resolve hostnames to IP addresses can help you troubleshoot network communications problems.

◄

The hosts file is missing from this process because the contents of the hosts file are automatically loaded into the local DNS cache. The system does not have to query the hosts file.

NetBIOS Names Still Linger

In the 1980s and 1990s, NetBIOS names were the only names used for Windows (and DOS) computers using Microsoft networking. *NetBIOS* stands for Network Basic Input Output System and is a method used to provide single-word names for computer names. The trend is to move away from NetBIOS and toward full DNS implementations (because DNS has become the standard of the Internet).

Many services still require NetBIOS names. You will have to check with your application vendors to find out which ones need it for your environment. Because some applications require NetBIOS, it is still part of the Windows name resolution process; however, NetBIOS name resolution has been moved to the end of the process. It is the last set of methods used to resolve a hostname.

When you attempt to connect to a remote system using a one-word hostname, Windows assumes that you want to append the primary DNS suffix to the hostname to create the FQDN. This primary DNS suffix is typically the AD domain name to which your computer is joined. The system uses the FQDN to resolve the hostname to an IP address. Only after it exhausts the DNS options does it fall back to NetBIOS name resolution.

Namespace Hierarchies

The hierarchical structure of an organization can be represented in AD using different methods. You can use a single domain and represent the organization's hierarchy using OUs, or you can use separate domains to represent the hierarchy. When you use separate domains, you are creating a namespace hierarchy.

As an example, you can create a corporate domain called company.local. It will become the root namespace. Next, you could create a domain for each department. The results could include such domains as:

    sales.company.local
    marketing.company.local
    manufacturing.company.local
    executive.company.local

Now, you could further break some departmental domains into functional domains. So, you could create functional domains such as the following:

inside.sales.company.local

outside.sales.company.local

In this case, the sales.company.local domain is referenced as a child domain of the company.local domain. Company.local would be referenced as the parent domain. Furthermore, the domain inside.sales.company.local is a child domain to sales.company.local and a grandchild domain to company.local.

When you're creating hierarchical namespaces that will contain AD domains, you need to understand the trusts that are established between these domains. In an AD environment, all child domains trust their parent domain, and all parent domains trust their child domains. These trusts are *transitive,* which means that they pass through or transfer to other trusts. Notice in Figure 5.8 that the company.local domain trusts the sales.company.local domain, which trusts the inside.sales.company.local domain. Therefore, company.local trusts inside.sales.company.local through the transitive trust chain.

> **Although DNS domain names can be several levels deep, you should avoid creating deep domain trees just because you can. Fewer domains with shorter full domain names are easier to manage.**

> **Trust relationships allow a user in one domain to be granted access to resources in another domain. They do not automatically provide access to resources without intentional granting of that access.**

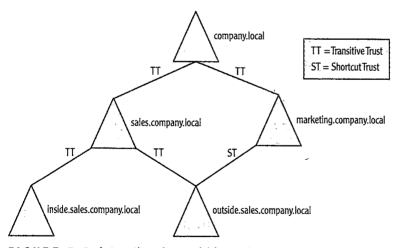

FIGURE 5.8 Automatic and manual (shortcut) trust relationships

In Figure 5.8, you can see that a direct two-way trust relationship exists between the marketing.company.local domain and the outside.sales .company.local domain. These manual or shortcut two-way trust relationships provide improved authentication performance when users from one domain access resources in the other domain. Normally, the authentication would have to travel up the transitive trust path to the root domain and back down to the marketing.company.local domain. The shortcut trust allows authentication to occur with less network traffic and in a shorter time frame.

Exploring Sites and Replication

For you to understand the functionality of AD, the final topics you must explore are the concept of sites and the process of replication. AD sites are part of the *physical topology* of AD. Replication is important because it allows objects to be synchronized among multiple domain controllers within a domain.

> *Physical topology* is a reference to the routers and switches that comprise your network and the possible WAN links between networks.

AD Sites

Microsoft defines a *site* as a group or collection of well-connected computers. When an organization is small enough to have a single location and only that one location, the entire network is typically the AD site. In larger organizations, multiple locations are likely to exist, and each location may be configured as a separate site. Sites are built from three primary components:

Subnets   The IP subnets are used to define the sites. A site includes one or more IP subnets. For example, at one location, you may use the 10.10.10.0 and 10.10.11.0 subnets, while at another location you use the 192.168.1.0 subnet. These IP subnets are the core of AD sites.

> Site links may be assigned a cost. When two links are available between sites, the AD replication engine will use the least-cost link to send the replication traffic.

Site links   Site links define the connections between sites. They can be configured with varying costs and can be used to define the replication schedule between the sites.

Bridgehead servers   The bridgehead servers are the servers at either end of the site links. All intersite replication (replication between sites) occurs through bridgehead servers.

Technically, a site is a collection of IP subnets specified to be part of a site. The IP routing infrastructure is completely ignorant of the real physical location of things, but you can indicate that a site exists through the Active Directory Sites and Services tool.

Sites can support a single domain across sites, or you can implement multiple domains that exist at all sites. A DC must exist for each domain at each site in order to truly implement multiple domains across multiple sites. Figure 5.9 shows multiple sites with single domain.

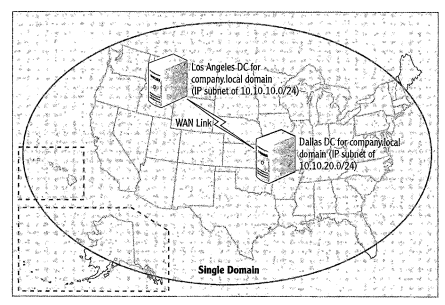

FIGURE 5.9 Multiple sites within a single domain

You can install a single domain with DCs at multiple physical locations that are separated by some distance without configuring an AD site; however, many benefits can be achieved through the use of sites. For example, when you define sites you can create Group Policies that apply only to a specified site rather than applying the policies to the entire domain. Additionally, you can control replication so that your WAN bandwidth is not consumed with replication traffic.

AD Replication

AD replication occurs in two ways. The first is *intrasite replication*. This replication occurs within an AD site. Intrasite replication is completely configured automatically. You do not have to configure anything for the DCs to replicate among themselves. The service responsible for intrasite replication is the Knowledge Consistency Checker (KCC). It builds the replication topology within the site, ensuring that no more than three hops exist between any two DCs whenever possible.

The second type of replication is *intersite replication*. This replication occurs between AD sites. The Inter-Site Topology Generator (ISTG) process determines the bridgehead servers to use for replication between sites. You can control the schedule for replication of intersite communications. This control allows you to restrain replication to when user-based communications do not require

As an added benefit, user logons will be processed by a local domain controller as long as one is available. This reduces WAN traffic as well.

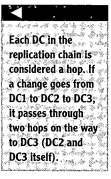

Each DC in the replication chain is considered a hop. If a change goes from DC1 to DC2 to DC3, it passes through two hops on the way to DC3 (DC2 and DC3 itself).

the WAN links or at least when these communications are reduced. The main benefit is that you can prevent AD replication from consuming all of your WAN bandwidth, which may be required for other day-to-day functions such as user functions.

Starting with the release of Windows 2000 and the introduction of AD, a multi-master replication model is used. Earlier domains used a single-master model with a Primary Domain Controller (PDC) and a Backup Domain Controller (BDC). In this older model, only PDCs could make changes to the domain database. With the AD multi-master replication model, any DC can make changes to the database. The DC that modifies the database becomes the master replicator for that change or the master server for that change.

PDC SERVER VERSUS THE PDC EMULATOR ROLE

Do not confuse the PDC server with the PDC Emulator role in AD domains. The PDC Emulator role in modern domains is responsible for password changes and replication with NT 4.0 BDCs in Windows 2003 domains. Windows 2008 domains no longer support NT 4.0 BDCs.

All domain objects are replicated to all DCs within the domain; however, some objects are stored in a special part of the AD called the Global Catalog (GC). The GC contains a partial replica of all objects in the domain. It contains a reference to every user and group with a small subset of attributes. This is done to allow faster searches of the forest. Universal groups are stored in the GC and are stored only there.

In a domain with multiple DCs, not every DC will also host the GC role. By default, only the first DC is configured as a GC. If you want more DCs to act as GC servers, you will have to enable the GC role on the additional DCs. This provides fault tolerance so that the GC is always available even if a DC goes down. In an environment with only two DCs, each DC should run the GC.

THE ESSENTIALS AND BEYOND

Active Directory (AD) is the Microsoft networked directory services. It contains users, groups, organizational units (OUs), computers, printers, and servers. AD has both a logical and a physical architecture. The logical architecture includes domains, domain trees, forests, and OUs. The physical architecture includes the AD sites and the servers that build the domain (the DCs). DNS provides the namespace for AD domains. AD domains look like Internet website domain names, such as company.local. AD sites provide improved control over replication and Group Policies for each location on your WAN. AD replication includes intrasite (within the site) replication and intersite (between sites) replication.

ADDITIONAL EXERCISES

▶ Draw a diagram representing a small company with two locations. Assume that one domain will be used but an AD site will be defined for each location. Note the IP subnets that will be used at each site.

▶ List four object types that may be stored in an AD database.

▶ Research the different functional levels available for domains and forests in Windows Server 2008 and Windows Server 2008 R2.

▶ Open the hosts file and view the contents on a Windows machine.

To compare your answers to the author's, please visit www.sybex.com/go/winadminessentials.

REVIEW QUESTIONS

1. What is the last method attempted for hostname resolution before a Windows client gives up and returns an error indicating that the hostname could not be resolved?

    A. Network broadcast   **C.** DNS server

    B. Lmhosts   **D.** hosts

2. True or false: By default, AD does not have containers for storing user accounts and groups; you must create organizational units to hold them.

3. What process is used to ensure that all copies of the AD database are synchronized across AD servers?

    A. Replication   **C.** Name resolution

    B. Authentication   **D.** IP address mapping

4. What is the trust boundary in AD networks?

(Continues)

THE ESSENTIALS AND BEYOND *(Continued)*

5. Which of the following server types are implemented in most organizations to support AD DS operations and client connections? (Choose two.)

   A. DNS **C.** SharePoint

   B. IIS **D.** DHCP

6. Define a domain tree.

7. Define an AD site.

8. What can be created directly between two child domains in different paths of an AD domain hierarchy in order to improve authentication efficiency?

   A. Global Catalog **C.** Transitive trust

   B. Site link **D.** Shortcut trust

9. How many domains must be implemented at a minimum when you want to implement AD and support three locations on your WAN?

   A. 1 **C.** 6

   B. 3 **D.** 9

10. True or false: You cannot use the AD Recycle Bin feature until your entire forest is in the Windows Server 2008 R2 functional level?

CHAPTER 6

Configuring Active Directory

In the preceding chapter, you learned about the parts and pieces of the AD architecture. In this chapter, you will see how you can install AD on a single server. Configuring AD begins with the installation of the server role. Before you install and configure the server role, you always should perform key planning steps to ensure that the installation results in a useful AD implementation. For this you will need to understand the AD installation planning process. Next, you'll need to understand the steps required to install AD starting from the DNS server up to the point where you can begin to create user accounts. This chapter provides all the instructions you'll need to get an AD installation up and running.

The following topics will be addressed in this chapter:

▷ **AD installation process**

▷ **Installing DNS**

▷ **Installing the AD DS role**

▷ **Running the DCPROMO Wizard**

Planning an Active Directory Installation

An AD installation should be well planned. In a production environment, installations should always follow planning.

The AD installation process is not as simple as installing the Active Directory Domain Services (AD DS) server role, configuring it, and hoping for the best. In this section, you will learn how to carefully plan the installation steps before you begin executing them.

Microsoft recommends an AD installation planning flow that looks like Figure 6.1. Notice that it proceeds through four initial steps and ends with a summary step called Detailed Design. Steps 1 through 4 are high-level steps, which include the forests and the domains. Included in step 5 is organizational unit planning, determining the number of domain controllers (DCs), DC placement, Global Catalog (GC) placement, Operations Master role placement, and planning the site design. The following sections describe the decisions you must make during high-level planning steps and the detailed design step.

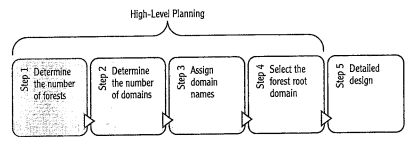

FIGURE 6.1 The AD planning process

High-Level Planning

The first high-level planning step is determining the number of forests required. AD deployments support both single and multiple forests. You may consider implementing multiple forests for any of the following reasons:

Multiple schemas are required.   A single schema is shared across a forest. It is possible that two or more applications could conflict with each other when they attempt to modify the same schema. You can create application forests so that they have a dedicated schema and eliminate such conflicts.

Separate forest administrators are required.   You may be implementing AD in an organization that is a collection of divisions or child organizations. Each organization may require complete separation of administration. Because the Enterprise Admins group can administer any domain in the forest, you may be required to create separate forests in order to provide truly separate administrative security boundaries for all divisions.

Legal or organizational policies demand it.   All domains in a forest trust all other domains in that forest through the inherent transitive-trust paths. Remember from the last chapter that all domains trust the domains below them and the domain above them in a domain tree. All the domains in a domain tree trust each other when they are in the same forest. The result, due to the fact that these trusts are transitive trusts, is that every domain trusts every other domain within a forest. For regulatory or policy reasons this may not be ideal. You can create distinct security boundaries by creating a separate forest.

A resource forest is needed. A resource forest is a forest that contains shared items that all users of all forests will require. For example, Exchange email servers may exist in a resource forest. Typically, resource forests are required only in implementations that demand multiple forests for one of the other previously listed reasons.

With this information, you can determine whether a single forest or multiple forests are required. If you determine that multiple forests are required, you may need to consider having trusts between forests. For example, if a user in one forest needs to access a resource in another forest, you may have to create a trust relationship in the remote forest to avoid having to create separate user accounts for the user in each forest in which he requires access.

After you have defined your forest needs, you can determine the number of domains you will require within the forest or forests. Several reasons exist for creating separate domains, including the following:

Replication Traffic Reduction If the domain will be very large (exceeding 100,000 objects), you may have to create a separate domain to reduce replication traffic. Large domains result in high amounts of replication traffic due to the fact that more frequent changes are occurring in a large domain. Whenever you want to reduce the network replication traffic for a single domain, you can achieve this through the implementation of more domains.

Improved Control over Replication Traffic When you have separate domains, you have even better control over replication traffic from the perspective of traffic flow across slow links. AD uses a compression algorithm on slow links that usually takes care of any problems; however, you can often eliminate the need for most replication traffic across slow links by creating separate domains at each location.

Frequently Changing Attributes Even in smaller domains, if object attributes are changed frequently, replication traffic can become excessive. You may have to create smaller domains in a highly dynamic environment.

Preservation of Legacy AD Installations Applications are not always upgradeable, and this can impact your AD planning. If you have an older application that runs on Windows Server 2003 and requires that version of AD, you may have to keep the Windows Server 2003 AD domain around while installing a newer Windows Server 2008 or later domain to take advantage of new features. The older Windows Server 2003 domain will effectively become an application domain.

◄ A resource forest may also be used in a high-security environment to allow service isolation.

◄ One option to explore is to create forest trusts between forests so that all of the domains in each forest automatically trust all of the domains in the other forest through the forest trust.

◄ An environment that frequently requires objects to be added, removed, or changed is referred to as being *dynamic*.

Another commonly encountered reason for creating separate domains is simply to mirror the organization. Stated differently, AD is often installed with a single domain for each division or department, assuming a separate forest is not required. Although organizational units (OUs) can also be used for this purpose, larger companies often use domains so that they can further divide the domains into logical administration structures through the use of OUs; while Microsoft discourages this practice, it is not uncommon in real production environments.

> Remember, OUs are administrative containers used to simplify the management of AD objects by providing a folder-type hierarchy for the objects.

When you are finished selecting the appropriate number of forests and domains, you are ready to move on to step 3 and name the domains. Organizations use many different methods for domain naming. Some organizations allow the Information Technology group to use whatever domain names they desire. In these environments, you often see names like Mordor.local, Stellar9.local, and DeepSpace.local. While these domains are fine for single domain deployments, they are not very descriptive and can be problematic for future growth or for multidomain deployments. For this reason, two primary naming methods are common in organizations that enforce policies for domain naming:

Specific Domain Names   For example, the root domain may be something like WidgetsRUs.com or GHI-INC.com. The domain name is based on the organization name.

Generic Domain Names   For example, the root domain may be something like corp.com or primary.local.

Whether you use specific domain names or generic domain names, you will have to decide whether you want to use Internet-based top-level domains (TLDs) or private top-level domains. Private top-level domains include the .local and .private domains. Internet-based top-level domains include .biz, .cc, .com, .org, and .net, among many others.

> You will learn more about choosing a top-level domain name later in the section of this chapter titled "Preparing to Install DNS."

It is also important that you consider the NetBIOS name that will be used for the domain. Windows Server 2008 and 2008 R2 domains still support NetBIOS domain names for backward compatibility. The domain names mentioned in the preceding paragraphs are DNS names. DNS names look like *company.local*, whereas NetBIOS names simply look like *company*. NetBIOS domain names are one-word domain names that can be up to 15 characters long. DNS domain names can have up to 255 characters in the entire FQDN. When you're selecting the DNS name, it is best to choose one mapping directly to a NetBIOS name for simplicity. For example, WidgetsRUs.com can map directly to the NetBIOS domain name of WidgetsRUs.

The final high-level planning task is the selection of the forest root domain. In a single domain deployment, the one domain is the forest root domain as well.

In large environments, it is common to have an empty forest root domain when deploying multiple domains. Some engineers recommend against using this practice because of the potential for increased complexity, but it is still in common use today. The forest root domain is used for Enterprise Admins and Schema Admins group provisioning and management, and nothing more. These two groups will contain users or groups who should have forest-wide administrative capabilities. Once you select a forest root domain, which is the first domain you install in the forest, you cannot change the name of that domain. For this reason, you should think carefully about the domain you select. More often than not, the root of the tree is selected, which would be something like *company*.com.

> ◀
>
> When you deploy a domain, you deploy a forest. A domain is part of one forest in every deployment; however, a single forest can have multiple domains.

Detailed Design

In the fifth step, several subtasks must be performed to create the detailed design for the domain, as shown in Figure 6.2. They include OU planning, determining the number and placement of domain controllers (DCs), assigning Global Catalog (GC) placement, selecting Operations Master role placement, and planning the site design.

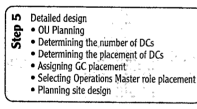

Step 5   Detailed design
- OU Planning
- Determining the number of DCs
- Determining the placement of DCs
- Assigning GC placement
- Selecting Operations Master role placement
- Planning site design

FIGURE 6.2 The detailed design subtasks

An OU is really a container used to store users, computers, and other domain objects. When planning an OU architecture, you should take into account two primary considerations:

Administrative Delegation   Think of an OU as a folder. Just as you can set permissions on a folder to allow users to manage files and folders within that folder, you can assign permissions to OUs to allow users to manage users, computers, and other objects in those OUs. Assigning permissions to the OU is called administrative delegation. For example, you can delegate the ability to reset passwords for user accounts to an individual who is not a member of the Domain Admins group.

Group Policy Application   Group Policies may be linked at several levels in the AD topology. They may be linked to domains, sites, OUs, and local machines that are AD domain members. When a Group Policy is linked to a container, it is applied to that container and to all objects within the container by default. As an example, assume you have an OU named Marketing and another OU named Sales. You could use Group Policies to deploy a marketing application to the Marketing OU computers or users. You could also deploy a sales application to the Sales OU computers or users. The point is that you create separate OUs so that you can configure the objects therein differently or deploy different software to them through Group Policies.

You will learn the details of Group Policy processing and implementation in Chapter 8.

After considering these two primary purposes for OU creation, you can begin planning an OU structure. The structure you choose may be based on your organization's hierarchy (which also reflects administrative needs), or it may be based on administrative needs alone. It is common to mix the two and first create OUs for each department or division in your company and then create administrative OUs in each departmental OU. Figure 6.3 shows an example of this mixed OU hierarchy.

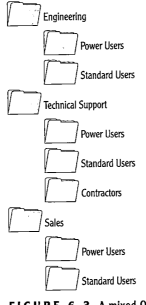

FIGURE 6.3 A mixed OU hierarchy

A mixed OU structure like the one in Figure 6.3 allows you to administer departments differently and to administer groups within those departments based on their needs. In this case, the sub-OUs are all based on permission capabilities. Power Users can be granted more capabilities than Standard

Users. Contractors can be administered differently from either Power Users or Standard Users. Alternatively, you can create OUs for each department and then sub-OUs for job roles within those departments. You may even choose to create top-level OUs for each location within a campus (not to be confused with sites) and then create sub-OUs for the departments within these location OUs. As you can see, you have extensive flexibility when creating an OU structure.

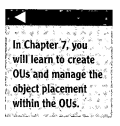

In Chapter 7, you will learn to create OUs and manage the object placement within the OUs.

The next detailed planning task is to determine the number of DCs. As a best practice, always start with two DCs and add additional DCs as needed. Two DCs are considered the minimum number for fault-tolerant purposes. If you have only one DC and that DC fails, users will be unable to log on. Additionally, you must consider each site on the network. Consider deploying two DCs per site in order to provide local logon capability and retain fault tolerance within the site in the event of a single server failure.

Additional DCs should be added as the workload demands it. For example, if you have two DCs and logons are processing slowly, you may have to add additional DCs to improve logon performance. Because there is so much variability in Windows Server environments, no specific algorithm can be used to determine the number of users that can be supported by a single domain controller. Windows Server can run on a server machine with specifications ranging from a dual-core processor to eight or more quad-core processors. Additionally, the server machine could have 4 GB of RAM or 32 or more GB of RAM. This means that in each environment you must evaluate the hardware profile of the servers to be deployed in order to determine the number of users each of those servers can support. A single server can certainly support 10,000 users or more as long as it has sufficient processing power, memory, and network throughput.

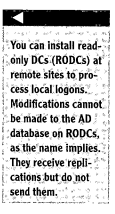

You can install read-only DCs (RODCs) at remote sites to process local logons. Modifications cannot be made to the AD database on RODCs, as the name implies. They receive replications but do not send them.

In addition to determining the number of DC servers required, you must plan the placement of those DCs. Microsoft defines DC locations as hub locations and satellite locations. *Hub locations* are the centralized locations where DCs are located, and these DCs serve many users within the organization while often acting as replication partners to satellite locations. *Satellite locations* are those DC locations serving fewer users (typically, a branch office location) and are often connected to a hub DC.

Administrators also often place DCs as close to users as possible. For example, you could install a DC on each floor of a building that is managed by a single switch or a cluster of switches. This would provide very close access to DCs and lower bandwidth consumption across the LAN or WAN for things like Group Policy processing and application installs (assuming the installation files are replicated to each DC). However, this model requires that replication traffic pass across the network from subnet-to-subnet, which may be a greater traffic cost than the logons as the traffic continues throughout the day.

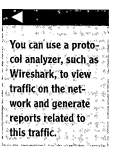

You can use a protocol analyzer, such as Wireshark, to view traffic on the network and generate reports related to this traffic.

The next two subtasks address specialty roles of the DCs:

▶ The Global Catalog (GC) role

▶ Site design planning

The GC contains a partial replica of all objects in every domain in the forest. This subset of data is used to provide faster searches of the directory. The GC also contains the Universal Groups and their membership lists. In a forest that contains a single domain deployment, Microsoft recommends that all DCs in the domain be configured as GC servers. In this situation, no additional requirements for storage, CPU usage, or replication traffic are generated by adding the GC role because all of the domain information is contained on each DC anyway. In large multiforest deployments, you will select a few DCs in each forest to play the role of the GC. In environments this large, the GC data set can become quite large and may cause heavy replication traffic. You should also know that some applications store data within AD, such as Microsoft Exchange. These applications may place increased demands on the required number of GC servers.

You must also choose the location for the Operations Master roles. The following guidelines can be used:

In smaller installations, you can leave the Operations Master roles on the default DC, which is the first DC installed.

PDC Emulator Role   Configure a DC with accessibility from all areas of the domain to play this role. When passwords are changed, users can log on immediately when this server is available.

RID Master Role   This DC can be less powerful and even unavailable at times. It gives out RIDs in pools of more than 500 to every other DC.

Infrastructure Master Role   This DC should be performing well because it is responsible for the synchronization of all group membership updates.

Schema Master Role   This DC will make all changes to the schema. Because the schema is not frequently modified, it can be a less powerful server. You must ensure it is online before you can change the schema.

Domain Naming Master Role   This DC must be online when you create or remove a domain or site.

Even with the preceding information, Microsoft recommends that you keep your Operations Master role plan simple. They suggest leaving a single-domain forest set to the defaults, which means that all Operations Master roles are on the first DC installed. In a multidomain, single-forest deployment, Microsoft recommends leaving all Operations Master roles on the first DC in the root domain and leaving them on the first DC in each additional domain (for the domain-specific roles). As you can see, following these recommendations will impact the AD installation process. You should always install the DCs that will contain the Operations Master roles first. Otherwise, you will have to manually move the roles after the installation is complete.

The final subtask is to plan the site design. In this task, you will define sites for each physical location where replication should be managed. You should understand that AD sites are not for replication only; they are also used to locate the nearest resources to a client for services such as user logon and the Distributed File System (DFS). In most network deployments, you will create an AD site for each physical location. Within a site there is an expectation of highly available bandwidth in order to support the frequency of intrasite replication. Whenever two locations are connected by a low-bandwidth connection, they should be broken into separate sites within AD. Sites may be connected with links not owned by your organization. For example, you could connect with a T1 line or with a different connection type, but have the connection use a leased line for data transfer. Even though you could allow replication to occur automatically, it is usually best to manually configure sites so that you can control the replication.

Because sites are based on IP subnets or collections of IP subnets, it's important that you have a good IP addressing plan. You must associate each site in AD with its corresponding subnets in order for client machines to use them appropriately. To learn more about IP addressing and planning an IP network, see *Microsoft Windows Networking Essentials* (Darril Gibson, Sybex, 2011).

> DFS is covered in detail in Chapter 11. It allows you to display distributed network resources to users as if they were in one location and to replicate resources out to multiple locations.

Installing Active Directory

After you've worked through the planning process, you're ready to begin installing AD. The installation process typically involves three phases as represented in Figure 6.4.

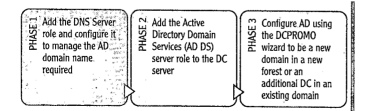

FIGURE 6.4 The three phases of AD installation

In the first phase, you must add the DNS Server role to a server if it does not already have DNS installed and configured within the environment. The DNS Server role is the component that allows a Windows server to act as a DNS server and provide hostname resolution for clients. If you are adding the DNS Server role to a new server, you will need to configure the server to act as the primary server for the zone you want it to manage. The zone that you configure will be for the namespace of your first AD domain. For example, if you plan to install a domain named company.com, you would create a zone with the same name on the DNS server.

The second phase is the addition of the AD DS Server role. Like other server roles, it is installed from within Server Manager. You will find the instructions for adding the AD DS Server role to a Windows Server 2008 R2 server in the section titled "Installing the AD DS Role."

The remainder of your high-level planning efforts will be put to good use in the final phase, AD configuration. A wizard will guide you through the process of configuring your first DC to meet your needs. This process is explained in the section titled "Running the DCPROMO Wizard."

LARGE AD INSTALLATIONS

Installing multiple domains or even multiple forests is more time-consuming than represented in this section. However, it is not really more complex. A domain is created by installing and configuring a DC. A forest is created when the first domain is installed. Therefore, large AD deployments really just require the installation of multiple DCs.

For example, imagine you want to install an AD deployment like the one represented in the following image:

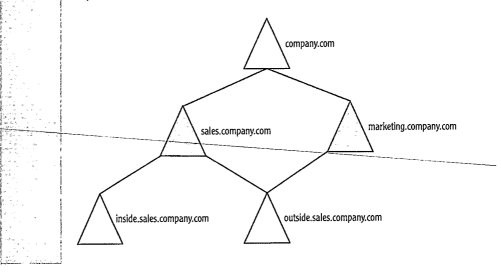

LARGE AD INSTALLATIONS *(Continued)*

You would first install the DC for the company.com domain at the root of the forest. Next, you would install the DCs for the sales.company. com domain and the marketing.company.com domain. You would continue this process for each domain. Do you see that the installation is not more complicated, but that it is more time-consuming? Don't be afraid of large-scale AD deployments. They are just like smaller deployments from an installation perspective. You just have to make the right decisions at the right moments in the Installation Wizard. Your plan will provide you with everything you need to make these decisions.

Preparing to Install DNS

Before you install the DNS Server role, you should spend some time planning your DNS infrastructure. With a solid plan, you can then add the DNS Server role to the appropriate server and configure the DNS zone it will manage.

First, you should ensure that you have a proper DNS domain name for your AD domain. If you plan to use a public DNS domain name, you will need to register it with the InterNIC (Internet Network Information Center) to avoid problems later. If you register the domain, no one else can set up a website with the same domain name. The InterNIC tracks registered domain names and resolves domain name transfer disputes. Many companies offer domain name registration on the Internet, and the following list is just a partial listing of these domain name registrars:

- ▶ GKG.net
- ▶ GoDaddy.com
- ▶ 1HostAustralia.com
- ▶ AdoptADomain.net
- ▶ AllDomains.com
- ▶ DomainPro.com
- ▶ FastDomain.com
- ▶ Internetters.co.uk
- ▶ NameWeb.biz

As you plan your domain name, you have to select a top-level domain name. The top-level domain is the right-most portion of the domain name. For example, if the domain name is company.biz, the top-level domain is .biz. Several top-level domains are available for use. You should register a valid Internet domain name for your AD domain even if you do not plan to use that domain name on the Internet. The reason is simple: if you register the domain name, you own it and you will avoid conflicts with other companies who may want that domain name for Internet use.

Many administrators use the .local top-level domain as a private domain name for temporary testing. This is fine for testing temporary installations or for learning purposes; however, it should not be used for a production network because there is no guarantee that the .local top-level domain will not be used in the future on the Internet.

At the time of writing, the only top-level domains that have been reserved and are guaranteed not to be used on the Internet are as follows:

The reserved top-level domains (TLDs) are documented in RFC 2606.

.localhost   Used for loop back to the local DNS server. Any other use may conflict with existing applications and services.

.test   Used to test current or new DNS-related code in development environments.

.example   Used in documentation or examples. The domain names of example.com, example.net, and example.org are also reserved.

.invalid   Used to specify that the domain names are clearly invalid. Although you could use this reserved top-level domain internally, it could confuse your users and might not work with all DNS clients.

THE TRAINING.LOCAL DOMAIN

In this chapter and the remaining chapters, the domain named training .local will be used for all demonstrations. Remember, it is only a useful domain name for testing and learning environments. In the remaining sections of this chapter, you will install and configure a domain and the DC for that domain. The training.local domain name is only an example and is not intended to be used within any production environment.

In later chapters, this domain will be extended to support an OU hierarchy for delegated administration. It will also be used for Group Policy application and for user and group management. If you plan to follow along with procedures in future chapters, it is important that you install the domain as this chapter describes.

(Continues)

THE TRAINING.LOCAL DOMAIN *(Continued)*

If you do not have a physical server with Windows Server 2008 R2 running, you can download a VHD file that includes the trial edition of the operating system. A VHD is a virtual hard drive that is used with a virtualization application such as Virtual PC or VMware Player to run an operating system as a virtual machine. The VHD files available from Microsoft are designed to work only with Virtual PC and Hyper-V. You will find the location of the VHD files here: `http://www.microsoft.com/windowsserver2008/en/us/try-it.aspx`.

The trial edition of the Windows Server 2008 R2 DVD is available here:

> `http://technet.microsoft.com/en-us/evalcenter/ee175713.aspx`.

Adding the DNS Server Role

The DNS Server role is added to a Windows Server 2008 R2 server by using the Server Manager console. To launch the Server Manager and add the DNS Server role, follow these steps:

1. Log on to the server as an administrator.

2. Click Start ≻ All Programs ≻ Administrative Tools ≻ Server Manager.

3. Select the Roles node in the left pane (which is called the Console Tree) of Server Manager.

4. Click the Add Roles link to launch the Add Roles Wizard.

> **◄**
>
> Alternatively, you can click Start and then right-click on the Computer shortcut and select Manage.

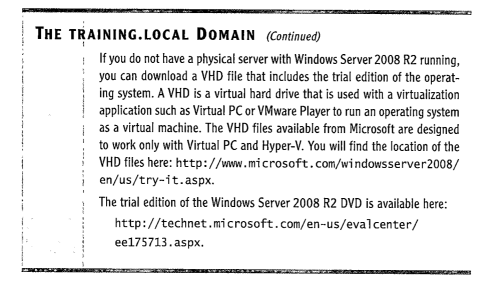

5. If the Before You Begin screen is displayed, click Next to select the DNS Server role.

6. On the Select Server Roles page of the wizard, select the DNS Server role by checking the box next to it.

> If you are presented with a warning dialog stating that you have no static IP addresses, be sure to configure the IP address with a static address before continuing.

7. Read the overview information presented on the DNS Server page of the wizard and, when ready, click Next to continue.

8. On the Confirm Installation Selections page, click Install to add the DNS Server role.

9. On the Installation Results page, click Close to exit the wizard.

After you perform this procedure, the Server Manager interface will change to reflect the newly added DNS Server role, as shown in Figure 6.5. If you no longer need the role, you can remove it by clicking the Remove Roles link. Click the Go to DNS Server link in the DNS Server section of the Roles page to view the DNS Server role administration interface. Close the Server Manager when you have finished adding roles.

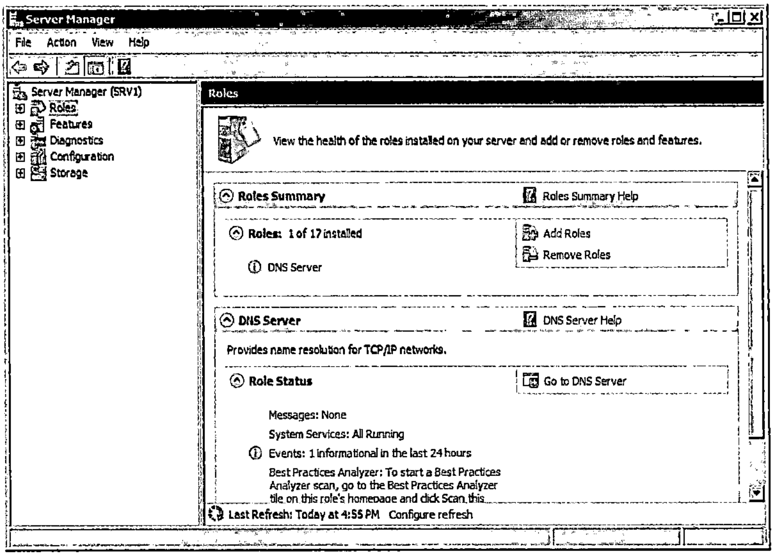

FIGURE 6.5 The Server Manager Roles page after the DNS Server role is added to a Windows Server 2008 R2 server

Configuring the DNS Zone

The preceding section showed you how to add the DNS Server role; however, it still is not configured to provide hostname resolution for the DNS zone training.local. To configure the DNS zone, follow this procedure:

1. Click Start ➢ All Programs ➢ Administrative Tools ➢ DNS.

2. When the DNS Manager loads, double-click on the server name in the left pane to expand the local server.

3. Because you want to create a forward lookup zone to resolve hostnames to IP addresses, right-click on Forward Lookup Zones and choose New Zone.
   You may have to click on the Forward Lookup Zones node before the right-click action will work.

4. In the New Zone Wizard, click Next to begin creating the forward lookup zone.

5. On the Zone Type page, choose the Primary Zone because this is the first DNS server to manage the training.local zone.

A *forward lookup zone* resolves hostnames to IP addresses. A *reverse lookup zone* resolves IP addresses to hostnames.

If you add another DNS server for fault tolerance later, you will configure it to be the Secondary Zone server.

6. After selecting Primary Zone, click Next.

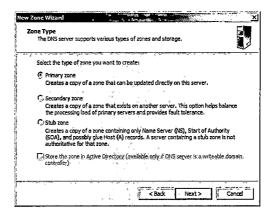

7. On the Zone Name page, enter the Zone Name value of **training.local**, as shown in the following image.

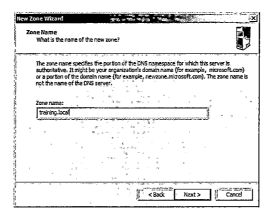

8. On the Zone File page, accept the default file for zone storage (training.local.dns) and click Next.

9. On the Dynamic Update page, select to Allow Both Nonsecure And Secure Dynamic Updates so that clients can automatically register their hostnames and IP addresses with the DNS server, and then click Next.

> ▶
>
> **You cannot select only secure dynamic updates until after AD is installed. After AD is installed, you can change this to Allow Only Secure Dynamic Updates.**

10. On the Completing the New Zone Wizard page, click Finish to create the zone.

After following these steps, you will see a new child node (named `training .local`) in the Forward Lookup Zones node. You may want to create a reverse lookup zone as well, so that you can discover the hostname belonging to a known IP address. Instructions for creating a reverse lookup zone can be found at:

`http://technet.microsoft.com/en-us/library/cc753997.aspx.`

Configuring the IP Settings and Primary DNS Suffix

Now that DNS is up and running on the server, you need to configure the server to use the DNS service. To do this, you will have to modify the IP configuration on the server. The following procedure will reconfigure the server to use itself as a DNS resolution server:

1. Click Start, right-click on Network, and select Properties.

2. In the Network and Sharing Center, click the link that reads Change Adapter Settings in the left navigation panel.

3. Right-click on the network adapter, usually named Local Area Connection, and select Properties.
   You can alternatively hold down the Alt key and double-click to view the Properties dialog.

> As a shortcut for steps 1 and 2, click Start and type *ncpa.cpl* into the Search field and then press Enter. You'll get to the same screen you see after step 2.
> ◄

4. In the Properties dialog, double-click on the Internet Protocol Version 4 (TCP/IPv4) item to modify the IP configuration.

5. Set the Preferred DNS Server IP address to the same value as the IP Address value of the local server, as in the following screen (your IP addresses may vary), and then click OK to save the changes.

6. Close all remaining windows.

In addition to changing the IP settings on the server, if you want the server to be able to browse the Internet, you will have to tell it where to look for Internet name resolution servers. You could do this with a secondary DNS server, but you should do it in the DNS Server role so that that server can resolve local and Internet hostnames for clients. You can do this in the DNS Manager by right-clicking on the server node and selecting Properties. In the Properties dialog, select the Forwarders tab and add a valid Internet DNS server, such as the Google DNS server at 8.8.4.4, which they provide for public use. Figure 6.6 shows this configuration.

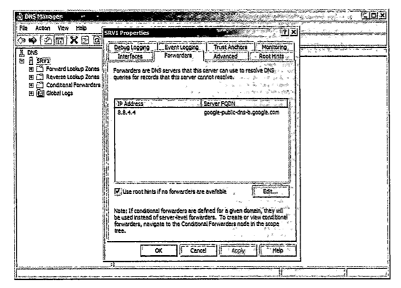

FIGURE 6.6 Forwarders configured in the DNS server

The final task before installing the AD DS role is to configure the primary DNS suffix on the server. The primary DNS suffix is used to define the FQDN of the server. The server name (hostname) is the first part of the FQDN, and the primary DNS suffix is the second. To configure the primary DNS suffix to be training.local, follow these steps:

1. Click Start, right-click on Computer, and select Properties.

2. Click the Change Settings link in the Computer Name, Domain, and Workgroup Settings section.

3. On the Computer Name tab, click the Change button.

4. In the Computer Name/Domain Changes dialog, click the More button.

5. Enter the value **training.local** in the Primary DNS Suffix Of This Computer field, as shown in the following image.

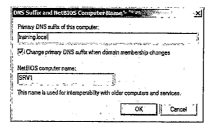

6. Click OK and close the remaining dialogs with the OK buttons.

7. When prompted to restart your computer, click Restart Now.

UNDERSTANDING THE PRIMARY DNS SUFFIX

The primary DNS suffix is appended to a one-word name when connections are requested using a one-word computer name. This includes connections requested from any command or operation. An example would be a PING command attempt executed against a one-word computer name like computer25. First, the connection is assumed to be DNS-based, and the primary DNS suffix is added to the one-word name. In the training.local domain, this would become computer25.training.local. If the FQDN cannot be resolved, the primary DNS suffix is removed and the connection is made as a NetBIOS name.

After rebooting the server, you should log on as an administrator and verify the configuration. You can verify DNS operations by opening the DNS administration tool and viewing the training.local forward lookup zone. The zone should now contain a Host (A) record for the local server. You can also verify operations by pinging an Internet website such as www.sysedco.com with the Command Prompt PING command to verify Internet DNS name resolution. If the domain name is resolved to an IP address, you know that DNS name resolution is working properly and you are ready to begin installing the actual AD DS role.

Installing the AD DS Role

Installing the AD DS Server role is one of the simplest tasks in the AD deployment process. The server role installation requires no configuration; however, you will not have an active AD deployment until you run the DCPROMO Wizard after installing the AD DS role. The next section titled "Running the DCPROMO Wizard" provides instructions for creating the AD domain named `training.local`. The following steps are used to add the AD DS role to a Windows Server 2008 R2 machine:

1. Log on to the server as an administrator.

2. Click Start All Programs Administrative Tools Server Manager.

3. Select the Roles node in the left pane by clicking on it.

4. Click the Add Roles link in the Roles Summary section of the Role screen.

5. If the Before You Begin page is displayed, click Next to continue with the Add Roles Wizard.

6. On the Select Server Roles page, select the Active Directory Domain Services role by clicking the box next to it.

7. If prompted to Add Features Required for Active Directory Domain Services, click the Add Required Features button.

8. Click Next to continue with the Add Roles Wizard.

9. On the Active Directory Domain Services page, read the provided information and click Next when you are ready to continue.

10. On the Confirm Installation Selections page, review the roles and features to be installed and click Install when ready.

11. When the installation completes, review the information on the Installation Results screen and click Close.

12. Close the Server Manager to complete the installation.

> You should only install server roles that are required on the target server. Installing unnecessary roles may reduce the performance of the server and increase the server's attack surface.

◀

As you can see, the installation of the AD DS role is very simple. You didn't need a plan to install the role, but the plan is important when you configure the role, which you will do in the next section.

Running the DCPROMO Wizard

One final task is required to get AD up and running on your server. You must run the DCPROMO Wizard to configure the domain and install the local server as a DC for the domain. You can run the DCPROMO Wizard from within Server Manager or from the Start menu's Search field. If you want to run DCPROMO from Server Manager, simply open the Server Manager, expand the Roles node, click on the Active Directory Domain Services node, and then click the link that reads Run the Active Directory Domain Services Installation Wizard (dcpromo. exe), as shown in Figure 6.7.

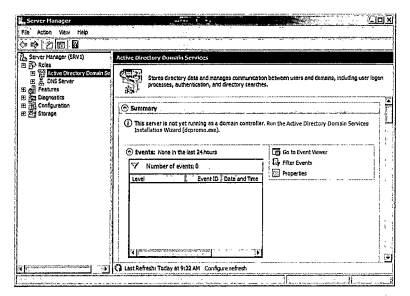

FIGURE 6.7 Viewing the Server Manager interface that allows execution of the DCPROMO Wizard

To run the DCPROMO Wizard and configure the `training.local` domain using the Start menu's Search field on Windows Server 2008 R2, follow these steps:

1. Click Start, type **dcpromo** in the Search field, and press Enter.
   The Active Directory Domain Services Installation Wizard will start.

2. On the Welcome to the Active Directory Domain Services Installation Wizard page, select Use Advanced Mode Installation and then click Next.

3. Read the provided information on the Operating System Compatibility screen.

This screen informs you that some compatibility issues may exist with old Windows NT 4.0 servers. Note the Knowledge Base article referenced for more information.

4. Click Next to continue.

5. On the Choose a Deployment Configuration screen, select Create a New domain in a New Forest because you are creating the first domain, which will be named `training.local` for the DNS name and `training` for the NetBIOS name.

6. Click Next to continue.

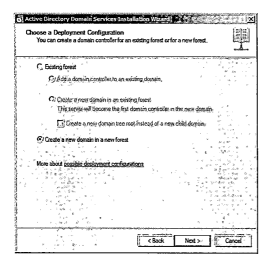

7. On the Name the Forest Root Domain screen, enter **training.local** in the FQDN of the Forest Root Domain field and click Next.

The wizard will verify the availability of the domain name and forest root name before continuing.

8. On the Domain NetBIOS Name screen, accept the default NetBIOS name TRAINING and click Next.

9. On the Set Forest Functional Level screen, choose the Forest Functional Level of Windows Server 2008 R2 and click Next.

The wizard will examine the DNS configuration, and this may take some time. Do not be alarmed by the delay.

In a lab environment, you can use the latest features. In a production environment, be sure to use a functional level that is compatible with your existing domains, applications, and client platforms.

10. On the Additional Domain Controller Options page, read the provided information and click Next.

Because you installed and configured DNS before running the wizard, you know it is configured for your needs.

11. On the Create DNS Delegation screen, select No, Do Not Create the DNS Delegation.

12. If you want to learn more about DNS Delegations, click the DNS Delegations link; otherwise, click Next to continue.

Root forest DNS zones, like `company.com` or `training.local`, do not require delegation records within their parent zones (which are TLDs). Only child domains in AD require the parent delegation records.

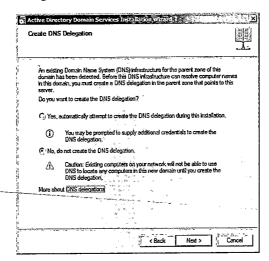

13. On the Location for Database, Log Files and SYSVOL screen, note that you can change the default locations, but accept all the defaults and click Next to continue.

14. On the Directory Services Restore Mode Administrator Password screen, enter **Password1** in both the Password and Confirm Password fields.

    Alternatively, you can enter a password of your choosing, but be sure you remember the password. For a lab scenario such as this, Password1 is easy to remember.

15. When finished, click Next.

16. On the Summary screen, review your selections and click Next to begin the AD installation and configuration process.

    The server must be rebooted when installation completes. You can optionally check the box that reads Reboot On Completion so that the server will reboot automatically.

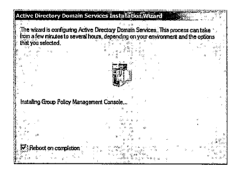

17. If you are alerted that "The DNS zone could not be created because it already exists," simply click OK.

    This is normal because you created the DNS zone before running the wizard.

18. If you did not choose the Reboot On Completion option after step 16, select the option to reboot the server.

When the server reboots, you will find that AD is installed and operational. At the first logon after the reboot, you will notice that you are logging on to the domain and not the local server machine. You can log on with the same password that was used for the local Administrator account before installing AD.

To verify that AD is running and accessible, open the Active Directory Users and Computers application in Administrative Tools on the Start menu. You should see the `training.local` domain with child nodes under it, including a Users container containing the Administrator and Guest user accounts. Only the Administrator account is enabled by default, as shown in Figure 6.8. The down arrow icon on the Guest account indicates that it is disabled. Your AD installation is now complete.

By default, the domain Administrator account password will be the same as the local machine's Administrator account password before you installed AD. This is true only of the first DC configured in the domain.

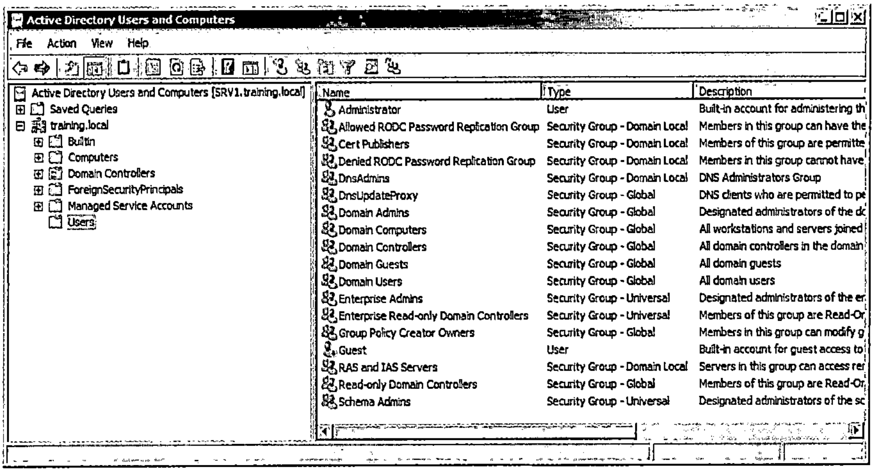

FIGURE 6.8 Viewing the Active Directory Users and Computers application after AD installation

THE ESSENTIALS AND BEYOND

Active Directory (AD) installation begins with planning. A well-thought-out plan considers the forests, domains, and domain trees and ensures that an architecture is selected that will support the needs of today and the demands of the future. The actual installation process for your first domain controller (DC) involves the proper installation and configuration of DNS, the addition of the Active Directory Domain Services (AD DS) Server role, and the configuration of AD DS through the DCPROMO Wizard. Before you configure DNS, be sure to have a clear plan for the domain names you will deploy in your environment. Carefully select the forest root domain, because it cannot be changed later. When installation is complete, you will be able to log on as an administrator of the AD domain. In this chapter, you installed the `training.local` AD domain.

(Continues)

THE ESSENTIALS AND BEYOND *(Continued)*

ADDITIONAL EXERCISES

▶ Download Virtual PC 2007 (Windows XP or Vista) or Windows Virtual PC (Windows 7) and install it on a machine with 3 GB of RAM or more.

▶ Download the Windows Server 2008 R2 trial VHD for use as a virtual Windows server and add it to Virtual PC 2007 or Windows Virtual PC.

▶ Install AD from start to finish, using the instructions in this chapter. Use the `training.local` domain so that you can perform the procedures in later chapters based on this domain.

To compare your answers to the author's, please visit www.sybex.com/go/ winadminessentials.

REVIEW QUESTIONS

1. What is the first step in planning an AD deployment according to Microsoft?

    A. Determining the number of domains required

    B. Determining the number of DCs required

    C. Determining the number of forests required

    D. Determining the location of the DCs

2. True or false: You can have multiple schemas in a single AD forest.

3. Which one of the following is not a valid reason for creating a separate domain?

    A. Reducing replication traffic

    B. Preserving legacy AD installations

    C. You have more than 1,200 users

    D. Improving control over replication traffic

4. What domain will be the forest root domain in a multiple-domain installation with a single forest?

5. What are the two primary reasons for creating an OU? (Choose two.)

    A. Reducing replication traffic

    B. Administrative delegationns

    C. Group Policy application

    D. Creating a trust boundary

6. Define a forest trust.

7. Define a resource forest.

(Continues)

THE ESSENTIALS AND BEYOND *(Continued)*

8. How many domain controllers should a domain have at a minimum, regardless of the size of the domain?

   A. 1   **C.** 3

   B. 2   **D.** 4

9. What are the two placement locations that Microsoft defines for domain controllers (DCs)? (Choose two.)

   A. Edge   **C.** Internal

   B. Hub   **D.** Satellite

10. True or false: The Global Catalog contains an entire replica of the domain databases for every domain in the forest.

CHAPTER 7

Managing Active Directory

Windows Server ships with several tools for managing Active Directory (AD) installations. These tools allow you to create user accounts, groups, and other objects within the AD deployment. They also allow you to manage the architecture for sites, domains, and trust relationships. In this chapter, you will begin by exploring the different AD management tools available to you. Then you will move on to discover how you can work with user accounts and groups. This includes understanding user and group management the Microsoft way, which is with the AGDLP model. Finally, you will learn more about organizational units than you did in preceding chapters.

You will learn about all of these important concepts and skills as you consider the following topics:

▷ **Exploring AD management tools**

▷ **Working with users and groups**

▷ **Understanding organizational units and containers**

Exploring AD Management Tools

Some tools allow you to work with both the architecture and object management.

The AD management tools fall into two categories: architecture management and object management. The architecture management tools allow you to configure the AD architecture for sites, replication, Operations Master roles, and administration. The object management tools allow you to create and work with users, groups, computers, printers, and other AD objects. Additionally, the object management tools allow you to create and manage organizational unit hierarchies. This section introduces the primary AD management tools and their purposes.

Understanding the AD Architecture Management Tools

Three toolsets are used to manage the AD architecture:

- ▶ Active Directory Sites and Services
- ▶ Active Directory Domains and Trusts
- ▶ Active Directory Module for Windows PowerShell

As a beginning Windows Server administrator, you are not likely to be called upon to work with these tools; however, understanding the roles they play in architecture management will be useful.

The Active Directory Sites and Services tool is used to create and manage sites. You first create a site that will be linked with one or more IP subnets. For example, you could create a site named BRANCHOFFICE. You could then define subnets and link them with the site. For example, you could define the subnet of 10.10.20.0/24, which indicates that the network address is 10.10.20 and the remaining octet (the last field) would be available to host addresses. Figure 7.1 shows the Active Directory Sites and Services tool.

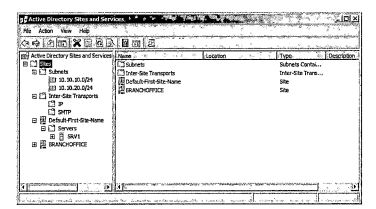

FIGURE 7.1 The Active Directory Sites and Services tool showing multiple sites and subnets

If you plan to use the default site-to-site replication configuration, you really need not do more; however, if you want to control the replication, you can create new Inter-Site Transports to define the schedule of replication and the frequency within that schedule. You can also configure SMTP for replication to remote sites without active WAN connections. The changes to the AD database can be sent to the remote site by using email messages. SMTP is not normally used unless a very slow WAN link is in place. Standard IP communications are used on faster WAN links for replication.

The Active Directory Domains and Trusts tool is used to create trust relationships and manage the domain functional level. If the domain is operating at a functional level lower than the highest level supported by the DC operating system, you can raise the level to the highest level supported. It is important to know that you cannot roll back to an earlier functional level after the domain has been raised to a higher functional level. This is because the newer functional levels actually change the schema of the AD domain. Always exercise caution when raising functional levels.

You also can manage the Domain Naming Operations Master role using Active Directory Domains and Trusts. Figure 7.2 shows the Active Directory Domains and Trusts tool with the Operations Master dialog open. You can only move the Domain Naming Operations Master role to another DC within the same forest, and you must be logged on as a member of the Enterprise Admins group to perform this action.

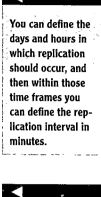

You can define the days and hours in which replication should occur, and then within those time frames you can define the replication interval in minutes.

The three domain-specific Operations Master roles (RID pool, PDC, and Infrastructure) are configured in Active Directory Users and Computers.

FIGURE 7.2 Viewing the Operations Master dialog in Active Directory Domains and Trusts

By default, transitive trust relationships exist that allow communications between all domains within a forest; however, you may want to create shortcut trusts directly between domains within a forest or even create a forest trust between two separate forests. The Active Directory Domains and Trusts tool is used to manage and create these trust relationships.

The final architecture management tool is actually a collection of tools or commands. The Active Directory Module for Windows PowerShell provides dozens of cmdlets for general AD administration. Several cmdlets are available for AD architecture management, including:

> **A cmdlet is a command in the Windows PowerShell interface. Think of cmdlets as traditional commands at the DOS prompt or Windows Command Prompt.**

`Get-ADDomain` Retrieves the AD domain information from the domain to which the currently accessed machine belongs. Figure 7.3 shows the output of this command.

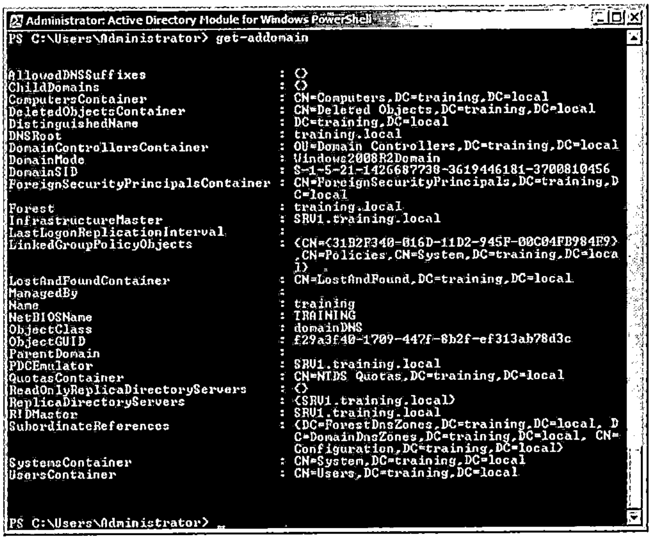

FIGURE 7.3 Using the Get-ADDomain cmdlet included in the Active Directory Module for Windows PowerShell

`Get-ADForest` Retrieves the information about the forest specified or, if no forest is specified, the forest to which the currently accessed machine belongs.

`Get-ADDomainController` Retrieves the information about the DC specified or, if no DC is specified, the currently accessed DC.

`Get-ADRootDSE` Retrieves the root of a directory server information tree. This provides information about the configuration and capabilities of the directory server.

`Set-ADForest` Used to modify global parameters in the forest.

`Set-ADForestMode` Used to set the forest functional level.

`Set-ADDomain` Used to modify global parameters in the domain.

`Set-ADDomainMode` Used to set the domain functional level

Understanding the AD Object Management Tools

The AD object management tools have been enhanced with Windows Server 2008 R2. You can use the Active Directory Users and Computers (ADUC) tool, which has been in Windows Server for a very long time. You can also use the new Active Directory Administrative Center, shown in Figure 7.4. Finally, you can use the Active Directory Module for Windows PowerShell.

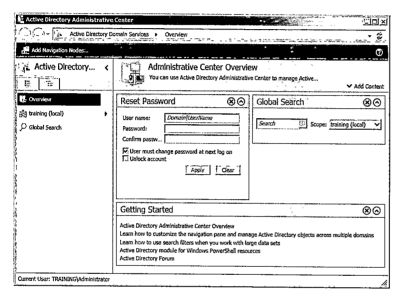

FIGURE 7.4 The Active Directory Administrative Center

New to Windows Server 2008 R2, the Active Directory Administrative Center (ADAC) lets you manage common AD administration tasks, including:

- ► User management

- ► Group management

- ► Computer management

- ► Organizational unit management

- ► Domain and forest functional-level management

The ADAC is built completely on Windows PowerShell cmdlets. This means that any change you make in ADAC actually calls on a PowerShell script to do the work.

The traditional tool for AD object management is ADUC. It is the most commonly used tool for AD management because you'll spend most of your time creating and managing users and groups. Using ADUC, you can perform nearly all object management tasks required, including:

▶ All tasks performed in ADAC

▶ Advanced delegation and permission management

▶ Creating queries to display subsets of the AD information

▶ Saving, exporting, and importing queries

▶ Perform Group Policy processing planning with Resultant Set of Policy

You will learn more about Resultant Set of Policy planning in Chapter 8.

The final object management toolset is the Active Directory Module for Windows PowerShell. This same module that is used for architecture management tasks can be used to manage AD objects such as users and groups.

The following Windows PowerShell cmdlets are used to work with computer objects in the domains:

```
New-ADComputer

Get-ADComputer

Remove-ADComputer

Set-ADComputer
```

The following Windows PowerShell cmdlets are used to work with user objects in the domains:

```
New-ADUser

Get-ADUser

Remove-ADUser

Set-ADUser
```

The following Windows PowerShell cmdlets are used to work with group objects in the domains:

```
New-ADGroup

Get-ADGroup

Remove-ADGroup

Set-ADGroup
```

The following Windows PowerShell cmdlets are used to work with group memberships in the domains:

    Get-ADGroupMember

    Remove-ADGroupMember

The following Windows PowerShell cmdlets are used to work with other objects in the domains:

    New-ADObject

    Get-ADObject

    Remove-ADObject

    Set-ADObject

In Figure 7.5, the New-ADUser command is being used to create a new user.

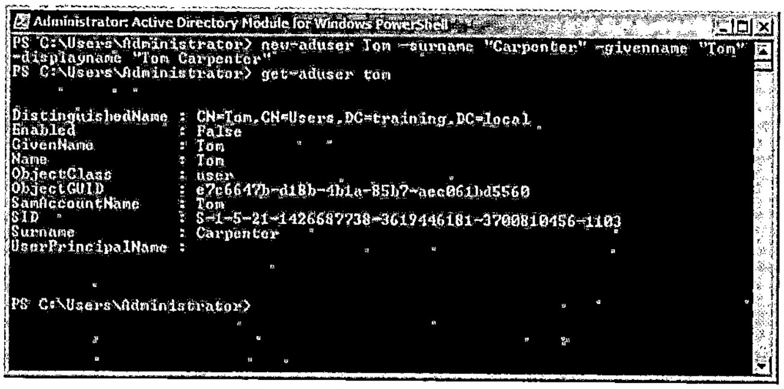

FIGURE 7.5 Creating a new user in the Active Directory Module for Windows PowerShell interface

Working with Users and Groups

Now that you are aware of the different management tools available to you for AD administration, you need to understand the difference between user accounts (users) and groups, the two primary objects you'll work with in AD. Additionally, you should understand the Microsoft-recommended model for user and group management.

User Account Types

Two account types can be created in Windows-based networks: local accounts and domain accounts.

Local accounts are created in the local database on a Windows computer. The Windows computer may be running Windows Server operating systems or Windows client operating systems. Both operating systems support local accounts. Local accounts are created by using the Computer Management interface on the machine. You should create local accounts in the following scenarios:

▶ When you need local accounts on Windows clients that are not part of a domain

▶ When you need accounts locally on Windows clients that are part of a domain so that users can log on locally instead of to the domain

▶ When you have a stand-alone Windows server that is not part of a domain

▶ When you have a service that must run as a user, but you do not want to run the service with a domain account

Domain accounts are created and stored in the AD database. They are used by users to log on to the domain and by services that must run in the context of an account with domain access. You cannot create domain accounts unless you have first created a forest and within it, a domain. Additionally, you must have the permissions required to create domain accounts. The Domain Admins group has sufficient permissions to create domain accounts. For more information on the different groups built into the AD installation, see the section titled "Working with Groups."

Both domain and local accounts have user profiles, which store the settings and files that are specific to the user. You can store user profiles for domain accounts on a network server; these profiles are called *roaming profiles* or *mandatory profiles*.

When using roaming profiles, you should ensure a consistent environment so that different versions of the same software do not overwrite settings and cause application failures.

Roaming Profiles   Can be modified by the user and are stored on the network so that they can be accessed from any Windows client.

Mandatory Profiles   Cannot be modified by the user, but they are stored on the network as well.

Local account profiles are stored on the local machine only because they do not participate in a domain. Only domain user accounts support roaming or mandatory profiles. Because the domain accounts profiles may be stored on a server, users can roam from machine to machine and take their settings with them. Domain accounts can also use local profiles. In many cases, local profiles are preferred for domain accounts—for example, when users never roam from machine to machine.

Creating User Accounts

Creating a user account is a simple and straightforward process. You will need a few pieces of information to create a new account, including:

User Logon Name   The name entered in the Logon field to log on to the network. This is called the User Logon Name (pre-Windows 2000) in the User Creation dialog.

User First Name   The user's given name.

User Last Name   The user's surname.

User Principal Name   The username that looks like an email address and is the real identity behind the scenes. This is called the User Logon Name in the User Creation dialog.

Password   The initial password used for the account.

> ◄
>
> The User Principal Name (UPN) is formatted based on Internet standards and, therefore, looks like an email address.

You can define additional account properties after creating the user account, but these properties are required when initially creating the account using the wizard.

To understand the account creation process, assume you want to create an account with the following parameters:

- ▶ User Logon Name: FredR
- ▶ User First Name: Fred
- ▶ User Last Name: Redrock
- ▶ User Principal Name: FredR@training.local
- ▶ Password: Password1

To create this account, use the following procedure:

1. Select Start ➣ All Programs ➣ Administrative Tools ➣ Active Directory Users and Computers.
   This step will be abbreviated to "Launch ADUC" in future procedures in this chapter.

2. Expand the training.local domain in the left pane.

3. Select the Users container.

4. Right-click the Users container and select New ➣ User.

5. On the first screen of the New Object - User dialog, enter the appropriate values in the fields, as shown in the following image, and then click Next.

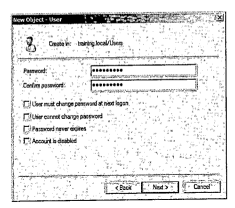

6. Enter **Password1** in both the Password and Confirm Password fields.

7. Deselect the User Must Change Password At Next Logon option, as shown in the following example, and click Next.

In production environments, you will usually leave the User Must Change Password At Next Logon value checked so users can personalize the password.

8. Click Finish to create the account.

After completing this process, you will have a new user account for Fred Redrock in the Users container. In production environments, it is common to create user accounts within organizational units instead of built-in containers, such as Users, but the Users container works fine for small environments. In the section titled "Understanding Organizational Units and Containers," we will explore the built-in container and discuss in detail each organizational-unit-creation process.

Now that you have created the Fred Redrock account, you can explore its many properties. When you double-click on a user account in ADUC, you will see the Properties dialog for that account, as shown in Figure 7.6. As you can see, several tabs are provided with many properties on each tab. The following sections explain each tab and its purpose.

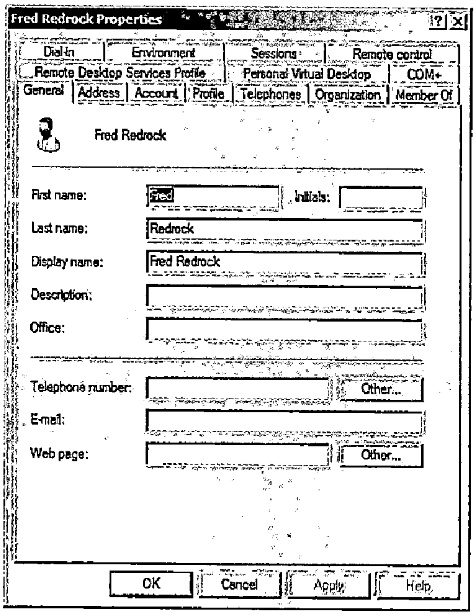

FIGURE 7.6 The Fred Redrock Properties dialog

General   The General tab is used to configure basic account settings, including a description, telephone number, email address, web page, and user display names.

Address   The Address tab is a nontechnical properties tab. It allows you to specify the street or P.O. Box address of the user, including city, state, and zip code settings.

Account   The Account tab is used to configure settings specific to account operations. These settings include the UPN and NetBIOS logon names, the allowed logon hours, the machines to which the user may log on, the account lockout status, and various additional account options. You can also set an account expiration date on this tab.

Profile   The Profile tab includes the user profile path, the logon script, and the Home folder settings. The user profile path is used to enable networked roaming user profiles. The logon script is used to specify a process that should run each time the user logs on to the network and may include batch files, executables, or Windows PowerShell scripts. The Home folder is intended to be the default location for user data. Although you can still manage these settings on this tab, most of the settings are managed through Group Policy.

Telephones   In addition to the telephone number that can be set on the General tab, the Telephones tab allows you to set a home, pager, mobile, fax, or IP phone number, and you can use it to add notes to describe the numbers.

Organization   The Organization tab provides fields for information related to organizational hierarchies and positions. You can enter the user's job title, department, and company on this tab. You may also specify the user's manager and view any other user's who are managed by the current user as direct reports.

The direct reports are built automatically based on the configuration of each user's manager. You do not have to enter the direct reports' information.

Member Of   The Member Of tab is used to manage group memberships from the user account perspective. Group memberships can also be managed from the Group Properties dialog box. You can set a primary group on this tab, but the primary group is required only for older Macintosh clients or Portable Operating System Interface (POSIX) applications, both of which are rare in modern networks.

Remote Desktop Services Profile   The Remote Desktop Services Profile tab is used to set up a separate user profile for accounts that use a Terminal Services server or access a server with Remote Desktop enabled. You can specify the profile path as a network path. You can also specify a separate Home folder for Remote Desktop Services connections, or you can indicate that this account is denied the user permissions to log on to Remote Desktop Session Host servers.

You will learn more about Remote Desktop Services and Terminal Services in Chapter 12.

Personal Virtual Desktop   The Personal Virtual Desktop tab is used to assign a specific virtual machine to the user account for the user's virtual Desktop. Personal virtual Desktops require the deployment of the Remote Desktop (RD) Virtualization Host on a Hyper-V server. RD Virtualization Host is a new role service included with Windows Server 2008 R2. You cannot use this feature with Windows Server 2008 servers.

COM+   COM+ partitions allow applications to be organized in logical containers. These applications run independently of configurations in other partitions. The partition is the configuration boundary. In most cases, COM+ partitions are deployed for web-based applications. The application can be configured differently for different pools of users and then placed into different partitions. The

COM+ tab allows you to select the appropriate COM+ partition for the current user account, if applicable.

Dial-in The Dial-in tab is used to configure remote network access properties for both dial-in users and VPN connections. You can set network access permissions to allow access, deny access, or use the Network Policy Server role on a Windows Server 2008 or later server to determine access. For true dial-in users, you can define a caller ID value for verification and require callbacks to the user's telephone number. Additionally, you can assign static IP addresses and static routes to control the reachable destinations for remote connections.

Environment The Environment tab is relevant only to Remote Desktop Services connections. You can specify a program to start automatically at logon, and you can control whether client devices (drives and printers) show up in the Remote Desktop session.

Sessions The Sessions tab is relevant only to Remote Desktop Services connections. You can use it to set properties for the connection (session), including:

- ▶ Set the delay timer to end a disconnected session.
- ▶ Set the delay timer to end active or idle sessions.
- ▶ Disconnect or end sessions when the active or idle timer expires.
- ▶ Allow sessions to be reconnected from any client or from the original client only (called the originating client in the user Properties interface).

Remote Control The Remote Control tab is relevant only to Remote Desktop Services connections. On this tab, you can designate whether to allow remote control. Remote control allows an administrator to take over the user's session for troubleshooting purposes or to demonstrate an action. You can also define whether the administrator can only view the session or also interact with the session.

Group Types and Scopes

Groups are used to manage multiple users and other groups as a unit. You can create a group, place one or more users in the group, and then assign permissions to the group. Those permissions are then applicable to every user in the group. Windows servers support multiple group types with different scopes of operation.

The first groups to consider are domain groups. They are created in ADUC and include three types: domain local, global, and universal. You should understand the scope of each group so you can select the appropriate group type for your needs.

Domain Local　Domain local groups can include members from any domain in the forest. These groups are used to assign permissions within a domain. They cannot be assigned permissions to resources outside of the domain in which they are created. Domain local groups can include the following members:

- ▶ Domain local groups from the same domain
- ▶ Global groups from any domain
- ▶ Universal groups from any domain
- ▶ User accounts from any domain

Global　Global groups have a forest-wide scope. They can be assigned permissions for any resource in any domain in the forest, and they can include the following members:

- ▶ Global groups from the same domain
- ▶ User accounts from the same domain

Universal　Universal groups can include members from any domain in the forest. They can also be assigned permissions to any resource in the forest. They should only be used when users or groups from multiple domains require access to shared resources. Universal groups are stored in the Global Catalog, and they can include the following members:

- ▶ Universal groups
- ▶ Global groups from any domain in the forest
- ▶ User accounts from any domain in the forest

> If you cannot create universal groups in your domain because the option is grayed out or disabled, the domain functional level is not high enough to support them.

Next are local groups, which are stored in the local database of a Windows machine. Windows clients and servers support local groups. You can use local groups to assign permissions to local user accounts, domain user accounts, or domain groups. This is useful if you have to share a resource on the local machine and you simply want to create a group that has access to the resource. When you need to grant access to another user or group, you simply add them to the local group.

> Local groups can contain only accounts and groups from the forest in which the local machine participates.

Finally, there are security and distribution groups. When you create domain local, global, and universal groups, you have the option of setting the group type to either security or distribution. A security group is a group that may be assigned permissions. A distribution group is a group that may not be assigned permissions. When you create a group to manage permissions, it must always be created as a security group. Distribution groups are useful for email lists and other purposes not requiring permissions.

DISTRIBUTION GROUPS AND ADMINISTRATION

After more than 20 years in the IT industry, I have seen many methods of administrative automation. Automating administrative tasks is important today because fewer support technicians are expected to manage more and more devices. In most organizations, you will support from two to four devices for each user. These devices include IP phones, mobile phones, tablet devices, laptop computers, desktop computers, and virtual devices such as personal virtual Desktops. With all of these devices to support, automation is very important.

While the most common use of distribution groups is certainly email distribution lists, administrative automation can benefit from them as well. You can create distribution groups for administration purposes only. Then you can apply Windows PowerShell commands only to users who are in specific distribution groups. For example, you could create a distribution group named FloorOneUsers and another called FloorTwoUsers. Then, you could execute commands against only those users on floor one or floor two of your building. Distribution groups take up less space in the AD database than security groups, so it is more efficient to use them when you do not need the extra feature of permission management.

Working with Groups

You should create groups only if one does not exist that meets your needs. Several groups are built into the Windows operating system. You should review the built-in groups of the domain to determine if one of them will meet your needs. This section begins by providing descriptions of the built-in groups, after which you will learn to create your own groups when required.

Table 7.1 lists the built-in groups included with Windows Server 2008 R2 and their descriptions. Use this table as a reference to determine whether an existing group has the capabilities you require.

TABLE 7.1   The Built-in Groups Included with Windows Server 2008 R2

Group Name	Group Type	Description
Domain Admins	Security Group – Global	This group can perform all administrative tasks within the domain.
Domain Guests	Security Group – Global	Place guest accounts in this group so you can control them differently than other domain users.
Domain Users	Security Group – Global	Every user in the domain is a member of this group and cannot be removed.
Enterprise Admins	Security Group - Universal	This group can perform all administrative tasks throughout the forest.
Enterprise Read-only Domain Controllers	Security Group - Universal	All members are read-only DCs in the enterprise.
Group Policy Creator Owners	Security Group - Global	This group can manage group policy settings in the domain.
RAS and IAS Servers	Security Group - Domain Local	Servers placed in this group can access and manage remote access properties of user accounts.
Read-Only Domain Controllers	Security Group - Global	All members are read-only DCs in the domain.
Schema Admins	Security Group - Universal	This group can modify the schema for the forest.
Account Operators	Security Group - Domain Local	These members can administer domain user and group accounts.

TABLE 7.1   *(Continued)*

Group Name	Group Type	Description
Administrators	Security Group - Domain Local	These members have complete unrestricted access to the computer or domain.
Backup Operators	Security Group - Domain Local	Members can perform backup and restoration procedures.
Certificate Service DCOM Access	Security Group - Domain Local	This group can connect to enterprise Certificate Authorities.
Cryptographic Operators	Security Group - Domain Local	This group can perform cryptographic operations.
Distributed COM Users	Security Group - Domain Local	This group can launch and activate distributed COM objects.
Event Log Readers	Security Group - Domain Local	These members can read the Event Viewer log files.
Guests	Security Group - Domain Local	By default, these members have the same permissions as the Users group, unless the Guest account is further restricted.
IIS_IUSRS	Security Group - Domain Local	This group is used by the IIS web server service.
Income Forest Trust Builders	Security Group - Domain Local	This group can create incoming one-way trust relationships.

(Continues)

TABLE 7.1 *(Continued)*

Group Name	Group Type	Description
Network Configuration Operators	Security Group – Domain Local	These members can perform administrative tasks limited to network configuration.
Performance Log Users	Security Group – Domain Local	This group can schedule and work with performance logs and traces.
Performance Monitor Users	Security Group – Domain Local	This group can access performance counter data on the local and remote machines.
Pre-Windows 2000 Compatible Access	Security Group – Domain Local	This group is used for backward compatibility, providing read access to all users and groups in the domain.
Print Operators	Security Group – Domain Local	This group can administer printers in the domain.
Remote Desktop Users	Security Group – Domain Local	This group can log on remotely using the Remote Desktop Client.
Replicator	Security Group – Domain Local	This group is used to support file replication in a domain.
Server Operators	Security Group – Domain Local	These members can administer servers in the domain.
Terminal Server License Servers	Security Group – Domain Local	This group can update licensing information for user accounts.

TABLE 7.1 *(Continued)*

Group Name	Group Type	Description
Users	Security Group - Domain Local	This group has limited access to the servers and domain.
Windows Authorization Access Group	Security Group - Domain Local	These members can access low-level authorization attributes for user accounts.

The Everyone group is an additional dynamic group of which every user is a member—even anonymous users.

When you determine that no built-in group meets your needs, you must create a custom group. To create a group, follow this procedure:

1. Launch ADUC.

2. If necessary, expand the `training.local` domain and then select the Users container.

3. Right-click on the Users container and select New ➤ Group. Alternatively, you can click the New Group icon on the toolbar. It is the icon with two users on it and a yellow star.

4. Enter the Group Name and the pre-Windows 2000 Group Name if it is different.

5. Select the Group Scope and Group Type and then click OK.

Group Management

As you probably noticed, you can put some groups inside of other groups as members. When you do this, you are performing *group nesting.* Group nesting can be very helpful for administrative management, but you need to be careful not to get too complicated. Here are a few tips that will help you avoid potential problems:

▶ Avoid nesting groups at more than three or four levels. If you have a group in a group that is in a group that is in a group, the processing cycles required to extract the groups and determine the permissions will be much more intensive on the servers.

▶ Focus on keeping it simple as possible. In addition to creating performance problems, deep group nesting adds complexity to the configuration and may make it more difficult to administer the users and groups.

▶ Remember that different group scopes allow different nesting options. Domain local groups can contain all three AD group types: domain local, global, and universal. Global groups can contain only other global groups. Universal groups can contain either global or universal groups.

> ▶
>
> All group scopes can contain user accounts as well as groups.

To simplify group nesting and group planning, Microsoft recommends the AGDLP model as the permission management standard. This model suggests that you should place user accounts (A) in global groups (G) and then make the global groups members of domain local groups (DL). Finally, you should assign permissions (P) to the domain local groups. Of course, scenarios will exist that demand exceptions to the model, but AGDLP should be the basic model you use. You will benefit from its simplicity when you implement it.

Understanding Organizational Units and Containers

Within AD, several containers exist by default. They are often called built-in containers because they cannot be removed or renamed. However, you can place objects within the built-in containers. The following default containers (both built-in containers and OUs) exist in a typical AD installation:

Domain   This is the domain itself. In the example, it is `training.local`.

Builtin   This container holds the default service administrator accounts and several default groups.

Users   This container is the default location for newly created user accounts and groups within the domain.

Computers   This container is the default location for computer accounts created within the domain.

Domain Controllers   This is actually an OU, but it is created by default.

Containers are used to provide logical management of the objects in the AD database. You may want more flexibility than these default containers provide, so Microsoft provides organizational units (OUs).

OUs provide several benefits, including:

► The ability to customize the container names

► The ability to create a hierarchy representing your organization (OUs can be nested in other OUs for a folder tree-like structure.)

► The ability to delegate administrative capabilities to a specific user account or group for an OU or hierarchy of OUs

► The ability to link different Group Policy Objects to different OUs

> The two most important reasons for creating OUs are administrative delegation and managing Group Policy Objects. You will learn more about Group Policy Objects in Chapter 8.

OUs can contain several object types. The most common object types include:

► Other OUs

► Computers

► Users

► Groups

► Printers

► Contacts

► Shared Folders

Creating OUs is a simple process. To create an OU, follow this procedure:

1. Launch ADUC.

2. Expand the training.local domain.

3. Right-click on the training.local domain and select New ➢ Organizational Unit.

   Alternatively, you can click on the New Organizational Unit button on the toolbar. It is the one with the yellow folder and the yellow star.

4. Enter the OU name and accept the default option to Protect Container From Accidental Deletion and then click OK.

You can create child OUs by performing the same procedure against the parent OU. In other words, you right-click on the OU instead of the domain and select New ➢ Organizational Unit.

THE ESSENTIALS AND BEYOND

Active Directory management includes four core tasks: architecture administration, user account management, group management, and organizational unit management. You can use the Active Directory Sites and Services, Active Directory Domains and Trusts, Active Directory Users and Computers (ADUC), or the Active Directory Module for Windows PowerShell to manage the architecture. You can manage user accounts with ADUC or the AD Module for Windows PowerShell. The same tools can be used to manage groups and users. For organizational unit (OU) management, you must plan the OU structure (as discussed in Chapter 6, "Configuring Active Directory") and then implement it using the simple OU-creation process. You can also delegate administrative capabilities, such as password resetting, to users and groups that are not part of the Domain Admins or Account Operators groups.

ADDITIONAL EXERCISES

▶ Create an OU named Sales in the training.local domain, and then create two child OUs within the Sales OU named Management and Sales Professionals.

▶ Create a domain local security group named Sales.

▶ Create a global distribution group named Campus A.

▶ Create two users with different names, and then add one to the Sales group and the other to the Campus A group.

(Continues)

THE ESSENTIALS AND BEYOND (Continued)

To compare your answers to the author's, please visit www.sybex.com/go/winadminessentials.

REVIEW QUESTIONS

1. Every user in the domain is an automatic member of which group?

   A. Domain Admins   **C.** Domain Users

   B. Domain Guests   **D.** Domain Accounts

2. True or false: Machine local groups can contain accounts and groups from any domain in the forest.

3. What kind of group can a global group contain when you are nesting groups?

   A. Global groups   **C.** Universal groups

   B. Domain local groups   **D.** Machine local groups

4. The Sessions tab of the user Properties dialog is used only when you are configuring the account for use with what service?

5. On what tab of the user Properties dialog can you set the home directory path for the user?

   A. General   **C.** Account

   B. Address   **D.** Profile

6. Define a distribution group.

7. *AGDLP* stands for what?

8. What can be created to display a subset of the objects within AD using the Active Directory Users and Computers tool?

   A. A query   **C.** A subset data type

   B. A filter   **D.** A subset group

9. What tool is used to manage delegated administration?

   A. Active Directory Domains and   **C.** Active Directory Sites and
          Trusts   Services

   B. Computer Management   **D.** Active Directory Users and
                                               Computers

10. True or false: The Domain Naming Operations Master role is managed in the Active Directory Domains and Trusts tool.

CHAPTER 8

Group Policy Management

Microsoft first released a technology known as Group Policy back in 2000 with the release of Windows 2000 Server and the first version of Active Directory. Since that time, the Group Policy component of Windows operating systems has grown considerably with each new operating system release. Windows Vista and Server 2008 introduced a completely new feature of Group Policy known as Group Policy Preferences, which was further enhanced in the Windows 7 and Windows Server 2008 R2 releases. Group Policy provides different features and capabilities for managing and administrating machines in your environment, depending on the operating systems you run. However, the good news is that even with multiple systems types in use, Group Policy works basically the same way regardless of the operating systems you run.

Group Policy is used to centrally manage Windows computers from the perspectives of configuration, software deployment, and restriction. In this chapter, Group Policy is explained so that you can understand its purpose and operations. You will learn about Group Policy through the following topics:

▷ **Understanding Group Policy**

▷ **Defining the Group Policy hierarchy**

▷ **Touring the Group Policy Management Console**

▷ **Creating a Group Policy Object**

Understanding Group Policy

Group Policy has been in Windows for more than a decade. The feature allows you to centrally manage and control many aspects of Windows clients and servers that are members of Active Directory domains. To fully understand and implement Group Policy, you will need to explore five important topics:

 ▶ Group Policy defined

 ▶ Group Policy requirements

▶ Group Policy management tools

▶ Group Policy sections and categories

▶ Supporting different Windows client versions

Each topic is addressed in this section.

Group Policy Defined

The first thing you should know about Group Policy is that it is not a direct reference to groups, which you learned about in the preceding chapter. Although groups can be given permission to apply a policy, the term *group* in Group Policy does not reference an administratively created group; rather, the word references a collection of policy settings. The following definitions should help clear up any confusion about Group Policy terminology:

Group Policy   The infrastructure that enables the creation and application of a collection of settings that are used to control or configure Windows computers.

Group Policy Processing   The method by which Group Policy settings are downloaded and applied to Windows computers.

Group Policy Object (GPO)   A collection of settings that can be applied to Windows computers by linking the GPO to a container.

Group Policy Setting   A single setting, within a GPO, that controls or configures a Windows computer. Group policy settings are applied in the "Policies" section of the GPO.

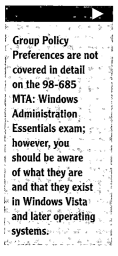

Group Policy Preferences are not covered in detail on the 98-685 MTA: Windows Administration Essentials exam; however, you should be aware of what they are and that they exist in Windows Vista and later operating systems.

Group Policy Preferences   A simple method for configuring settings using GPOs with dialog boxes similar to those in the local Windows GUI interface. Unlike policies, preferences may be changed by users to override the administrator's preference settings. The Group Policy Preferences are defined in the "Preferences" section of the GPO.

Preference Item   The same as a policy setting, but in relation to Group Policy Preferences.

Group Policy is a solution that allows you to control and configure Windows computers on the network. By using Group Policies, you can control the machines in your environment in multiple ways, including disallowing some functions that may be allowed by default. For example, you can disable Registry editing so that normal users cannot damage their machines by improperly deleting or modifying Registry entries. You can disallow access to various Control Panel applets, and you can limit the operating system in many other ways. You can also distribute software to the systems in your environment, and set the default settings for other configuration settings through preferences.

Group Policy is configured by creating GPOs and linking them to containers. The containers store AD objects such as user accounts and computers. When you link a GPO to a container, the policy settings within it apply to all users and computers in the container. If you like, you can change the default permissions so that the GPO applies only to specific users or computers in the container.

The Registry is the configuration setting database for Windows operating systems and applications.

GROUP POLICIES DON'T APPLY TO GROUPS

It may seem odd, but Group Policy Objects (GPOs) do not apply directly to groups. However, if you think about it, you will see why they don't. Does a group log on to a computer? No, users log on to computers. This is why GPOs apply to users and computers and not to groups.

Now, are you ready for the deep revelation? Groups can be used to control how GPOs are applied. By default, all GPOs apply to all users and computers in the linked container—the site, domain, or organizational unit (OU). You can edit the permission on the GPO so that it applies only to a specific user or computer. This is where groups come into play. You can place all the users in a group that should receive the settings in the GPO. Then, you simply edit the permission on the GPO so that only that group may apply it.

The ability to control GPO application through groups is very useful for software distribution. Group Policy provides a feature for the distribution and automatic installation of Microsoft Installer (MSI) installation files. This allows you to install and configure software on Windows computers.

For example, assume you have a software application that must be installed on 13 computers in the Accounting department. However, there are 60 users and computers in the Accounting OU. You do not have enough licenses to install the application on all 60 computers used by the 60 users. What do you do? You can create a GPO that deploys the software and link the GPO to the Accounting OU. Next, you can create a group called AccountingSoftware and add the 13 users to the group. Finally, you can modify the permissions on the GPO so that only the AccountingSoftware group can apply it. You have successfully distributed the software to the 13 targeted individuals within the OU.

Group Policy Requirements

To use Group Policy on the network, the first thing you'll need is an Active Directory (AD) installation. If Active Directory isn't running, you can't use Group Policy to centrally configure and control your Windows computers. Chapter 5, "Active Directory Infrastructure," and Chapter 6, "Configuring Active Directory," explained the planning and installation processes for AD.

Older Windows operating systems use a technology known as System Policies. System Policies were the precursor to the more powerful Group Policy in use today.

Next, you must have a Windows computer running Windows 2000 or later. Earlier versions of Windows, including Windows NT and Windows 95, 98, and ME, do not support Group Policy. Windows servers and Windows clients can process GPOs from the AD network as long as they are running Windows 2000 or later.

Of course, the Windows computers must be able to access the DCs running AD, and they must be members of the domain. Each DC will contain a copy of the GPOs. The GPOs are synchronized on all DCs automatically using replication. The GPO settings are stored in the SYSVOL share on the DCs. If the Windows computers are to access the DC, the network must be configured to allow it. Two important network requirements must be in place. The first is the proper IP configuration, and the second is an active DNS server. Both of these items are required for general AD functionality. If you can log on to the domain, in most cases, GPOs will be processed without problems.

The final requirement for GPO processing is the assignment of proper permissions. By default, when you link a GPO to a container, all users and computers in that container will have the permissions to process it. However, you may need to change these permissions so that only the appropriate users can process the GPO.

Group Policy Management Tools

Three primary tools exist for Group Policy management. Two of the tools are for managing AD GPOs, and the other is for managing local Group Policy. The tools are:

- ▶ Group Policy Management Console (GPMC)
- ▶ Windows PowerShell
- ▶ Local Group Policy Editor (GPEDIT.MSC)

The GPMC is the most commonly utilized tool for Group Policy management. It provides a GUI for administration of GPOs and reporting on GPO processing, as shown in Figure 8.1.

The GPMC interface is covered in detail in the section of this chapter titled "Exploring the GPMC Interface."

FIGURE 8.1 The Group Policy Management console

Windows Server 2008 and later support Group Policy management through Windows PowerShell. To use the Group Policy cmdlets in PowerShell, you must first import the GroupPolicy module. To do this,

1. Execute the following command at a PowerShell prompt:

   ```
   Import-Module GroupPolicy
   ```

2. After importing the module, execute the following command to see all of the Group Policy cmdlets:

   ```
   Get-Command -Module GroupPolicy
   ```

The results of the command are shown in Figure 8.2. Windows Server 2008 provides cmdlets for creating GPOs, linking GPOs, deleting GPOs, and reporting on GPOs, among other tasks. You can do almost anything in the Windows PowerShell that you can do in the GPMC.

FIGURE 8.2 Windows PowerShell with the GroupPolicy module imported

When you must configure local Group Policy settings on a machine, use the GPEDIT.MSC console. This console provides direct access to Group Policy settings and allows the configuration of multiple local GPOs on Windows Vista and later machines. GPEDIT.MSC is shown in Figure 8.3.

You will learn to configure settings using GPEDIT.MSC in the section of this chapter titled, "Configuring a Local Group Policy Setting."

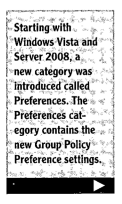

FIGURE 8.3 The Local Group Policy Editor (GPEDIT.MSC)

Group Policy Sections and Categories

Starting with Windows Vista and Server 2008, a new category was introduced called Preferences. The Preferences category contains the new Group Policy Preference settings.

When you create a GPO, you are creating a policy that can apply to computers or users or both. On Windows machines, users have profiles that maintain their settings. Policy settings from a GPO that are inherited by a user account in Active Directory will apply to users when they log on and specifically impact these profiles. Policy settings that are inherited by computers apply to all users who log on to the machine. These two sections (computer and user) are referred to as nodes within the GPO.

It is important to understand that the computer and user nodes contain many different policy settings and some of the same settings. Within the computer and user nodes are categories, which are also known as *child nodes*. These categories include:

- ▶ Software settings
- ▶ Windows settings
- ▶ Administrative templates

Within each category are further subcategories. Some settings exist in both the computer node and the user node. For example, you can distribute software to either a computer or a user in the Software Settings subcategory of the GPO. However, many more settings in each section are different between the two.

The settings in Administrative Templates are all unique to the section. For example, no policy setting in the Computer Configuration ➤ Administrative Templates category is identical to a setting in the User Configuration ➤ Administrative Templates category. This is because the computer-section administrative template–based policies apply to the HKEY_LOCAL_MACHINE section of the Windows Registry. The user-section administrative template–based policies apply to the HKEY_CURRENT_USER section of the Register. For this reason, even if the policy setting has a similar name and description, it applies to a very different part of the system Registry. Figure 8.4 shows the Group Policy Management Editor with the Default Domain Policy GPO loaded. Notice the different subcategories within the Administrative Templates category in the computer and user sections.

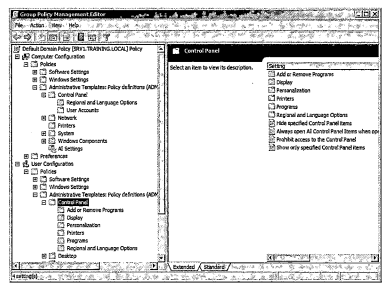

FIGURE 8.4 The Group Policy Management Editor showing the differences between the computer and user sections

Between the computer and user sections, more than 100 categories exist within GPOs for Windows 7 and Windows Server 2008 R2. If you open the local Group Policy Editor (GPEDIT.MSC), you can browse through these categories and the policy settings they contain. In most cases, the settings are described very well and you can understand what you can do with these settings through the descriptions. You can download helpful documents that explain the GPO categories and policy settings from the following location:

http://go.microsoft.com/fwlink/?LinkId=54020

You should also visit the Windows Server Group Policy home page:

http://technet.microsoft.com/en-us/windowsserver/bb310732.aspx

At the Windows Server Group Policy home page, you will find explanations of the various components that make up Group Policy and videos demonstrating the application of GPOs.

Supporting Different Windows Client Versions

The final issue an administrator must address is the support of multiple Windows clients for Group Policy. In this case, any Windows machine is a client whether it runs a server or client version of the operating system, because all Windows machines download the appropriate GPOs and apply them to their local systems. Older clients support fewer policy settings than newer clients. As an administrator, you must determine how to address this issue. The good news is that Microsoft has made it simple.

To support all Windows clients, simply use a *management machine*—a Windows computer with the appropriate software installed to create and manage GPOs— running the newest version of the Windows operating system. For example, if your management machine runs Windows 7, you will be able to create GPOs with proper settings for Windows 2000 through Windows 7 client operating systems and Windows 2000 through Windows Server 2008 server operating systems.

If an administrator wants to use a Windows 7 computer as the management machine, she must install the Remote Server Administration Tools (RSAT) on the system. The RSAT tools for Windows 7 can be downloaded here:

http://go.microsoft.com/fwlink/?LinkId=167131

After the administrator installs the RSAT tools, the GPMC will be available on the local machine and can be used to create the GPOs. Figure 8.5 shows the concept of using a Windows 7 management machine for Group Policy administration. The Windows 7 machine is used to create GPOs for Windows XP, Windows Vista, and Windows 7 clients, as well as Windows servers. The GPOs are still stored in AD, but they support all the newest policy settings because they are created on a newer operating system.

> It does not matter what version of AD you are running. You can create GPOs with Windows 7 and deploy them to Windows Server 2003 domains, and they will be processed properly.

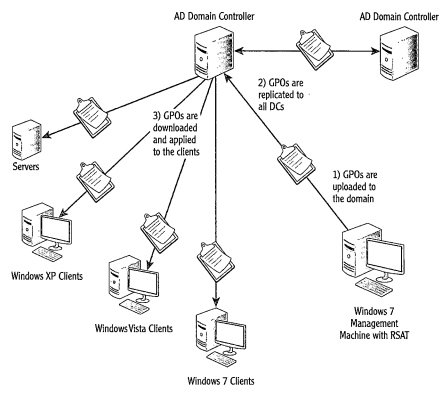

FIGURE 8.5 Using a Windows 7 management machine for Group Policy administration

Defining the Group Policy Hierarchy

Group Policy supports layers of application. You can link GPOs to different containers, and each container will represent a potential layer of application. The containers include the site, the domain, and each OU in a hierarchy. In this section, you will learn about how Group Policy processing works and the hierarchy of application. You will also learn about the two major sections within a GPO.

Group Policy Processing

Multiple GPOs could be downloaded by a client for processing. Administrators must understand the processing order of these GPOs. The default processing order is easy to understand. It starts at the local machine and moves to the highest level within AD, the site, and then down to the domain and finally through OU architecture to the deepest nested OU. The order is as follows:

1. Local Group Policy

2. Site GPOs

3. Domain GPOs

4. OU GPOs in order of hierarchy

All GPO settings are applied cumulatively to the client. For example, imagine you have the GPOs linked as defined in Table 8.1. The first policy setting to apply will be the one local setting for disabling Registry editing tools. The next policy settings will be applied from the Site A GPO. Then the Default Domain Policy GPO will apply. The Marketing GPO will apply next, and finally the Marketing Management GPO will apply.

When using default GPO processing, the last application of a policy setting wins any conflicts. For example, disabling a policy setting at the OU level over-rides the enabling of the setting at the domain level.

TABLE 8.1   Example GPO Hierarchy

Group Policy Object	Policy Setting or GPO	Linked Target/Container
Local Policy Settings	Prevent Access to Registry Editing Tools	Local Machine
Site	Site A GPO	Site A
Domain	Default Domain Policy GPO	Domain
OU	Marketing GPO	Marketing OU
OU	Marketing Management GPO	Management child OU under the Marketing OU

The default processing of policy settings is hierarchical and cumulative, but you can do two important things to change this processing. First, you can con-figure a GPO to be enforced. When a GPO is enforced, lower-level GPOs cannot override the higher-level GPO's settings when a conflict occurs. Second, you can configure a container, such as an OU, to block inheritance. This means that the OU will not allow the application of any GPOs above it in the hierarchy. When a lower-level container is configured to block inheritance and a higher-level GPO is configured as enforced, the enforced setting takes precedence and the higher-level GPO will still be applied, regardless of the block inheritance configuration. It is assumed that a higher-level setting would be configured by a more powerful administrator and the enforced configuration should be honored.

The enforced option was called "no over-ride" in earlier ver-sions of Group Policy.

The actual engine that processes the different settings in GPOs is the client side extension (CSE). CSEs are updated periodically to allow enhancements to the Group Policy functions. CSEs are Dynamic Link Libraries (DLLs) that reside on the Windows computers. The logon process calls on these DLLs to apply GPOs when the user initially logs on to the computer. They are also called during a refresh, if new policy settings are discovered. A policy setting refresh involves checking for new policy settings from the network and applying them as required.

When Windows 2000 was released, nine CSEs were included out of the box. The release of Windows XP added two more CSEs, and Windows Vista added five more. In Windows 7 and Windows Server 2008 R2 systems, five additional CSEs were added for GPO processing. In addition to all this, twenty-one CSEs are used for Group Policy Preference processing, which can only be used on Windows 7 and Windows Server 2008 R2 systems. In the end, the total is thirty-eight CSEs in Windows 7 and Server 2008 R2 systems.

> By default, Group Policy settings are refreshed every 90 minutes with a 30-minute randomization. This means that clients will refresh within a random range from 90 to 120 minutes.

Local Group Policy

Local Group Policy can be configured in two ways on Windows Vista and later machines. The first method is the traditional flat model of local Group Policy. You simply run the GPEDIT.MSC console and apply policy settings. The second method is the multiple local GPO (MLGPO) model, and it requires the loading of a special console through the Microsoft Management Console (MMC). To create a console with the Group Policy Object Editor loaded:

1. Log on to a Windows 7 client as an administrator.

2. Click Start, type mmc into the Search field, and press the Enter key.

3. Click File Add/Remove Snap-In to add the Group Policy Object Editor.

4. Select the Group Policy Object Editor from the list of available snap-ins and click the Add button.

5. In the Select Group Policy Object dialog, click Finish to accept the Local Computer GPO.
   You are returned to the Add or Remove Snap-ins dialog.

6. Select the Group Policy Object Editor snap-in again and click Add.

7. In the Select Group Policy Object dialog, click Browse to select a specific GPO to edit.

8. In the Browse for a Group Policy Object dialog, select the Users tab, then click on the Non-Administrators GPO, and click OK.

9. Click Finish to add the snap-ins to the list.

10. Repeat steps 6 through 9, this time selecting the Administrators GPO from the Users tab of the Browse for a Group Policy Object dialog.

11. Repeat steps 6 through 9, this time selecting a specific user's GPO, such as Tom's, from the Users tab of the Browse for a Group Policy Object dialog.

Figure 8.6 shows an MMC configured per the preceding steps. Make sure you understand the processing order for these multiple GPOs. The first policies to apply are the Local Computer Policy settings, which include both computer and user settings. Because only one computer can exist on a local machine, this is the only level where MLGPO applies computer settings.

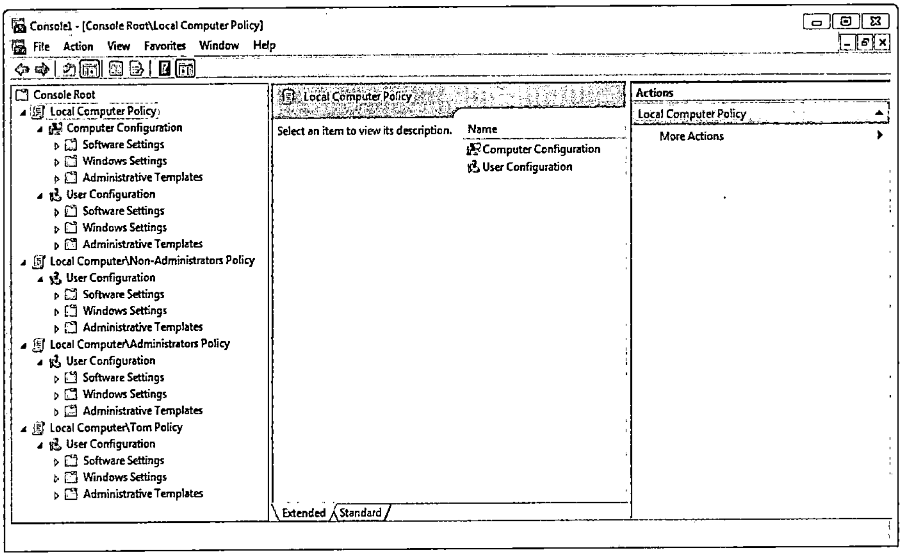

FIGURE 8.6 An MMC configured for management of MLGPO

The next level to be applied is the Administrators/Non-Administrators policy level. A user is either an administrator or not. If the user is an administrator, the Local Computer\Administrators policy is applied. If the user is not an administrator, the Local Computer\Non-Administrators policy is applied. Only one of these policies is applied to the user, depending on their administrative group memberships. The Administrators/Non-Administrators policy level can override the settings in the Local Computer policy level for user settings.

The final level to be applied is the Local Computer\"Username" policy. This policy is specific to a user and is applied only to the named user. These settings can override Administrators/Non-Administrators level settings and they can override Local Computer policy settings. Using MLGPOs, in this way, provides

> MLGPO can be used on domain computers and nondomain computers, but it is mostly used on non-domain computers.

flexibility in policy setting application for non-AD environments. This functionality is useful even in large organizations for computers that do not participate
in the domain, such as roaming laptop computers and branch office desktops
without WAN connections to the corporate headquarters.

Touring the Group Policy Management Console

The primary tool for Group Policy management is the Group Policy Management
Console (GPMC). The GPMC was first introduced as a downloadable add-on and
is included in Windows Server 2008 and later. With the GPMC, you can create
GPOs, link the GPOs to containers, and manage those GPOs. Additionally, you
can analyze GPO processing with the GPMC using the Resultant Set of Policy
(RSoP) feature of the tool. In this section, you will tour the GPMC and learn
about the features it offers.

Exploring the GPMC Interface

The GPMC has a default display that includes four sections (see Figure 8.7). The
standard menus and toolbars are the same across all MMC consoles. The console
tree pane, on the left, is used to navigate through the sections or features of the
console. The GPMC has several nodes that are used to manage Group Policy. The
content pane is where reports are displayed and information about the selected
item in the console tree is displayed.

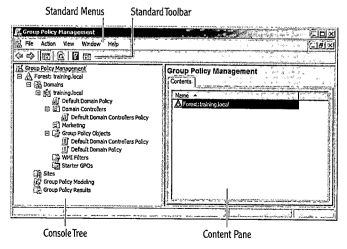

FIGURE 8.7 The GPMC interface defined

Within the console tree are the following nodes and child nodes:

► **Forest:** This is the root node for the forest. You can select different forests to manage multiple forests when they are available.

▸ **Domains:** This child node of the Forest node contains all domains in the forest.

▸ **Domain Name:** The container for all Group Policy–related items linked to the domain. In Figure 8.7, this container is named `training.local`.

▸ **Domain Controllers:** This child node of the domain name node contains references to all GPOs that apply to the Domain Controller's OU.

▸ **OU Names:** These child nodes of the domain name represent each of the OUs in the Active Directory and contain references to all GPOs that are linked to the named OU. In Figure 8.7, Marketing is a named OU.

▸ **Group Policy Objects:** The container of all of the GPOs in the domain.

▸ **WMI Filters:** A node used to define filters based on Windows Management Instrumentation. For example, you can allow a GPO to apply only to machines matching specific hardware-resource requirements.

▸ **Starter GPOs:** A node used to create starter GPOs or GPO templates.

▸ **Sites:** This child node of the Forest node contains all sites configured in the forest.

▸ **Group Policy Modeling:** This child node of the Forest node is used to simulate GPO processing based on defined scenarios.

▸ **Group Policy Results:** This child node of the Forest node is used to report actual results for real users and groups in the forest.

Understanding the GPMC Features

The GPMC supports many features that simplify administration tasks. Among these features are:

Importing and Exporting GPOs   You can import GPOs for application within the domain. This allows you to reuse GPOs that were created in other domains and reduce work effort. Of course, you must first export the GPOs from the other domain.

Copying and Pasting GPOs   You can copy a GPO that is linked to one container (site, domain, or OU) and paste it to another container. This is faster than manually linking the GPOs in many cases. Simply right-click on the GPO in the Group Policy Objects container and select the Copy option. Then right-click on the target container and select Paste.

Backing Up and Restoring GPOs   The GPMC allows you to right-click on a GPO in the Group Policy Objects container and select Backup to back up to a folder. In the future, you will be able to right-click on the GPO and select Restore From Backup to restore the backup of the GPO.

Searching for Existing GPOs   In very large environments, you may have hundreds of GPOs. You can right-click on the Forest node and select Search to locate GPOs anywhere in the forest. You can search based on GPO Name, GPO Links, Security Groups, and on the existence of User Configuration and Computer Configuration settings within the GPO.

Reporting capabilities   When you click on a GPO or GPO link, you can select the Settings tab in the content pane to view reports on the settings within the GPO. These reports are HTML-based and provide a simplified view of all applied settings in the GPO.

Group Policy Modeling   Group Policy Modeling allows you to simulate Resultant Set of Policy (RSoP) data for planning Group Policy deployments before implementing them in the production environment. You can specify users and the groups to which they belong and the OUs in which they exist to see what policy settings they would receive.

Group Policy Results   Group Policy Results allows you to obtain RSoP data for viewing GPO interaction and for troubleshooting Group Policy deployments. This information is based on actual users in actual containers within the domain.

Creating a Group Policy Object

Now that you understand Group Policy and the tools used to manage it, you can create a GPO. The process for creating a GPO is as follows:

1. Determine the policy settings that should be configured in the GPO.

2. Create the GPO.

3. Link the GPO to the appropriate container.

4. If necessary, modify the permissions of the GPO.

The following sections provide instructions for working through these steps. In addition, you will learn to configure a local Group Policy setting on a Windows Server.

Determining Policy Settings

The first step is to determine the policy settings that should be configured in the GPO. The following guidelines will help you to determine the policy settings that should be included in a given GPO, as well as more general Group Policy planning.

▶ Create a GPO for any policy settings that must always be enforced for all users in the domain and link it to the domain. Designate the GPO as enforced so no other GPO can override the settings.

▶ Create a GPO for any policy settings that must always be enforced for all users in a site or an OU just as you did for the domain.

▶ Use as few GPOs as possible without sacrificing your needs. Do not create a single GPO for each policy setting. Instead, combine the policy settings into a fewer number of GPOs for improved processing performance and reduced network bandwidth consumption.

▶ Remember that you can use security groups to filter the application of GPOs to only users in specified groups.

▶ Create a test environment for staging the GPOs before you deploy them in the production domain.

In the following exercise, you will create a single GPO that prevents access to Registry editing tools. This section provides the steps for configuring only one setting; just remember that a GPO can apply multiple settings. To configure more settings in a single GPO, open the GPO and configure the rest of the settings using the same procedure you used to configure the first GPO.

Creating the GPO

Creating the GPO is a very simple process in GPMC. To create a GPO that is named NoReg and applies the Prevent Access to Registry Editing Tools policy, follow this procedure:

1. Log on to the Windows Server 2008 R2 server as an administrator.

2. Select Start ➢ All Programs ➢ Administrative Tools ➢ Group Policy Management.

3. Expand Forest: training.local ➢ Domains ➢ training.local ➢ Group Policy Objects.

4. Right-click on the Group Policy Objects node and select New.

5. Enter NoReg in the Name field of the New GPO dialog. Accept the default (none) for the Source Starter GPO option and click OK.

6. You will return to the GPMC. Right-click on the NoReg GPO and select Edit.

7. In the Group Policy Management Editor, expand User Configuration ➢ Policies ➢ Administrative Templates ➢ System.

8. With the System child node selected, double-click on the policy setting named Prevent Access To Registry Editing Tools in the content pane.

9. In the Prevent Access To Registry Editing Tools dialog, select the Enabled radio button, accept all other defaults, and click OK.

10. Close the Group Policy Management Editor. The changes to the GPO will be saved automatically.

> You could also perform these steps on a Windows 7 management machine with RSAT installed.

At this point, you have created a GPO in the domain for preventing access to Registry editing tools; however, you have not linked the GPO to any container. You will learn to do that next.

Linking GPOs to Containers

GPOs are independent objects that can be linked to multiple containers. In the preceding section, you created a GPO that is configured to prevent access to Registry editing tools. Now, you will link this GPO to the domain so that it applies to all users. To link the GPO to the domain container, follow these steps:

1. Open the GPMC if it is not already open.

2. Expand Forest: training.local ➤ Domains ➤ training.local in the console tree.

3. Right-click the training.local domain node, and select Link an Existing GPO.

4. In the Select GPO dialog, click the NoReg GPO to select it and then click OK.
   You will return to the GPMC. Notice the new link to the NoReg GPO in the domain.

Modifying Permissions on the GPO

When you link a GPO to a container, the default permissions on the GPO will allow for all members of the Authenticated Users group to download and apply the GPO. This is the default security filtering setting. You can change this so that only specific users or groups can download and apply the GPO. Through such security filtering, you can limit the scope of the GPO to specific users or groups instead of all users within the linked container. To modify the default permissions on the GPO linked in the preceding section, follow these steps:

> **If you want the GPO to apply only to a specific group, remember to remove the default Authenticated Users group in Security Filtering after adding the specific group.**

1. Open the GPMC if it is not already open.

2. Expand Forest: training.local ➤ Domains ➤ training.local in the console tree.

3. Select the NoReg GPO in the console tree.

4. Use the Security Filtering section in the content pane to change the default security permissions.

Configuring a Local Group Policy Setting

At times, you may want to apply a Group Policy setting to a single specific machine. You may not be concerned with MLGPO or domain policies. For example, if you need to disable the Solitaire (SOLITAIRE.EXE) application on a single Windows 7 computer, you could accomplish this on the local machine by using the local Group Policy. To disable solitaire on a Windows 7 Professional client machine, follow this procedure:

1. Log on to the Windows 7 machine as an administrator.

2. Click Start, type GPEDIT.MSC in the Search field, and press Enter.

3. In the Computer Configuration section, expand Windows Settings ➢ Security Settings ➢ Software Restriction Policies.

4. Right-click on the Software Restriction Policies node, and select new Software Restriction Policies,

On Windows 7 Enterprise and Ultimate editions, you may use the Application Control Policies (AppLocker) instead of the Software Restriction Policies if you like.

5. Right-click on the Additional Rules node, and select New Hash Rule to create a software restriction rule based on a *hash* (mathematically computed unique identifier) of the application executable.

6. Click Browse to locate the SOLITAIRE.EXE application.

7. Navigate to C:\Program Files\Microsoft Games\Solitaire, select the SOLITAIRE.EXE file, and click Open.

8. In the New Hash Rule dialog, accept the default Security Level setting of Disallowed and click OK.

9. Close the Local Group Policy Editor.
   The changes will be saved automatically.

Administrators who support AD domains should avoid local Group Policy as much as possible. Domain-based Group Policy is much easier to centrally manage. However, the availability of local Group Policy is beneficial for smaller environments as well as on machines that do not participate in the domain.

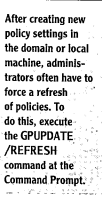

After creating new policy settings in the domain or local machine, administrators often have to force a refresh of policies. To do this, execute the GPUPDATE /REFRESH command at the Command Prompt.

THE ESSENTIALS AND BEYOND

Group Policy allows you to centrally control and configure Windows computers that participate in your AD network. You can utilize local Group Policy on stand-alone servers and clients that are not members of an AD domain. Group Policy Objects (GPOs) contain policy settings, and they can be linked to one or more containers within an AD. The GPOs are created using the Group Policy Management Console (GPMC), which can be used to create, apply, and update the GPOs. It can also be used to determine how the GPOs will be applied to a specific user or group. GPOs are processed in the order from local policies,

(Continues)

THE ESSENTIALS AND BEYOND *(Continued)*

to site GPOs, to domain GPOs, to OUs in order of hierarchy. By default, the last GPO to be applied can override previously applied GPOs if any settings conflict. You can configure a GPO as "enforced" to indicate that lower-level GPOs cannot override it. You can also block inheritance at the OU level to indicate that higher-level GPOs should not apply.

When creating multiple local GPOs (MLGPOs), you have three levels of application:

Local Policy Settings   The local policy settings apply first, and they can contain both user and computer configuration settings.

Administrator/Non-Administrator Level   The Administrator/Non-Administrator policy settings apply next and a single user receives only administrator or nonadministrator GPO settings, depending on administrative group membership.

Specific User Level   The final policy settings to be applied are those in the specific user GPO—if one exists.

The Administrator/Non-Administrator level and specific user-level GPOs contain only user configuration settings.

You can use the Group Policy Management Console (GPMC), the local GPEDIT.MSC console, or Windows PowerShell to work with Group Policy. To use Windows PowerShell, you must import the GroupPolicy module with the Import-Module cmdlet.

ADDITIONAL EXERCISES

▶ Use the local GPEDIT.MSC Editor to prevent access to the Command Prompt on a Windows 7 client.

▶ Create a GPO named SalesDept and link it to the Sales OU. If the Sales OU does not exist, create the OU using Active Directory Users and Computers first. Enable the following policy settings in the GPO:

```
User Configuration\Policies\Administrative Templates\
Control Panel\Display\Hide Settings Tab
```

```
User Configuration\Policies\Administrative Templates\
Control Panel\Personalization\Prevent changing screen saver
```

▶ Execute the GPUPDATE /FORCE command to refresh Group Policy immediately.

▶ Using the GPMC, view the settings in the Default Domain Policy GPO.

To compare your answers to the author's, please visit www.sybex.com/go/winadminessentials

(Continues)

REVIEW QUESTIONS

1. What version of Windows Server must the DCs be running to support Group Policy settings that are new in Windows 7?

   A. Any version that supports Group Policy
   C. Server 2008

   B. Server 2003 R2
   D. Server 2008 R2

2. True or false: You can create GPOs and link them to multiple containers.

3. What must be added to a Windows client so that you can use it as a Group Policy management machine?

   A. RSAT
   C. Remote Desktop Client

   B. MMC
   D. GPEDIT.MSC

4. What must you use to work with MLGPO on a Windows 7 client?

5. Which of the following tools provide a GUI for Group Policy management? (Choose all that apply.)

   A. GPEDIT.MSC
   C. Windows Command Prompt

   B. Windows PowerShell
   D. GPMC

6. Define a GPO.

7. Define Group Policy Preferences.

8. What command must be executed before you can use the Group Policy cmdlets in Windows PowerShell?

   A. Import-Module GroupPolicy
   C. Import-Cmdlets GroupPolicy

   B. None, the cmdlets are there by default
   D. Get-Cmdlets GroupPolicy

9. What must exist in order to use centralized Group Policy provisioning for Windows clients?

   A. Active Directory
   C. Exchange Server

   B. SQL Server
   D. System Center Configuration Manager

10. True or false: You have created an MLGPO configuration. Policy settings are configured for the local policy, the administrative users, the nonadministrative users, and for Joe. When Joe logs on, the administrative users policy overrides his specific policies.

CHAPTER 9

Application Servers

Windows servers are often used as application servers, which provide application services to the network. For example, Windows Server 2008 and 2008 R2 can be used to provide database services, mail services, collaboration services, monitoring services, and threat management services. You must simply install the proper add-on software to provide the service.

In this chapter, you will learn about the different application server types as you explore the following topics:

▷ **Understanding Application Servers**

▷ **Database Servers**

▷ **Mail Servers: Using Microsoft Exchange Server**

▷ **Collaboration Servers**

▷ **Monitoring Servers**

▷ **Threat Management Servers**

Understanding Application Servers

Application servers are servers implemented to support applications. For example, you cannot use Microsoft Outlook to check email without an email server. As another example, you cannot use a custom application to process data in a networked database without a server to provide access to that database. Application servers exist so that network-based applications can use them for data access, business logic, and collaboration.

Application servers are typically identified by the following characteristics:

▶ *They are dedicated to application processing.* They are not used for traditional Windows server functions such as domain logon or file and print services.

▶ *They are optimized for the execution of procedures that support other servers or client applications.* These procedures can be compiled programs or scripts.

▶ *They are accessed by multiple clients.* Users may access the application server directly through a local application or indirectly through another server application.

When developing applications, programmers have three basic options:

Localized Application Logic   In this case, all logic exists in the local application and no dependency on application servers exists. The application is installed on the local machine, and all data and processing logic exist on that machine.

Distributed Application Logic   In this case, some logic may exist in the local application and the remaining logic exists in one or more application servers.

Centralized Application Logic   In this case, the business logic is completely housed in application servers. An example of this latter case is a web-based application. The browser displays the pages, but all processing takes place on the application servers.

When all or part of the business logic is on application servers, several benefits can be realized, including:

Improved Security   Security can be improved because the local applications do not store business logic. This means that it is more difficult to circumvent security measures by hacking the client application. Additionally, security can be more easily managed because all data access is controlled through the application server instead of the client.

Improved Performance   If the application design allows small requests to be sent to the server and fine-tuned results to be received from the server, network traffic can be reduced. Many client applications with the entire logic within themselves pull all of the data from a database table and then process it locally. The resulting intense network activity can reduce the performance for other users of the network.

Improved Data Integrity   Just as security management is improved, data integrity management is improved as well. Because the code is centralized, you can modify it and immediately impact the application. If you detect an error that is causing improper data results, you can fix it quickly. Localized application logic requires the redistribution of the compiled application to all clients.

Application servers often serve other servers. A user application may communicate with one server that calls on yet another server for data access or business logic processing. This is often called a *multi-tier solution.*

Although application servers can improve security, they also make it easier to create holes. Because the application logic is on the server, a security flaw can be exploited more easily than a flaw in a client.

WEB APPLICATION SERVERS

You may have noticed that web application servers are not covered in this chapter. There is a good reason for this. Although they are application servers, they are used so frequently that they warrant an entire chapter of their own. They are covered in Chapter 10, "Internet Information Services (IIS)," where the Internet Information Services (IIS) service is covered.

Web application servers provide the same benefits as the other application servers discussed in this chapter. They provide the potential for improved security, performance, and data integrity. They make the deployment of applications much simpler, but this simplicity must not cause carelessness. Administrators who become careless in the deployment of web applications open their networks to attacks. Web application servers are primary targets for attack in modern networks. Be sure to check with your web application vendor and implement security best practices. You'll learn more about security in Microsoft's web server solution in Chapter 10.

Database Servers

Database servers play a very important role on modern networks. In today's business world, the vast majority of database applications access their data across the network. In the past, many applications stored their data locally, but this is becoming less common every year.

Before we get too far into Microsoft's database server solutions, I want to state one fact clearly: *The database is not the database server, and the database server is not the database.*

It is not uncommon for a database administrator (DBA) to say, "I have to restart the SQL Server database." What he really means is that he needs to restart the SQL Server service, which manages access to the database. The database is separate from the database management system. SQL Server is the database management system that runs on Windows servers. Databases can be detached from one SQL Server instance and then attached to another. In fact, you can attach Excel spreadsheets, Access databases, and virtually any data source that you can connect to with Open Database Connectivity (ODBC) drivers to a SQL Server as a linked server object. Once the link is made, the SQL Server service can manage access to that data source (via the ODBC or other connection type) for your users.

To help you better understand the relationship applications have with a database server, I am going to explain three kinds of database applications:

▶ Localized applications

▶ Client/server applications

▶ N-tier applications

First, however, I will explain the different versions of Microsoft's SQL Server product.

Microsoft SQL Server

Microsoft SQL Server is the database application software offered for Windows servers from Microsoft. It is a relational database management system (RDBMS), which means that it supports databases including schemas, tables, and data records in those tables that may be related to data records in other tables. SQL Server comes in several editions. The following editions are available for SQL Server 2008:

Standard   Microsoft suggests that the Standard Edition is best used for departmental applications. It includes important features for data management and business intelligence (BI). This is a paid license edition.

Enterprise   The Enterprise Edition has all of the features of Standard Edition. It adds special features such as the resource governor for better control of resource consumption by databases, data and backup compression for optimization of storage, transparent data encryption (TDE) to allow for data encryption without requiring modifications to client applications, and unlimited virtualization. This is a paid license edition.

Workgroup   The Workgroup Edition is similar to the Standard Edition; however, it has important limitations. The Workgroup Edition can only use up to 4 GB of RAM, while the Standard Edition can use up to 64 GB. The Workgroup Edition only supports up to 2 CPUs, while the Standard Edition supports up to 4 CPUs. Additionally, the Workgroup Edition has very limited support for the SQL Server Integration Services component in that it can import and export data only through a wizard. The Standard Edition can run advanced SSIS jobs for data processing automation. This is a paid license edition.

Web The Web Edition is intended only for use as a web application database server. This is a paid license edition.

Express The Express Edition is a very limited edition of SQL Server that can act as a database server accessed by remote computers, although it is intended more for localized application access. It supports a maximum database size of 10 GB and a maximum RAM utilization value of 1 GB. This is a free license edition.

Developer The Developer Edition is exactly the same as the Enterprise Edition, with the exception of licensing. You are not authorized to use the Developer Edition for production database servers accessed by users for business purposes. The Developer Edition is intended only for development and testing purposes. This is a paid license edition.

Compact The Compact Edition is used to embed a SQL Server database within applications. It is used mostly for mobile devices, but it can be used to embed SQL Server databases in applications running on desktop and laptop computers as well. This is a free license edition.

For more details about the different editions of SQL Server 2008, visit the following website: `http://www.microsoft.com/sqlserver/2008/en/us/editions-compare.aspx`. As a server administrator, you must be careful to select the appropriate edition so that the database server can meet your current needs and grow with your near future needs.

Database Application Types

The three primary kinds of database applications are localized, client/server, and n-tier applications. Localized applications will not be covered in detail here because our primary focus is on running SQL "servers" and not on SQL Server clients.

A WORD ABOUT LOCALIZED APPLICATIONS

You should know that a localized application usually talks to a local installation of SQL Server using a protocol called shared memory. The name says it all: the local application talks to the local SQL Server installation (usually SQL Server Express) without using the network interface card.

Client/server database applications, also called single tier, involve a client application communicating directly with the database in most cases. An example of a client/server application is a Microsoft Access front-end that communicates with a SQL Server 2008 back-end database. The SQL Server is the server and Microsoft Access is the client. Technically, an Excel data import from a SQL Server is a client/server application. Figure 9.1 shows an example of this model.

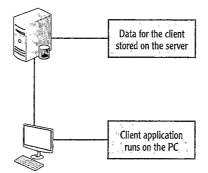

FIGURE 9.1 Client/server application

The example in Figure 9.1 shows an application communicating with a SQL server. Notice that the user interacts with the application as if everything is installed on her local machine. In fact, as long as the network is working and the database server is available, the user will usually feel as if the data is indeed in her computer. Of course, as you add more users—without increasing servers or the single server's capacity—they will likely notice a drop in performance; however, this drop should be minimal as long as the database server is well maintained and upgraded as needed.

An *n-tier database application* is an application that requires multiple levels (tiers) of communication in order to accomplish meaningful work. For example, a SharePoint server farm that includes one server for the database and another server for the website is an n-tier application or, more specifically in this case, a two-tier application. The user communicates with the web server (tier 1) and the web server communicates with the database on the user's behalf (tier 2). The *n* in n-tier is simply replaced with the number of links in the communication chain.

Figure 9.2 illustrates the SharePoint implementation. You can see the links or tiers in the application. Such an implementation provides several benefits. First, developers can change the database without necessarily rewriting all of the code at the web server. This benefit assumes a standard data access method was used between the web server and the database. Second, the developers can completely change the look and feel of the application without changing any of the data. In 3-tier, 4-tier, and more-tier implementations, the solution is even more componentized; and the result is greater flexibility in the solution over time.

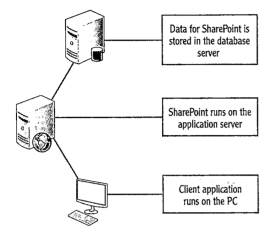

Data for SharePoint is stored in the database server

SharePoint runs on the application server

Client application runs on the PC

FIGURE 9.2 The n-tier application (SharePoint)

Finally, n-tier database applications are easier to scale. Single-tier applications are notoriously difficult to scale. Everything is resting on a single server. If the performance of the database becomes too slow, you are very limited in what you can do. With an n-tier application, you can distribute the data across several servers on the backend and absolutely nothing will change from the users' perspectives. No wonder developers love to use this model. It's not without its faults, but it certainly has its benefits.

Mail Servers: Using Microsoft Exchange Server

You can certainly perform email operations using Internet Information Services and the SMTP module, but for full mail server capabilities using Microsoft technologies, you will need the Microsoft Exchange Server product. In this section, you will learn about mail servers in general and the features of Microsoft Exchange Server in specific.

Mail servers support several protocols for communications. A protocol should be enabled only if it is required by a client application, and the fewer protocols you run on the network, the easier it will be to manage. The following protocols are often supported by modern mail servers:

Simple Mail Transport Protocol (SMTP)   SMTP is the most widely used email transmission protocol in the world. It is how the vast majority of email messages are sent on the Internet. By default, it works on port 25.

Post Office Protocol version 3 (POP3)   POP3 is frequently used to check email on Internet-based email servers. Microsoft Exchange can support POP3, but it is disabled by default. POP3 uses port 110 as the default communications port.

Internet Message Access Protocol (IMAP)   IMAP is another protocol that can be used to check email. While it offers more features than POP3, it still does not offer full support for Exchange Server features; therefore, it is disabled in Exchange Server by default. The default port used by IMAP is 143.

Messaging Application Programming Interface (MAPI)   MAPI is the primary protocol used for communications with Exchange Servers from Microsoft Outlook clients. MAPI is enabled by default on Exchange Server and uses dynamic ports for communications.

Exchange Server has evolved over multiple decades. Figure 9.3 shows the evolution of Exchange Server through different releases over the years. Exchange Server 2010 represents years of enhancements and added capabilities to Microsoft email and calendaring platform.

> IP-based communications used TCP and UDP ports to send data to the appropriate application on the receiving computer. Most services are configured using default port values.

> Microsoft Outlook is by far the most common desktop computer client used to check email on Exchange servers.

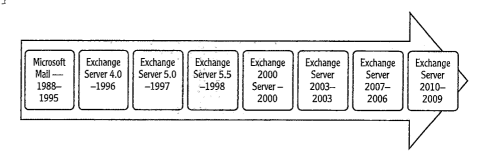

FIGURE 9.3 The Exchange Server evolution

Exchange Server features can be explored from several perspectives. The following sections explore Exchange Server design goals, roles, storage solutions, and mailbox management.

Exchange Server Design Goals

Exchange Server 2010 was designed with specific goals in mind: improved flexibility and reliability, enhanced anywhere access, and protection and compliance. These goals are further explained in the following sections:

Improve Flexibility and Reliability   Flexibility and reliability are provided through three major Exchange Server 2010 features:

> ► Flexible installation options
>
> ► Streamlined high availability and disaster recovery
>
> ► Simpler administration processes

An Exchange Server 2010 installation can be spread across many servers, and you can install only the needed components on a given server. High-availability capabilities are built into the system from the start. Administration is more consistent because the GUI management tools are based on Windows PowerShell cmdlets. Anything you can do in the GUI, you can automate in Windows PowerShell with scripts.

Enhance Anywhere Access   Anywhere access is improved through three features as well:

> ► More mobility options
>
> ► Email management tasks are improved
>
> ► Voicemail access may be integrated

You can access Exchange Server mailboxes from more client devices, such as Tablet PCs and web-enabled devices. Email management tasks are improved in the Outlook Web App interface for users. As with Exchange 2007, you can integrate voicemail access with the addition of other Microsoft products so that users receive their voicemails as email attachments.

Protection and Compliance   Exchange Server 2010 improves protection and compliance through two key features: built-in tools for meeting compliance requirements and improved security measures for sensitive information.

Exchange Server 2010 can be managed using the GUI tool called the Exchange Management Console (EMC) or from the command line using the Exchange Management Shell (EMS), which is a Windows PowerShell interface. The management interface you choose will be based on your proficiency with the tool and your

◄

Outlook Web App is the new version of Outlook Web Access in Exchange Server 2010; it allows users to access their email and calendars through a web browser.

administrative needs. For example, Windows PowerShell will be far superior to the EMC for automation. However, a single change to a user mailbox may be much faster through the EMC.

Exchange Server Roles

Exchange Server 2010 supports multiple roles. Each server can implement one or more of these roles. All roles can be installed on a single machine with the exception of the Edge Transport role.

Hub Transport   The Hub Transport role is used to move email around within your Exchange organization. At least one Hub Transport role is required.

Client Access   The Client Access role provides access to the Exchange organization and, therefore, to mailboxes for your users. At least one Client Access role is required. All clients connect through the Client Access role server to access their emails stored on the Mailbox role server.

Unified Messaging   The Unified Messaging role is an optional role. Unified Messaging brings voicemail, faxing, and emails together into the Exchange store for telephony integration. Exchange integrates with other software to provide the faxing solution, and this software must be acquired from third-party vendors.

Mailbox   The Mailbox role server contains the actual user mailboxes and their data. Multiple Mailbox role servers can be installed and database availability groups (DAGs) can be created for high availability.

Edge Transport   The Edge Transport role connects to the outside world for email transfer. The Edge Transport role should not be a member of your Active Directory domain for security reasons.

Management Tools   The management tools can be installed on the servers running the various Exchange Server roles, on a separate machine, or both.

> A database avail-
> ability group (DAG)
> is one of the primary
> new features in
> Exchange Server
> 2010 that provides
> high availability.
> ▶

Exchange Server Storage Architecture

Historically, Exchange Server has utilized storage groups to store mailboxes. Exchange 2010 removes this feature and implements mailbox databases and public folder databases. Mailbox databases can also be part of a database availability group (DAG). The DAG allows fault-tolerance without the need for clustering services. A DAG allows multiple databases to be online, and it allows client access server (CAS) role servers to direct user connections to an available copy of the database.

When compared with previous versions, Exchange Server 2010 makes the following important changes related to storage:

▶ *Storage groups are not supported.* The storage groups have been removed and mailbox databases exist as individual files, each with their own transaction logs.

▶ *Single instance storage is removed.* This feature allowed an email transmitted to ten users to be stored once and referenced in each mailbox for reduced storage consumption. Today, storage is less of an issue than performance, so this feature has been removed in favor of performance optimization changes.

▶ *Disk I/O is optimized.* According to some measurements, disk I/O has been reduced by as much as 70 percent from Exchange Server 2007.

Exchange Server 2010 systems use the Extensible Storage Engine (ESE) for data management. Data is stored in log buffers and transaction log files before being placed in mailbox databases. Mailbox databases are stored in *.EDB files. Each database has its own EDB file. When creating a mailbox database, your most important decision will be where to store it. When making this decision, you'll need to weigh two factors: performance and availabilty. You'll want to store the EDB files on well-performing storage devices such as RAID arrays or storage area networks (SANs). To help ensure availability, you might need to use RAID or a SAN as well.

Exchange Mailbox Management

Mailbox management in Exchange Server is more complex than it might first appear. In Exchange organizations, you manage mail recipients. Recipients can be any of several types:

▶ Outlook and other email accounts

▶ Distribution lists

▶ Group mailboxes

▶ Conference rooms

▶ Equipment

To create recipients, you must first create the account and then create the mailbox for the account. The accounts are created in Active Directory, and the mailboxes are created in the Exchange Management Console, although you can automate the process from either side.

When Exchange Server is installed, the Active Directory schema is modified to include the classes and attributes required by Exchange. These changes allow information to be stored within Active Directory for the Exchange organization. When Exchange is installed within an Active Directory domain, the Exchange Management Console can be used to create a mailbox and to create the Active Directory account at the same time.

Additionally, you can create contacts so that nondomain users can be listed in address books and distribution lists. A contact is an Active Directory object that cannot be used to log on to the domain; however, it can be configured as a recipient.

Creating mailboxes is a two-step process:

1. Create the Active Directory object

2. Create the mailbox

> **You can perform the mailbox and user-account creation steps at the same time in the Exchange Management Console, if desired.**

Collaboration Servers

When it comes to collaboration solutions, no product is growing faster than SharePoint. Microsoft SharePoint Server 2010 adds important features that allow SharePoint to meet the needs of many organizations right out-of-the-box. It also provides customization options to developers so they can expand the system to meet any organization's needs. The following sections introduce the SharePoint 2010 collaboration platform.

SharePoint 2010 Defined

SharePoint 2010 is a collection of products that serve as a business collaboration platform for organizations. SharePoint is a multi-tier application that relies on several other Microsoft technologies. For example, SharePoint requires a database and uses SQL Server for that database. SharePoint requires a web server and uses Internet Information Services for that web server.

SharePoint has often been called a content management system (CMS). A CMS is a system used to add, modify, approve, and delete content within websites. Although it is true that SharePoint is a CMS, it is much more than a simple CMS. SharePoint includes several features that take it far beyond the typical CMS. These features include:

▶ Access to external databases and data sources

▶ Built-in calendaring functions

- Discussion forum support capabilities

- File sharing through document libraries

- Advanced search functions and customization

- Microsoft Office application integration

- Customizations and feature additions through simple web parts

- Social tagging capabilities

- Business process automation through workflows

File sharing with document libraries is a key collaboration feature of SharePoint 2010, and Microsoft recommends using it to replace the older public folders offered in Exchange Server.

The preceding list does not include all the ways that SharePoint provides for customization of the content delivery method through the use of blogs, wikis, user profiles, versioning, surveys, and task lists. The point is that SharePoint is more than just a simple CMS. It is an entire-enterprise content-collaboration solution.

Businesses and organizations can use SharePoint for many purposes, including:

Standard Intranet Provisioning   SharePoint can be used to provide the traditional web services of a corporate intranet. It serves up web pages and documents for internal users.

Project Management   SharePoint is an excellent tool for centralizing project management information. Tasks can be managed from within SharePoint, and calendars can be associated with these tasks. Project workers can be notified when their tasks should begin and when they are due for completion.

Document Sharing   Everything from Excel workbooks to Adobe PDF documents can be stored in SharePoint document libraries. In some cases, SharePoint understands the document format and can offer special functions, such as data analysis for Excel workbooks. In other cases, SharePoint simply provides the storage location for the documents.

Resource Library Management   Resources such as images, media files, and other data resources can be managed using SharePoint resource libraries and external data lists.

Line-of-Business Integration   SharePoint can pull data from line-of-business (LoB) applications, such as SAP and J.D. Edwards, into reports, and lists in SharePoint sites. This allows users to view data from many different distributed systems.

Team Collaboration   The collaboration features of SharePoint include discussion forums, task lists, document libraries, and workflows. Each of these features adds to the collaboration capabilities of SharePoint and can be customized for the needs of the organization.

As you can see, SharePoint is a flexible application offering many different uses for the modern information-based organization.

SharePoint Editions

SharePoint 2010 comes in four different editions. When planning a SharePoint implementation, you must understand the different editions so that you can select the right one for your needs. The four editions are listed here:

> If you want to work with SharePoint in a lab or test environment, you can download SharePoint Foundation 2010 for free and work with it as long as you like.

SharePoint Foundation 2010   SharePoint Foundation 2010 is a free download. The only license required to use the product is the Windows Server operating system licensing. SharePoint Foundation 2010 provides the basic SharePoint features, but it does not include such features as social tagging, My Content, My Profile, enterprise wikis, Secure Store Service, and web analytics.

SharePoint Server 2010 Standard   SharePoint Server 2010 Standard Edition adds social tagging, My Content, My Profile, enterprise wikis, Secure Store Service, web analytics, and additional features as well. It is the entry-level licensed SharePoint product for businesses and organizations; however, SharePoint Server 2010 Standard Edition still lacks some features such as Visio Services, InfoPath Forms Services, Excel Services, and Access Services.

SharePoint Server 2010 Enterprise   To get the full feature set, the SharePoint Server 2010 Enterprise Edition must be purchased. The Enterprise Edition includes all the features of SharePoint Server 2010 Standard Edition as well as Visio Services, InfoPath Forms Services, Excel Services, and Access Services.

SharePoint Server 2010 for Internet Sites   SharePoint Server 2010 for Internet Sites can be purchased as either a Standard Edition or Enterprise Edition license. If you require the full feature set for an Internet-facing website, you will need the SharePoint Server 2010 for Internet Sites, Enterprise license. The SharePoint Server 2010 for Internet Sites license allows deployment of SharePoint for Internet websites, but only for a single domain with subdomains. For each additional domain set, you will have to purchase an additional license. An unlimited number of clients may access a SharePoint site hosted using the for Internet Sites licenses.

In implementation, the SharePoint Server 2010 editions are really just different licenses. The only installation difference is when selecting the appropriate license you plan to implement. During installation and configuration, you are asked to provide the Client Access License (CAL) product key. If you enter a standard CAL, you will enable the Standard Edition feature set. If you enter an enterprise CAL, you will enable the Enterprise feature set.

Monitoring Servers

While most application servers provide services that are ultimately consumed by users on the network, some application servers are really there to serve the network and other servers more than anything else. Monitoring servers fall into this category. A *monitoring server* is one that can monitor other servers or the network and trigger alerts for administrators if a problem occurs. They can even respond automatically to the problem and resolve it in many situations.

As an example, consider a server that monitors the services running on other servers. If a required service fails, the monitoring server may initiate a forced reboot on the server with the failed service. While the server will be down for a period of time, the failed service could possibly start again after the reboot, thereby restoring the service. This is an example of an automatic response from a monitoring server.

Microsoft offers several monitoring server solutions that may be useful, depending on your scenario. These solutions include:

System Center Virtual Machine Manager (SCVMM)   SCVMM is used in combination with Hyper-V to manage the virtualization environment running on Windows Server 2008 or Windows Server 2008 R2. SCVMM offers automatic provisioning and reprovisioning of virtual machines (VMs). This is a fancy way of saying that it can move a VM from one physical server to another in the event of a failure.

System Center Operations Manager (SCOM)   SCOM offers end-to-end service management. This simply means that it can monitor distributed services and notify administrative personnel when problems occur. SCOM can be used to monitor Windows servers in general, as well as SQL Server, Exchange Server, and even Windows clients.

System Center Data Protection Manager (DPM)   DPM is a centralized backup solution; however, it is also more. DPM is considered a monitoring solution because it performs backups regularly in the background. In most cases, file changes are backed up within minutes of the changes being made on the server; however, you can control the backup frequency.

In addition to these Microsoft monitoring solutions, third-party solutions can perform many similar functions. For example, if you use VMware ESX servers instead of Hyper-V virtualization server, you can use the VirtualCenter application to monitor and control the virtualization environment.

Threat Management Servers

Threat management servers are used to detect and, hopefully, prevent security attacks on your network. They are typically deployed at the egresses of the network, which are typically Internet connections. Microsoft offers the Forefront server solutions for threat management. Forefront products can integrate with other Microsoft products to provide security. Products that can be integrated include:

> Microsoft Forefront Threat Management Gateway is just one example of a threat management server. Several companies offer competing products.

▶ Exchange Server

▶ SharePoint

▶ Office Communication Server

▶ Endpoints (computers running Windows operating systems)

Microsoft Forefront Threat Management Gateway 2010 is deployed in the perimeter network and offers several features to help protect your users. These features include:

> Site-to-site VPN connections are made between two networks to allow traffic from multiple users to traverse the VPN. Remote access VPNs create a direct connection between a single client and the corporate network.

HTTPS Inspection   Provides the ability to inspect the contents of SSL encrypted traffic to look for potential malware

Email Security   Scans email messages for potential malware

Network Inspection System (NIS)   Scans network traffic for malware and other types of attacks

Web Malware Detection   Scans standard HTTP traffic for malware

VPN Support   Allows VPN connection to be created for site-to-site connections and remote access VPN connections

THE ESSENTIALS AND BEYOND

Application servers abound on modern networks. If you are preparing for the 98-365 Windows Administration Fundamentals exam, you will need to identify the different server types and the functions they provide to the network. Email servers allow users to send and receive emails. Database servers provide access to databases for user applications and other server applications. Collaboration servers allow users to share information, documents, and communications. Monitoring servers watch the activity on other servers or the network and respond based on their configurations. Threat management servers monitor the network and computers to ensure compliance with security policy and to prevent malware from entering the system.

ADDITIONAL EXERCISES

▶ Read about the planning and design process used to implement the Forefront Threat Management Gateway at:

   `http://technet.microsoft.com/en-us/library/cc441674.aspx`

▶ Download, install, and use the Exchange 2010 Mailbox Server Role Requirements Calculator to see the different requirements for the various Exchange Server roles.

▶ Install SQL Server Express 2008 R2 on a Windows server with the SQL Server Management Studio Express and explore the options provided in the administrative interface.

To compare your answers to the author's, please visit:

`www.sybex.com/go/winadminessentials`

REVIEW QUESTIONS

1. SMTP uses what port for network communications?

   A. 110   **C.** 21

   B. 25   **D.** Dynamic

2. True or false: The Developer Edition of SQL Server offers all the same features as the Enterprise Edition.

3. What is the default mail server communications protocol used between a Microsoft Outlook client and an Exchange Server?

   A. POP3   **C.** MAPI

   B. SIP   **D.** IMAP

4. What is an example of a Microsoft monitoring server?

(Continues)

THE ESSENTIALS AND BEYOND (Continued)

5.   What type of database application-server plan includes more than one server for a single application solution?

A. Localized   **C.** N-tier

B. Client/server   **D.** Web server

6. Define a mail server.

7. Define a collaboration server.

8.   What component of the Forefront Threat Management Gateway is responsible for scanning the network traffic for malware?

A. Email security   **C.** Network inspection service

B. Web malware detection   **D.** HTTPS inspection

9. Which one of the following is not a feature of SharePoint 2010?

A. Social tagging   **C.** Malware scanning

B. Access to external data sources   **D.** Document sharing

10.   True or false: A database server and a database are the same thing.

CHAPTER 10

Internet Information Services (IIS)

Web services are an important business demand in today's computing environments. On the Internet, they provide the websites we all enjoy browsing. The radical growth of Internet web services in the 1990s caused many companies to implement in-house solutions based on Internet technology. SOAP development is just one example of such technology. Hidden beneath applications, such as SharePoint and Outlook Web App (OWA), you will find the core web services.

   In this chapter, you will learn about web services and the solutions available on Windows servers to implement them. The principal concepts of web services are covered, including:

▷ **Understanding web services**

▷ **Internet Information Services**

▷ **Running an FTP server**

▷ **Configuring sites and ports**

▷ **Web server security**

Understanding Web Services

According to the World Wide Web Consortium (W3C), *web services* are defined as "a software system designed to provide a standard means of interoperating between different software applications, running on a variety of platforms and frameworks." A website is effectively a web service. It is a simple web service, but it meets the requirements of the web services definition. Web services have special characteristics that differentiate them from other server applications, such as:

Interoperability   Web services allow client access from different device types on different platforms. They even allow different applications on those platforms as long as those applications use the same communications protocols and standards as the web services, such as the Hypertext Transfer Protocol (HTTP) and the Extensible Markup Language (XML).

Extensibility   Web services typically support extensions through add-on modules and integration with other web services. For example, a website may provide content from multiple other websites using Really Simple Syndication (RSS). The web server may be extended using add-on components to add functionality like search or support for different development platforms and frameworks, such as Active Server Pages (ASP), PHP, or ASP .NET.

Loose Coupling   Web services are often called *loosely coupled*. This phrase simply means that the individual components of the system are not fully aware of the internal workings of the other components. For example, a web application that pulls information from a database is not concerned with the specific methods the database management system (DBMS) uses to retrieve the data. It requires only that the appropriate data be retrieved and transmitted back to it. Loose coupling may also result in decreased network throughput consumption because the requests typically contain less information when passed between the components.

A web service requires a foundation on which to be built. This foundation should provide a method for communicating with other web services and client applications. It should also provide a framework for the development of core service functionality. On Windows servers, these demands are provided by Internet Information Services (IIS) and the ASP or ASP .NET frameworks. IIS is the web server and application server that ships with the Windows client and server operating systems. ASP and ASP .NET are software development frameworks, which means that they provide access to prebuilt routines for many of the actions that applications must take to perform their intended functions.

> While ASP is still supported in Windows Server 2008 R2 installations of IIS, most new development is being done in ASP.NET, which has been available since January of 2002.

SOAP: AN EXAMPLE OF A WEB SERVICES SOLUTION

One of the most popular solutions for web service communications is the Simple Object Access Protocol (SOAP), although the acronym is no longer defined in the newest version of the specification and it is simply referred to as SOAP. SOAP is a specification, based on XML, which allows developers to build web services that can communicate with each other in a standard method. SOAP messages are sent between web services; they include one-way communications (notifications or alerts), request/response interactions, and peer-to-peer conversations.

SOAP also provides for n-tier web service topologies. SOAP nodes include the SOAP sender (the origination of the message), the SOAP receiver (the final destination for the message), and possible SOAP intermediaries.

(Continues)

SOAP: AN EXAMPLE OF A WEB SERVICES SOLUTION *(Continued)*

You do not have to master SOAP (or any other web services technology) to administer a Windows server running IIS, but it is helpful to be aware of the different solutions used within the applications you may choose to implement.

WWW, the common term used all over the Internet, stands for World Wide Web. The servers on the WWW offer web services to their clients. Many of these servers are single-tier implementations in that they are self-contained. Others are n-tier applications that rely on backend servers for things like database access, search processing, and other specialized services. The remainder of this chapter focuses on the Microsoft IIS server, which is the foundation on which you can run web services with Windows servers. For a detailed explanation of web services, see the "Web Services Architecture" document located at http://www.w3.org/TR/2002/WD-ws-arch-20021114.

Internet Information Services

Internet Information Services (IIS) has been in Windows Server for several versions. It was first introduced in the 1990s and has evolved rapidly since that time. As a web server, IIS is capable of offering simple websites to the Internet or the local network. As a web application server or web services server, it is capable of providing complex applications for both web browsers and custom client applications. In this section, you will learn about the basic process used to provide a web page to a client using IIS. You will also learn how to add the Web Server (IIS) role, which is the way you install the IIS service on Windows Server 2008 and later. Finally, you will learn about the management tool—IIS Manager—used to manage the web server.

> IIS 7.0 ships with Windows Server 2008 and Windows Vista. IIS 7.5 ships with Windows Server 2008 R2 and Windows 7.

Understanding How IIS Works

Because IIS is a web server, you must understand how a web server works in general to understand how IIS works in that role. A web server provides web pages to browsers that request them. More specifically, a web server is a server that is capable of responding to HTTP requests for files. These files may include Hypertext Markup Language (HTML), graphics (GIF, JPG, and PNG), media (audio and video), and scripting (ASP, PHP, etc.) files. The HTTP protocol defines the standard messages for communications between a web server and a web browser. Figure 10.1 illustrates the concept of web requests and responses between a web server and a web browser or web client.

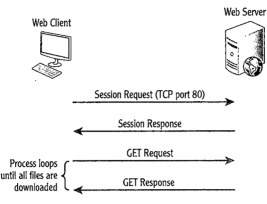

FIGURE 10.1 The HTTP request/response process

When a web client, such as a web browser, accesses a website, it must download several items. Websites are comprised of web pages, which in turn are comprised of text-based code files, image files, and media files. A single web page can contain dozens of image and media files. As an example, consider the basic HTML code listing in Listing 10.1. In this simple example, two image files are referenced in the web page. The first is the logo.gif file, and the second is the office.jpg file. For a web browser to display the web page represented in Listing 10.1, it will have to send three GET requests to the web server. First, it must get the web page text itself, which is the content in Listing 10.1. Next, it must get the logo.gif file. Finally, it must get the office.jpg file. The HTTP protocol is used to send each of these GET requests to the web server and then to transfer the files to the local machine.

Listing 10.1: Sample Web Page

```
<html>
<head>
<title>Sample Web Page</title>
</head>
<body>
<p>Welcome to our web page!
<img src ="/images/log.gif" alt="Our Company">
<p> We are glad you chose to visit us. The following image
shows our corporate offices:
<p><img src="office.jpg" alt="Company HQ" width="460" height="280">
</body>
</html>
```

The World Wide Web Publishing Service will be added to the list of services in the Services console on your server after IIS is installed. This service is the HTTP-compliant web server responsible for fulfilling GET requests and other HTTP actions. In addition to providing files to the requesting client, the web server can receive files from the client. The POST and PUT methods are used to send data from the client to the server. (For a complete listing of the HTTP methods available, search for and read *RFC 2616*, which defines the HTTP 1.1 standard.)

One of the key features in IIS is the use of application pools. An *application pool* is a collection of one or more worker processes responsible for running web applications. The application pool may contain multiple web applications, which can include websites, FTP sites, and custom applications. SharePoint 2010 is an example of a solution, based on IIS, that uses custom applications that run in application pools. On an IIS server with multiple websites, you can run each website in its own application pool, which results in greater stability for your web server because the failure of one application pool causes the failure of only the websites in that pool.

A *Request for Comment* (RFC) is a document used to develop Internet standards.

Adding the Web Server (IIS) Role

To install IIS on a Windows server, you will add the Web Server (IIS) role. The role is added in the same way as any other server role. Complete the following procedure to install it:

1. Launch Server Manager.

2. Select the Roles node in the console tree.

3. Click Add Roles in the content pane.

4. If the Before You Begin screen is displayed, click Next.

5. On the Select Server Roles screen, select the Web Server (IIS) role and click Next.

6. On the Web Server (IIS) screen, read the provided information that introduces you to the IIS server, if you desire, and then click Next.

7. On the Select Role Services screen, accept the default selection of role services and click Next.

8. On the Confirm Installation Selections screen, read the list of items to be installed and then click Install to begin the installation.

9. When the installation is complete and the Installation Results screen is displayed, click Close to exit the Add Roles Wizard.

You can add several other role services on this screen. You will learn to add these extra services after installation in the next section titled "Configuring IIS."

Immediately after the installation is completed, your Windows server will function as a web server. If you open your local web browser on the server and navigate to http://localhost, you will see a page like the one in Figure 10.2.

FIGURE 10.2 The default page displayed when accessing the web server immediately after installation

INTERNET EXPLORER ENHANCED SECURITY CONFIGURATION

Windows Server 2008 introduced a new feature called Internet Explorer Enhanced Security Configuration (IE ESC). When IE ESC is enabled, which is the default setting, you cannot browse websites unless they are in the Trusted sites zone. Internet Explorer uses zones to determine the level of trust to grant to a website. The sites in the Trusted sites zone are allowed to run with very few constraints. The IE ESC feature is enabled by default to help protect your server installation. You can disable IE ESC using the Server Manager. If you disable it, remember that you are exposing your server to a greater risk of accidental infection with malware. However, to disable it:

1. Launch Server Manager.

2. Select the root node, Server Manager (server_name), in the console tree.

3. Scroll down in the content pane until you see the section titled "Security Information."

(Continues)

INTERNET EXPLORER ENHANCED SECURITY CONFIGURATION

(Continued)

4. In the Security Information section, click on the Configure IE ESC link.

5. Turn IE ESC off for administrators or users or both by selecting the Off option.

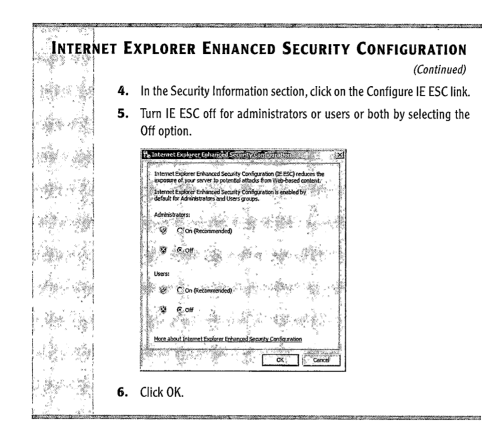

6. Click OK.

Configuring IIS

The primary tool used to manage IIS is the IIS Manager. The IIS Manager is an administrative console preconfigured to support IIS configuration and administration tasks. You can use the IIS manager to create and manage websites, create and manage application pools, and perform important maintenance tasks such as restarting the WWW Publishing Service. Figure 10.3 shows the IIS Manager.

One task you may have to perform is IIS component management. Two core components drive the majority of IIS operations:

Protocol Listeners The protocol listeners receive requests from clients, pass them onto IIS for processing, and then return the responses to the clients. The primary listener in IIS is the HTTP listener, which is driven by HTTP.sys. HTTP.sys provides listeners for both HTTP (cleartext communications) and HTTPS (encrypted communications). Additional listeners may be made available by third-party solution providers.

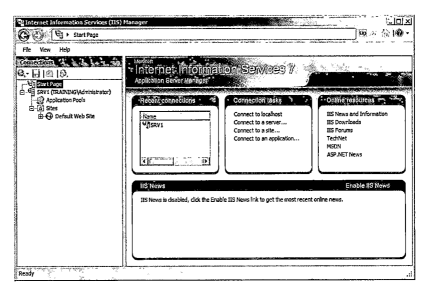

FIGURE 10.3 The IIS Manager administration interface

Services   The two services that provide the processing for IIS are the WWW Publishing Service (also called simply the WWW service or W3SVC) and the Windows Process Activation Service (WAS). The WWW service is the HTTP listener service. It receives the requests from clients and provides the responses to those clients. The WAS service is the processing service. It is responsible for managing application pools and the worker processes in those application pools.

An additional task that is common and often required is the restarting of the WWW service. If a website stops responding, you may need to restart the WWW service. To restart the service, follow this procedure:

1. Log on to the server as an administrator.

2. Launch the IIS Manager by clicking Start ➢ All Programs ➢ Administrative Tools ➢ Internet Information Services (IIS) Manager.

3. In the Connections pane on the left of the IIS Manager, click the server name on which you want to restart the WWW service.
    In Figure 10.3, the server name is SRV1 (TRAINING\Administrator).

4. In the Actions pane on the right, click Restart.

Modern web applications are often more complex than the simple static websites that were common on the early Internet. Today, websites use application code on the servers that render HTML documents for transmission to the

> You can manage the IIS services directly in the Services node of the Server Manager console; however, it is usually best to manage them from within IIS Manager to avoid configuration problems.

clients. IIS supports such code using ASP and ASP .NET; however, the default installation of IIS does not include these components. To add support for ASP and ASP.NET to the IIS installation, follow this procedure:

1. Log on to the server as an administrator.

2. Launch Server Manager.

3. In the console tree, expand Roles ➤ Web Server (IIS) and select the Web Server (IIS) node by clicking on it.

4. In the content pane, scroll down to the Role Services section and then click on the Add Role Services link.

5. On the Select Role Services screen, choose the Application Development role service and all the subitems within Application Development, as shown in the following image, and then click Next.

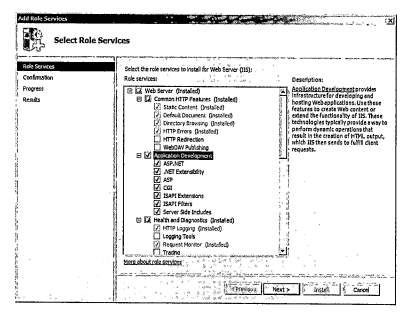

6. On the Confirm Installation Selections screen, click Install to begin the installation.

7. On the Installation Results screen, click Close to exit the Add Role Services Wizard.

After the Application Development role service is installed, you will see new objects in the IIS Manager. An entirely new section, named ASP .NET, will be displayed and a new item will be added to the IIS section, which is named ASP.

The ASP item allows you to configure settings for the older Microsoft web application development framework. The ASP .NET section allows you to configure settings for the newer web application development framework that is based on Microsoft's .NET framework.

Another common task you will have to perform as an IIS administrator on Windows Server 2008 64-bit servers is that of allowing 32-bit web applications. By default, IIS only allows 64-bit web applications to run. This prevents older ASP applications from working. It can also impact third-party applications. If you have a 32-bit application, you must ensure that the application pool in which it runs is configured to allow 32-bit code. To enable 32-bit applications for an application pool, follow this procedure:

1. Launch IIS Manager.

2. In the Connections pane, expand the server node that contains the application pool you want to configure.

3. Select the Application Pools node.

4. Click on the application pool you want to configure in the content pane.

5. Click the Advanced Settings link in the Actions pane.

6. Set the Enable 32-Bit Applications settings to True, as shown in the following image, and then click OK.

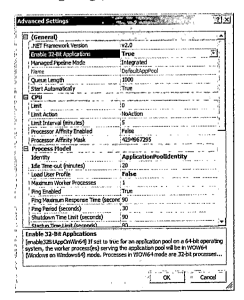

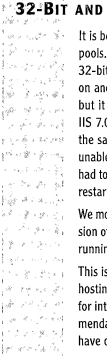

32-BIT AND 64-BIT WEB APPLICATIONS

It is best to run 32-bit and 64-bit web applications in separate application pools. In fact, if the organization's budget allows for it, it's best to run only 32-bit web applications on one server and only 64-bit web applications on another server. This is not necessarily a recommendation of Microsoft, but it is based on real-world experience. I have been involved in several IIS 7.0 and 7.5 deployments where 32-bit and 64-bit code was mixed on the same server; even with dedicated application pools for each, we were unable to get the desired stability when running with this configuration and had to configure frequent automatic refreshes of the IIS services (automatic restarting of the services).

We moved the 32-bit code off to a separate server, still running the same version of Windows and IIS, and found that the servers were more stable when running only 32-bit web applications or only 64-bit web applications.

This is certainly not a requirement and is not realistic as a solution for web hosting providers that host hundreds of sites on a single server. However, for internal servers that an organization manages itself, it is a good recommendation for achieving improved stability. With the heavy dependency we have on intranet applications today, stability is very important.

Running an FTP Server

The File Transfer Protocol (FTP) is used to copy files from one machine to another using the TCP/IP protocol suite. FTP is typically divided into two components: the server and the client. The FTP server provides for file uploads and downloads to and from a storage space.

Most FTP servers provide security features so that you can control the level of access granted to the users connecting to the server. The default transmission process, however, is a cleartext process. This means that the data is transmitted in such a way that it can be read by users or attackers who understand how to capture packets off the network with a protocol analyzer.

FTP clients can be simple command-line tools or powerful GUI applications with scheduling and scripting capabilities. Free FTP client applications, such as FileZilla shown in Figure 10.4, are readily available. Commercial FTP applications are also available. A command-line FTP client is installed or available for installation in every Windows operating system.

A *protocol analyzer* is a software application that can retrieve network packets from a network and potentially decode and display the information they contain.

FIGURE 10.4 The FileZilla FTP client application connected to `ftp.microsoft.com`

While Figure 10.4 shows that an FTP client application can function much like a local file manager, it is important that you understand FTP is not a file manager, but a file transfer solution. GUI FTP clients simply retrieve a directory listing from the FTP server and display it in the graphical interface. An FTP connection between a client and a server is initiated using the following basic process:

> This entire process is documented in technical terms and in much greater depth in *RFC 959*.

1. The client initiates a TCP connection to the server on port 21 (the default FTP port).

2. The server responds with a reply indicating it is ready for a new user.

3. The client initiates a login process and provides the username.

4. The server either responds with a successful login or requests a password, if required.

5. If the password is required, the client sends the password.

6. Assuming a correct password is entered, a connection is established, and the client can request the appropriate directory or file listing.

Once connected, the FTP servers support file transfers using different modes. The default mode is usually ASCII and is used to transfer text files. In binary mode, also called image mode, nontext data can be transferred. Binary mode should be used for any data for which the type is unknown. Even a text file transferred as binary data should be uncorrupted by the transfer; however, binary files transferred as ASCII data will usually be corrupted.

To set up an FTP server on Windows servers, you must add the FTP service to the server. After it is added, you can specify the directories you want to make available to FTP clients.

To add the FTP service to the server, following this procedure:

1. Launch Server Manager.

2. Expand the Roles node in the console tree.

3. Click the Web Server (IIS) role in the console tree.

4. Scroll down in the content pane until you see the Role Services section.

5. In the Role Services section, click the Add Role Services link.

6. On the Select Role Services screen, scroll down in the Role Services list until you see FTP Server.

7. Select the FTP Server role service, and ensure that the FTP Service and FTP Extensibility options are checked as well.

8. Click Next.

9. On the Confirm Installation Selections screen, click Install.

10. When the installation completes, click Close on the Installation Results screen.

To configure the FTP server, use the IIS Manager. You will need to create an FTP site and determine the user access permissions that should be allowed. To create an FTP site, follow this procedure:

1. Launch the IIS Manager.

2. Expand the server and Sites container, as shown in the following image.

3. Right-click on the Sites container and select Add FTP Site.

4. On the Site Information screen, enter the FTP Site Name you want, and select the local drive and folder you want to use as the content directory for the FTP site.

> If the folder does not exist, you can create the folder using the Make New Folder button while browsing for the content directory.

5. On the Binding and SSL Settings page, you can configure the local server's IP addresses that should be used for FTP and change the port from the default of 21, if you'd like.

   If you run only one FTP site, it will likely be on port 21.

6. On the Binding and SSL Settings page, select the No SSL option within the SSL section to disable support for secure FTP at this point, and click Next.

> You must have an SSL certificate installed on the server to use SSL with FTP. By default, no such certificate will be available in a default IIS installation.

7. On the Authentication and Authorization Information screen, you can configure the authentication type and define who can access the FTP server:

   a. Choose Anonymous authentication so that anyone can connect to this site.

   b. Choose All Users in the Authorization section to allow anonymous users to have access to this site as well as users with valid accounts.

   c. Select both the Read and Write permissions so that users can download and upload files.

8. Click Finish.

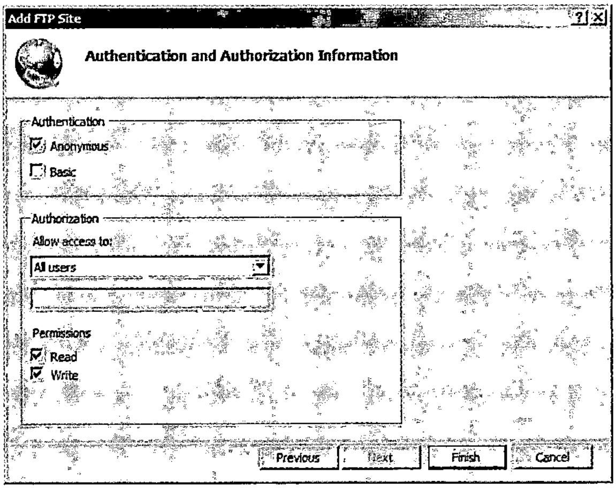

Figure 10.5 shows a Windows 7 Command Prompt accessing the FTP server running on Windows Server 2008 R2. The `ftp ip_address` command is used to create the connection. The password for an anonymous logon can be anything, but the tradition of the Internet is to use the user's email address as the password. Notice that the `dir` command is used to list the items on the FTP server. The available FTP commands can be retrieved by typing a question mark (?) and pressing Enter while connected to the FTP server.

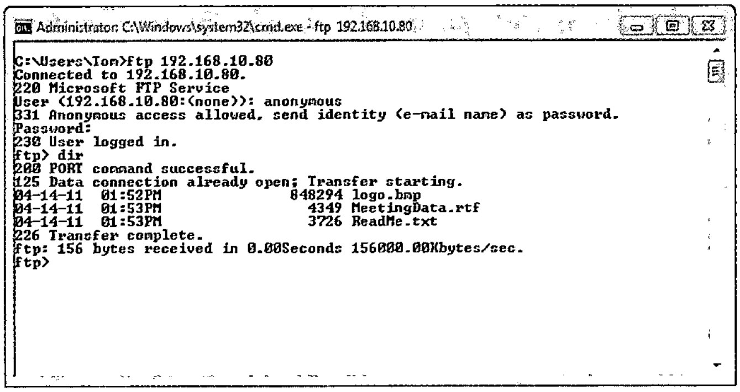

FIGURE 10.5 Connecting to the FTP server with a Windows 7 client

Configuring Sites and Ports

Creating a new website is similar to creating an FTP site. A site named Default Web Site is created automatically when you first install IIS. You can use this website and create new websites. It is common to create new websites with a port other than the default port of 80. To create a new website and use port 8080, follow this procedure:

1. Launch the IIS Manager.

2. Expand the server and Sites container.

3. Right-click on the Sites container and select Add Web Site.

4. In the Add Web Site dialog, enter the following information:

   a. A Site Name

   b. The Physical Path for the storage of the website content

   c. The Port value of 8080

5. Click OK.

The Site Name value will be displayed as a node within the Sites container.

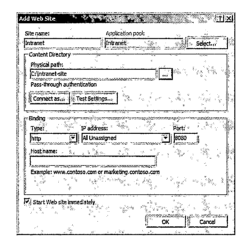

As an alternative to using custom ports, you can use host header mappings. Host header mappings use the DNS hostname to identify the appropriate site. This allows multiple sites to run on the same IP address and port with different hostnames. To accomplish this, you must perform two actions. First, you must create the host record in DNS. For example, you could add a host record for the intranet.training.local host to point to the IP address of the IIS server. Second, you must configure the site bindings to respond to port 80 with the defined host header. In this example, you would configure the host header as intranet.training.local, as shown in Figure 10.6.

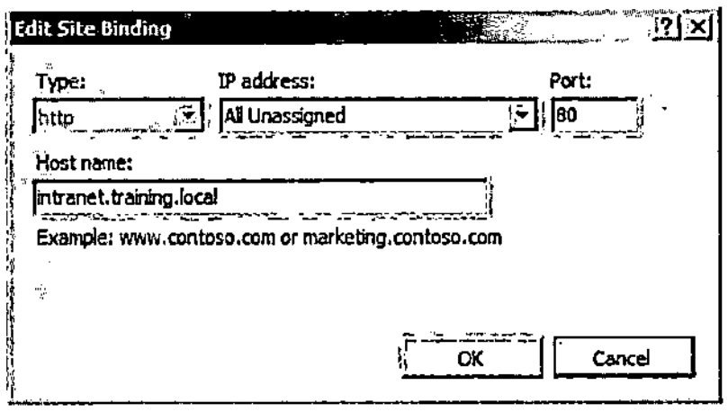

FIGURE 10.6 Configuring sites using host headers instead of custom ports

Web Server Security

When it comes to web server security, you'll need to pay special attention to two aspects. The first is *authentication*. You must determine who will be allowed to access your servers. The second is *encryption*. You must decide whether or not encryption is required and plan for its implementation when it is. The following sections provide an overview of the security solutions available in IIS on Windows servers.

Planning for Authentication

Authentication can be defined as "proving a person or object is who or what he or it claims to be." It should not be confused with *authorization*, which is defined as "granting access to a resource by a person or object." Authorization assumes the identity has been authenticated. If authentication can be spoofed or impersonated, authorization schemes fail. From this, you can see why authentication is such an integral and important part of network and information security. When an attacker exploits a weakness in your authentication system so that he is seen as an authenticated user, the authorization becomes irrelevant. Authentication must be strong if authorization is to serve its purpose.

Many different credential solutions are available for securing your networks. It's important that you select the right solution for your needs. While most web servers use passwords, it is possible to provide authentication for internal users using other means. The following three authentication methods are common:

- ▶ *Something you know:* a password or a personal identification number (PIN)

- ▶ *Something you have:* a smart card or a key

- ▶ *Something you are:* biometrics such as fingerprint scanners and retina scanners

IIS supports both authentication and authorization. When you define permissions on a site (web or FTP), you are defining authorization settings.

A smart card is a credit card–sized authentication device that includes identity information on the card in the form of a certificate.

A credential validation solution should provide a means of user or computer identification that is proportional to your security needs. You do not want to select a credential solution that places unnecessary burdens on the users and results in greater costs (of both time and money) than the value of the information assets you are protecting.

Sometimes, one type of authentication alone is not sufficient. In these cases, multifactor authentication can be used. Multifactor authentication is a form of authentication that uses more than one set of credentials. An example of a multifactor authentication process would be the use of both passwords and fingerprint scanners. Usually, the user places her finger on the fingerprint scanner and then is prompted for a password or PIN (personal identification number) code. The password may be used for network authentication, or it may be used only for localized authentication before the finger scan data is used for network authentication. However, in most cases the password and fingerprint scan data are used to authenticate to the local machine and then the network or just to the network alone. A common example of multifactor authentication would be your ATM card. You have the card and you know the pin (something you have and something you know).

DO YOU HAVE CRED?

Remember the word *credentials*? Consider other important "cred" words: *credit* and *credibility*. Do you see how they are related? They all have to do with having proof of something. When you have good credit, you have proof of your trustworthiness to pay debts. When you have credibility, you have proof that you are authentic, persuasive, and dynamic. When you have credentials, you have an object or the experience that proves your skill or identity. Authentication results in the verification of credentials.

The root of these cred words is the Latin word *credo*, which means "I believe." This original meaning is why the word *incredulous* means you are unwilling to believe. In summary, authentication uses credentials, and credentials are used to prove identity so that the system can "believe" you are who you say you are.

IIS supports five types of authentication for user access. When you select the authentication method, you should have a basic understanding of what it offers and how it works. The five types of authentication in IIS are listed here:

- ► Anonymous

- ► Basic

- Digest
- Forms
- Windows

Anonymous authentication is used when a website is a public access site. For example, the site may be available on the Internet or on a guest intranet. In such scenarios, you will have no method for establishing credentials with the guests browsing the SharePoint site and anonymous access must be allowed.

Basic authentication uses usernames and passwords and should be used only when an SSL connection (HTTPS) is established with the website. If SSL is used, the basic authentication process is encrypted in the SSL-secured connection. If SSL is not used, the credentials are transferred in a manner that allows them to be easily interception by an attacker. The credentials are sent in Base64 encoding, which is easily decoded without an encryption key. Once the credentials are sniffed from the network and decoded, the attacker can use them to log on as the valid user. This is why basic authentication should never be used without an SSL connection.

Digest authentication is based on RFCs 2617 and 2831. Digest authentication is based on secret keys. While Basic authentication sends the password across the network in an easily decodable form, digest authentication does not; the secret keys and passwords are not sent across the network in any form. Digest authentication should be used when the full encryption of HTTP communications is not required. SSL is preferred when full encryption is required.

Forms authentication uses a web page–based form to enter credentials for authentication. Forms-based authentication is used with popular IIS-based applications such as SharePoint and Exchange Server 2010 Outlook Web App.

Windows authentication uses the Active Directory Domain Services (AD DS) domain user database for authentication to the IIS server. The server and client must both support NT LAN Manager (NTLM) or Kerberos as the authentication protocol for Windows authentication to be used.

NTLM authentication is required by older client systems that are not Active Directory–aware. Such systems include NT 4.0 and Windows 98 computers, and even newer operating systems when they are not members of the domain. The IIS authentication process dictates that the authentication protocols be used in order from most secure to least secure. For this reason, you can enable both NTLM and Kerberos for your IIS installations. Kerberos will be used when it is available, and NTLM can be used when Kerberos is not available.

NTLM is not as secure as Kerberos, so you will want to use Kerberos as much as possible. When you must use NTLM, ensure that strong passwords are chosen. Such passwords are usually 7 or 14 characters long and include multiple character types. Due to an anomaly in the original NTLM authentication process, passwords of between 8 and 13 characters were less secure than passwords of 7 or 14 characters. While this problem has been resolved, many administrators still encourage users to use seven-character passwords. Today, with NTLM v2, eight-character passwords are actually more secure than seven-character passwords.

Kerberos authentication is the best method for internal IIS installations (websites used only by domain clients). The clients must have access to the Key Distribution Center (KDC), which is the domain controller in an AD DS environment. The KDC provides a Ticket-Granting Ticket (TGT) at initial user logon to the domain. The TGT is used to acquire Session Tickets (STs) for access to individual servers, such as IIS servers. The most important thing to remember is that Kerberos is more secure than NTLM and should be used by internal clients as much as possible.

Many browsers do not support NTLM or Kerberos authentication and will require the use of Basic authentication. If you must support such browsers for sites that require security, ensure that SSL is used.

Planning for Encryption

The last security topic we'll discuss in this chapter is encryption. The process of converting data from its normal state to an unreadable state is known as *encryption*. The unreadable state is known as *ciphertext* (or *cipherdata*), and the readable state is *plaintext* (or *plaindata*). The normal way to encrypt something is to pass the data through an algorithm using a key for variable results. For example, let's say you want to protect the number *108*. Here is an algorithm for protecting numeric data:

```
original data / crypto key + (3 x crypto key)
```

Using this algorithm to protect (encode or encrypt) the number *108* with a key of 3, produces this:

```
108 / 3 + (3 x 3) = 45
```

In order to recover the original data, you must know both the algorithm and the key. Needless to say, modern crypto algorithms are much more complex than this and keys are much longer, but this overview gives you an idea of how things work with data encryption.

IIS supports encryption of the communications between the server and connecting clients. The encryption is provided using a protocol called Secure Sockets Layer (SSL). When you connect to a website that begins with the HTTPS protocol identifier, such as https://somebankintheworld.local, you are creating a secure, encrypted connection with the server.

SSL encryption requires the use of certificates to provision keys for the secure communications. A *certificate* can be defined as "a digitally signed statement that contains information about an entity and the entity's public key" (*Dictionary of*

Information Security, Syngress Publishing, 2006). Certificates may be generated internally if the generating organization has implemented a *Public Key Infrastructure* (PKI), or they may be acquired externally through third-party organizations.

A PKI is an internal set of servers responsible for the creation, distribution, management, and revocation of certificates. Organizations that require hundreds or even thousands of certificates will typically implement a PKI. The certificates generated from the PKI are useful for internal web servers. They are not as beneficial for external public users because the certificates will not be trusted by those users' machines.

Third-party vendors offer certificates that are usually trusted by clients on the Internet. In order for a certificate provider to be trusted, the provider's certificate must be installed in the client machine. Certificates from popular certificate providers, such as VeriSign and Thawte, are provided in most operating systems out-of-the-box.

A *self-signed certificate* is another certificate option for web servers. If you use a self-signed certificate, all users will receive a security warning the first time they visit your site because the certificate will not be from a trusted source. However, the users may install the certificate in their local store on the first visit so they won't receive future warnings.

When a user accesses an HTTPS website, their machine validates the certificate. If it is from an untrusted party, the user receives a security warning.

These issues are important considerations when planning for encryption. Once you have chosen a certificate source, you can import the certificate into IIS and enable SSL for the appropriate site or sites.

To create a self-signed certificate, follow this procedure:

1. Launch IIS Manager.

2. Click on the server node in the Connections pane.

3. Double-click on Server Certificates in the content pane.

4. Click the Create Self-Signed Certificate link in the Actions pane.

5. Provide a name for the certificate, and click OK.

To import a certificate received from a third-party vendor, follow this procedure:

1. Launch IIS Manager.

2. Click on the server node in the Connections pane.

3. Double-click on Server Certificates in the content pane.

4. Click the Import link in the Actions pane.

5. Follow the prompts in the Import Wizard.

To create a certificate request so that you can receive a certificate from an internal PKI, follow this procedure:

1. Launch IIS Manager.

2. Click on the server node in the Connections pane.

3. Double-click on Server Certificates in the content pane.

4. Click the Create Certificate Request link in the Actions pane.

5. Follow the prompts in the Certificate Request Wizard.

After you have added a server certificate, you can enable SSL for a website. To enable SSL for a website, follow this procedure:

1. Launch IIS Manager.

2. Expand the server node and the Sites container in the Connections pane.

3. Click on the target site for which you want to enable SSL.

4. Click the Bindings link in the Actions pane.

5. Click Add to add a new binding that supports SSL.

6. Choose the type of HTTPS and the certificate to use for SSL, and click OK.

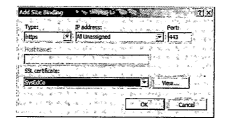

7. Click Close in the Site Bindings dialog.

After performing the preceding procedure, SSL will be available for the targeted site. If you want to require SSL, you will have to take one more action. Select the target site in the Connections pane and double-click on the SSL Settings option in the content pane. You will see a check box labeled Require SSL. Once this has been enabled, anyone who visits the site will have to use SSL in order to connect.

THE ESSENTIALS AND BEYOND

Internet Information Services (IIS) allows a Windows server to act as a web server and provide services for websites and other web applications. Using the IIS Manager, you can provision websites and even deploy FTP Server sites. IIS supports several different authentication methods, and you should be careful to choose the method that provides the greatest level of security without overburdening your users. Anonymous access is provided for public access website hosting. Encryption is supported and requires the use of SSL, which itself requires a certificate to provision encryption keys. A certificate may be acquired through internal PKIs, third-party certificate providers, or through the use of a self-signed certificate.

ADDITIONAL EXERCISES

▶ Create a website that maps to port 8060 on the server.

▶ Create a website that maps to port 80, but uses the hostname
  `intranet.training.local`.

▶ Create an FTP site that points to the directory `C:\ftpanon`.

▶ Create an FTP site that points to the directory `C:\ftpsecure` and requires user authentication.

To compare your answers to the author's, please visit

`www.sybex.com/go/winadminessentials`.

REVIEW QUESTIONS

1. What form of authentication, supported by IIS, uses pre-shared secret keys that are not sent across the network in any form?

   A. Basic   **C.** Digest

   B. Forms   **D.** Anonymous

2. True or false: IIS 7.5 first shipped with Windows Vista and Server 2008.

3. If a web page has six images and one HTML code file named `sales.html`, how many HTTP request operations are required to download the web page?

   A. 1   **C.** 6

   B. 2   **D.** 7

4. Name a characteristic of a web service.

(Continues)

THE ESSENTIALS AND BEYOND *(Continued)*

5. What two types of sites are created by right-clicking on the Sites container in IIS Manager?

    A. FTP   **C.** Joomla!

    B. SharePoint   **D.** Web

6. Define a protocol listener in IIS.

7. Define SSL.

8. How are FTP communications transmitted by default?

    A. With AES 128-bit encryption   **C.** As cleartext

    B. With AES 512-bit encryption   **D.** With 64-bit WEP encryption

9. Which one of the following is certain to occur if you use a self-signed certificate for an IIS website?

    A. Public users will receive a warning that the certificate could not be verified.   **C.** The encryption will be cracked in less than 90 minutes.

    B. The encryption will not work properly.   **D.** The authentication will fail.

10. True or false: Self-signed certificates are not supported in IIS.

CHAPTER 11

File and Print Servers

Access to shared data is an important component of modern business operations, and file servers (servers that provide a location for shared disk access) are among the oldest server types used on computer networks. In this chapter, you will learn about the file server features of Windows Server.

Network users need to store and print data. Historically, local printers were connected directly to users' computers. In the next phase of printing history, printers were made available on the network, but they were managed through internal management interfaces. Now, in modern networks based on Windows, centralized printer management can be implemented by configuring Windows print servers. Going beyond this, users can even print to printers and manage those printers using web-based interfaces. Of course, all of this is achieved using the interfaces, server roles, and roles services you've come to know throughout this book. Defragment your mind, because you'll be learning about all of these topics in this chapter:

▷ **Exploring File Servers**

▷ **Understanding DFS**

▷ **Understanding Print Servers**

Exploring File Servers

Windows file servers are simply Windows servers that provide shared folders to users and systems on the network that are used to store content. A file server can be implemented with advanced management tools provided through the File Services role, or it can be implemented using default installed interfaces and features. In this section, you will learn about the following important topics related to file servers:

- ► Understanding share permissions
- ► Understanding NTFS permissions
- ► Auditing files and folders

A shared folder is simply a folder on a Windows computer that has been configured for availability on the network.

▶

Understanding Share Permissions

Share permissions are used to control who can access shared folders from the network. The permissions dictate what capabilities users will have when connecting to the shared folders. Three share permissions exist, and they are defined as follows:

Read   Users with Read permission to a share may list and open documents and folders within the share, assuming NTFS permissions do not override the share permissions. NTFS permissions are defined directly on files and folders, while share permissions are applied to the access through the network share.

▶

NTFS permissions can override share permissions and are utilized for increased granularity in permission management. You will learn more about this in the next section.

Change   Users with Change permission can list and open documents and folders. They can modify documents, create new documents, and create new folders. They can also delete documents or folders. All of these actions may be taken as long as NTFS permissions do not override the Share permissions.

Full Control   Users with Full Control can do everything the Change permission allows, and they can manage permissions. When you have full control of a share, you can modify the permissions on that share. Typically, only administrators are given full control of a share. Like the other share permissions, Full Control may be overridden at the NTFS permission level.

Depending on the server version you are using and the way the server is configured, you may see these three permissions represented as Reader (read), Contributor (change), or Owner/Co-owner (full control). Under the hood, the permissions are still Read, Change, and Full Control. Microsoft simply changed their names in some interfaces to make them easier to understand for beginning administrators.

On Windows Server 2003 R2 and earlier, you can simply right-click on any folder and select Share to manage the share properties of the folder. Starting in Windows Server 2008, a new Sharing Wizard is enabled by default. When you right-click on a folder, you will see a Share With menu option and it will list two options: Nobody or Specific People. If you select Nobody, you are removing the share (although the folder will still remain on the hard drive). If you select Specific People, you will see the wizard shown in Figure 11.1. (I would call this the File Sharing dialog and not a wizard, but Microsoft calls it the Sharing Wizard.)

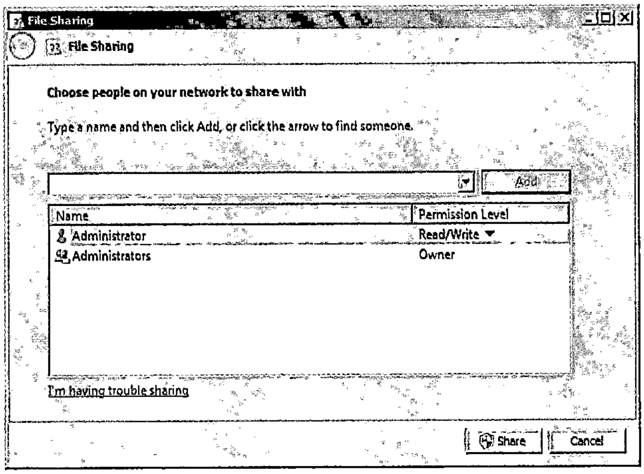

FIGURE 11.1 The Sharing Wizard enabled by default in Windows Server 2008 R2

You can disable the Sharing Wizard using the following procedure:

1. Open a drive so that an Explorer window is displayed similar to the following image:

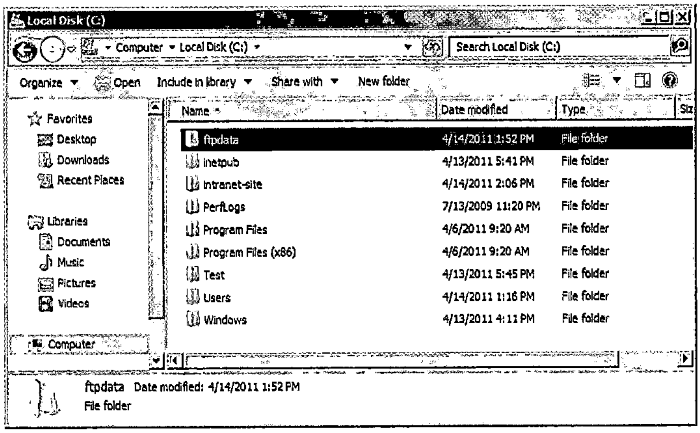

2. Click the Organize drop-down option and choose Folder and Search Options.

3. Click on the View tab.

4. Scroll down to the bottom of the Advanced Settings section and deselect Use Sharing Wizard (Recommended) as in the following image, and click OK.

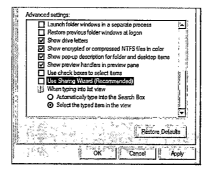

After the Sharing Wizard is disabled, when you right-click on a folder, you can select Share With ➤ Advanced Sharing to access the traditional Share tab on the Folder Properties dialog.

Understanding NTFS Permissions

NTFS permissions are defined on the local drive within the server. The drive must be formatted with the NTFS file system in order to use these permissions. The NTFS permissions apply when files are accessed locally and across the network. FAT32 does not support security permissions. NTFS permissions may be explicit or inherited:

> ▶ *Explicit permissions* are set on an individual folder or file.

> ▶ *Inherited permissions* are set through the parent object.

For example, by default a file inherits the permissions of the folder in which it is created. Subfolders also inherit the permissions of parent folders. This inheritance can be blocked, but it is the default behavior.

NTFS permissions are defined in Table 11.1. These permissions are called *standard permissions* because they are used for most access scenarios that you will need to configure. In addition to the standard permissions listed in Table 11.1, NTFS supports special permissions. The standard permissions are really a collection of special permissions that are frequently needed by users. The complete listing of special permissions and the standard permissions to which they map can be found at:

    http://technet.microsoft.com/en-us/library/cc732880.aspx

NTFS is the NT File System dating back to the first release of Windows NT Server. Evolving since that time, it is required for permission management on Windows drives accessed directly from the console.

TABLE 11.1 NTFS Standard Permissions

Permission Type	Description
Read	Users can read files.
Write	Users can read, modify, and create new files or folders.
Read and Execute	Users can read and execute files (such as .exe, .bat, and .com files).
List Folder Contents	Users can view the contents of a folder, but not read the contents of actual files.
Modify	Users can read, write, execute, and delete files and folders.
Full Control	Users can do anything, including take ownership and manage permissions. None of the other permissions in this table allow permissions to be managed.

UNDERSTANDING COMBINED PERMISSIONS

Combined permissions are derived from multiple security accounts or multiple security ID sources. For example, each user account and each group has a security ID. Combined permissions are those built from all the groups to which a user belongs and the user's account itself. For example, a user may belong to several groups. Permissions can be assigned to groups and to users; therefore, as the administrator, you must be able to determine how the permissions will apply if users access a resource with permissions specified for groups to which they belong and for their user accounts.

When dealing with share permissions or NTFS permissions individually, the general rule is that the most liberal permission set applies. For example, if you are given Read permission on a share as a user, but you are given Change permission through a group membership on the same share, the Change permission is more lenient and therefore will apply. If you are given NTFS Read permissions to the C:\Data folder as a member of the Accounting group and are given NTFS Read and Execute permissions as a member of the Management group, you will have Read and Execute permissions. The only exception to this "most liberal" rule is the Deny permission. Explicit denial to a resource overrides the granting of that permission through any other group membership or the user account.

Always remember that an explicit denial wins over granted permissions every time. If you explicitly deny Full Control permissions, the user will have no permissions on the resource at all.

◀

When dealing with the combination of both share and NTFS permissions that have been configured on the same resource, the most restrictive permission set applies. For example, if the share allows Change permission, but an NTFS permission on a folder in the share allows only Read permission, the user will have Read permission when accessing that folder through the share. You can think of the share as a permission pipe. By this I mean that you can never give the user more permissions than the share provides. If the share provides Read permission and a folder within the share provides Modify NTFS permission, the user will still have only Read access, because the share is limiting the permissions of the user. In the end, NTFS permissions can further restrict the permissions granted at the share, but they can never expand the permissions granted at the share.

USER RIGHTS VERSUS USER PERMISSIONS

User rights should not be confused with permissions. Permissions are granted on objects to allow the user to access those objects with different levels of capabilities. Rights are not granted on objects, but rather on actions. For example, a user may be given the right to change the system time. Without this right, the time will be set automatically in most environments based on a central time server and the time zone in which the user is located. By default, only administrators can change the system time, but users can change the time zone in newer versions of the Windows operating systems.

Another example is the right to shut down the system. By default all users can shut down the system if they are logged on locally. These rights are managed in Group Policy using the Computer Configuration ➤ Windows Settings Security Settings ➤ Local Policies ➤ User Rights Assignment node.

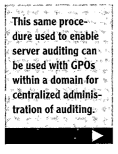

This same procedure used to enable server auditing can be used with GPOs within a domain for centralized administration of auditing.

Auditing Files and Folders

Windows Server supports auditing files and folders so that administrators can see who is accessing the data and who is attempting to access the data when they do not have permissions. Auditing is a very important part of security. Windows servers support auditing of successful and failed folder and file access.

Before you can audit a file or folder, you must enable auditing on the server. The following procedure will enable auditing for files and folders on a Windows Server 2008 R2 installation:

1. Click Start, type **gpedit.msc** in the Search field, and press Enter.

2. Expand Computer Configuration ➤ Windows Settings ➤ Local Policy ➤ Audit Policy in the Local Group Policy Editor.

3. Double-click on the Audit Object Access policy.

4. Select both Success and Failure in the Audit Object Access Properties dialog, and then click OK.

The preceding procedure will enable file and folder auditing, and only operating system folders will be tracked by default. To add data folders, you will have to enable auditing on the folder using this procedure:

1. Right-click on the folder and select Properties.

2. Select the Security tab.

3. Click the Advanced button.

4. Select the Auditing tab.

5. Click the Edit button.

6. Click the Add button, enter the user or group you want to audit, and click OK.

7. Choose the permissions you want to watch for and click OK.

Figure 11.2 shows the Advanced Security Settings dialog with auditing configured for a folder. After auditing is enabled and configured for a file or folder, the audit logs will be stored in the Event Viewer Security log.

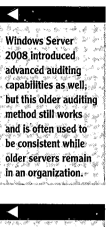

Windows Server 2008 introduced advanced auditing capabilities as well, but this older auditing method still works and is often used to be consistent while older servers remain in an organization.

Many administrators choose to audit only failures so that their security logs are smaller; however, this configuration is less secure because you cannot see when files and folders are accessed.

FIGURE 11.2 Auditing is configured on a folder on Windows Server 2008 R2.

Understanding DFS

The Distributed File System (DFS) is a Windows Server technology that provides replication and simplified access to dispersed folders and files on the network. You can look at DFS from three perspectives:

▶ It can provide simplified access to dispersed files and nothing more.

▶ It can provide localized access to files through replication.

▶ It can provide localized access to files through replication while also simplifying access to dispersed files and providing high availability.

The third option seems quite complex, but it will be easy to understand when you see the way DFS works. In the following sections, you will learn how DFS works, the recommended uses of DFS, and the process for creating a DFS namespace.

DFS offers what Microsoft calls WAN-friendly replication because it uses compression when transmitting data. The compression used is Remote Differential Compression (RDC).

Understanding How DFS Works

DFS is actually comprised of two components:

DFS Namespaces   A DFS namespace is a group of shared folders that may be distributed across multiple servers. The namespace provides a logical structure to the distributed shared folders and appears as a single, shared folder to users. When users access the namespace and select one of the shared folders in the namespace, it appears to be a subfolder within the share. In actuality, the folder the user is accessing may be in a share on a completely different server.

The DFS namespace is integrated with AD DS and takes advantage of site structures. The DFS namespace is replicated onto different servers within different sites, so when users click to request data they are automatically referred to the content that is stored on servers within their local sites whenever possible.

DFS Replication   DFS replication is the component responsible for synchronizing folders among servers participating within the DNS namespace. DFS replication has replaced an older replication scheme used in Windows servers called the File Replication Services (FRS). When domains operate in the Windows Server 2008 functional level, DFS replication is even used for replication of the AD DS SYSVOL folder, which contains Group Policy Objects (GPOs).

DFS replication was first introduced in Windows Server 2003 R2.

Figure 11.3 illustrates the two components of DFS. In the diagram, notice that the first step occurs when the user accesses a folder in the namespace. The DFS namespace server replies to the client computer with a list of referrals for actual folder locations. By default, this list will prioritize servers in the user's site so that the first target server in the list will be in that user's site. The administrator can override this by configuring different target priorities, but in most scenarios you will want the users accessing a server within their site. After the client receives the referral list, it will attempt to connect to the first server in the list. If that server is unavailable, it will move down the list until it finds one that is available or until it has exhausted the list.

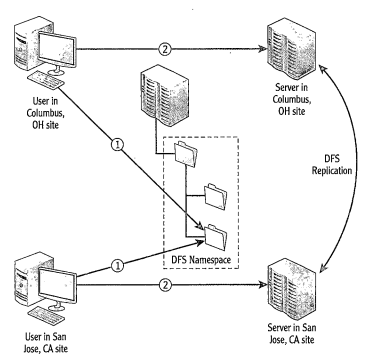

FIGURE 11.3 The DFS namespace and replication components

> You can use either the DFS Namespace role service or the DFS Replication role service independently. You are not required to use them together.
>
> ◀

Figure 11.3 also shows the DFS replication component. Notice that it is configured on the servers containing the actual target folders referenced by the DFS namespace. From this, you can see that the DFS planning process must define a minimum of two elements. First, it must define the DFS namespaces that will be required. Second, it must define the DFS replication requirements for the servers containing the shared folders participating in the namespace.

Starting in Windows Server 2008, DFS is a role service of the File Services role. You can install the File Services role and install the DFS Replication and DFS Namespace roles services at the same time, or you can install the DFS roles services later.

Planning for DFS Recommended Uses

Microsoft defines three key scenarios where DFS may be most useful. These scenarios are listed here:

Data Collection   Many organizations have data that is located in various branch offices. This data is important to the organization and has traditionally been created, managed, and archived locally. However, this process is error prone because local administrators with sufficient technical training may not be available. DFS can be used to replicate the data from the branch offices to a central hub site or corporate headquarters location. This is known as *data collection*. Once the data is replicated to the central site, it can be backed up by well-trained administrators.

Since the replication uses RDC, this results in the replication of only the modified data. Administrators may also configure replication schedules so that the data replication occurs during less active times on the network.

Additionally, DFS namespaces can be used with the DFS replication so that the branch office users typically access the data locally, but if their local servers fail, they can access the data on the central servers. After their local servers return to active operations, the clients can failback to their local servers.

> ▶
>
> Client computers older than Windows Vista must have a client failback hotfix applied in order to failback in these scenarios.

Data Distribution   Data distribution is the opposite of data collection. In this case, organizations need to localize data that is centrally created. A DFS namespace can be created and DFS replication can be used to replicate data from centralized locations to distributed branch office sites. Actually, DFS replication can distribute the data without the need for a DFS namespace; however, using a DFS namespace also provides for highly available access to the data. Whenever a local server fails, the clients that would typically use that server can access another server in the namespace.

Data Collaboration   Users in several branch offices may need to share files with each other. This can be accomplished with DFS replication as well. When using DFS replication for collaboration purposes, the users must be aware of latency issues. Depending on the replication configuration, it is possible for data synchronization among the participating sites to take several hours.

Several benefits are provided through data collaboration scenarios. The first is the ability to work with files from any location. For example, if DFS namespaces and DFS replication are used to enable the collaboration, a user may store a file in a folder participating in the DFS namespace. This folder may be on a local server at the user's site. Now, the user goes to another site with a local server participating in the namespace and in the replication. When the user accesses her file, she does not traverse the WAN to her normal site, but instead accesses the files at the local server.

An additional benefit is the ability to share files from one branch with another branch without having to send the files back to the corporate headquarters. Users can view and modify the files (assuming they have proper permissions) on the localized copy, and their changes will be replicated automatically to the other branches. DFS replication is a multi-master model, so changes can be made on any server participating in the replication process by default.

Creating a DFS Namespace

DFS namespaces are created using the DFS Management node in the File Services management tool. If you have not installed the File Services role, you should install it and select the Distributed File System role services as well. After the File Services role is installed and the Distributed File System services (both DFS Namespaces and DFS Replication) are installed, you can create a DFS namespace using the following process:

1. Click Start ➢ All Programs ➢ Administrative Tools ➢ DFS Management to launch the DFS Management tool.

2. In the console tree on the left, right-click the Namespaces node and select New Namespace.

3. Follow the steps in the New Namespace Wizard to create the namespace.

As you work through the New Namespace Wizard, you will be required to provide the following information:

▶ Name of the server to host the namespace

▶ Name of the namespace

▶ Namespace type

Three namespace types are available:

Standalone Namespace These namespaces do not require AD DS, and they can be larger than AD DS integrated namespaces in Windows 2000 Server mode.

Domain-Based Namespace These namespaces, in Windows 2000 Server mode, require AD DS; and they support replication and high availability. Standalone namespaces require Windows Server Clustering for high availability. Domain-based namespaces can provide high availability through the use of multiple namespace servers. Windows 2000 Server mode namespaces can support a maximum of 5,000 folders with targets.

Domain-Based Namespace   In Windows Server 2008 mode, these namespaces support more than 5,000 folders with targets, and they also support all other features of Windows 2000 Server mode namespaces.

For more detailed information about the different features supported by the different namespace modes, see:

```
http://technet.microsoft.com/en-us/library/cc732863%28WS.10%29.aspx
```

Understanding Print Servers

To manage the basics of print servers in a Windows environment, you'll need to understand these major factors:

► The basic print server functionality of Windows Server

► The use of printer pools

► The use of web printing

The following sections address each of these topics in turn.

Managing Basic Print Server Functionality

Windows servers can act as printer servers. A *printer server* is a server that queues print jobs and prints them to printers connected to the server via any of the following connections:

To get the complete feature set available for a Windows print server, add the Print and Document Services role to the server.

► FireWire

► Serial

► Parallel

► USB

► TCP/IP

A Windows server cannot act as the print server for a networked printer that is shared and managed by another Windows machine on the network.

Local printers can be used to print while logged on to the server's Desktop either locally or using a remote desktop solution (like Remote Desktop Services discussed in the next chapter). Shared printers connected to a server are still local printers on the server.

Network printers are printers that are connected to the network. They exist as a single device on the network — this is different from a Windows Server machine acting as a print server. When a Windows Server machine acts as a printer server, it may share multiple printers. A networked printer is usually a single, dedicated device with a single IP address on the network. While some advanced network printers may support multiple IP addresses, they are still single devices on the network. You can connect to a network printer using a TCP/IP connection and then share it from the Windows server. This allows the Windows server to manage the printer queue for the printer.

The printer queue stores the print jobs until they can be printed. You can manage the printer queue and print jobs in several ways.

Change a Print Job Priority   Print jobs have an associated priority value ranging from 1 to 99. The print job with the highest priority is printed before lower priority jobs. The default print job priority is 1.

Pause a Print Job   If a user prints an urgent job and other jobs are in the queue already, the administrator can pause the other jobs to allow the urgent job to process sooner.

Resume a Print Job   When the administrator pauses a print job, he has the ability to resume that print job.

Restart a Print Job   A print job may fail because of a printer problem. While the print job will attempt to continue where it left off, the administrator may need to restart the job from the beginning if the pages that the server thought were properly printed actually were not.

Cancel a Print Job   In some cases, a print job needs to be cancelled. A user may send a print job to the server and then realize he printed the wrong thing. The user may be able to call the Help Desk and have the print job canceled before printing resources are wasted.

It is important to provide the appropriate drivers for the printers you share from the server. To add additional drivers, follow this procedure:

1. Open the Printer Properties page.

2. Click the Sharing tab.

3. Click the Change Sharing Options button.

4. On the page that is displayed (shown in Figure 11.4), you can choose the Additional Drivers button to add drivers for 32-bit platforms.

The drivers installed on the server will work only on 64-bit clients.

Printers may also be installed using Group Policy. Assuming the appropriate drivers are on the printer server, they will be installed during deployment.

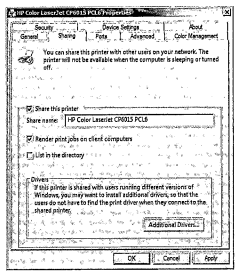

FIGURE 11.4 You can add additional printer drivers on The Change Sharing Options page.

You can also list a shared printer in AD DS if the print server is a member server. This allows users to search the network for printers and locate them based on their name, location, or properties. For example, a user may need to print a color print job. He could search for a printer in his building that supports color printing. Assuming one is listed in the domain database and he has print permissions for it, he can install the color printer that is displayed in the search results and then print to it.

Understanding Printer Pools

A *printer pool* is a collection of physical printers that appear as one logical printer on the network. The user installs a single local printer, but multiple printers are available on the server for processing the print jobs. On the server, several printers are installed and configured to participate in the printer pool.

The entire printer pool uses a central queue for print job management. Printer pools provide several advantages:

▶ Print jobs can be completed faster.

▶ If a single printer fails, the other printers can still provide printing services.

▶ Printing requests are load balanced among the printers in the pool.

The process for enabling printer pooling is simple:

1. On the server, install each printer that will be part of the pool.

2. Open the Printer Properties for a printer that will participate in the printer pool.

3. Select the Ports tab.

4. Check the Enable Printer Pooling check box.

5. Select each printer that will be part of the pool, as shown in the following image:

Network printers can be part of the printer pool. Simply add each printer as a new TCP/IP port.

6. Click OK to close the Printer Properties dialog.

Using Web Printing

Web printing requires that Internet Information Services (IIS) be installed on the print server, but it allows users to print using a web page to connect to the print server. Web printing is enabled by adding the Internet Printing role service to the Print and Document Services server role on the server.

After installing the Internet Printing role service, you can view the web-based interface for accessing and managing printers by navigating to http://*server_name*/printers, where *server_name* is the name of the printer server on which you have installed Internet Printing. Figure 11.5 shows this page and indicates an Error status for the printers.

If you click on a printer in the console, the status detail information will appear. Figure 11.6 shows the status detail, and you can see that an attempted print job originating from the Notepad application by the Administrator has an error. To cancel the errant print job, you can select the document and then click the Cancel link in the left column under Document Actions.

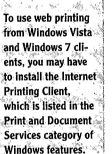

To use web printing from Windows Vista and Windows 7 clients, you may have to install the Internet Printing Client, which is listed in the Print and Document Services category of Windows features.

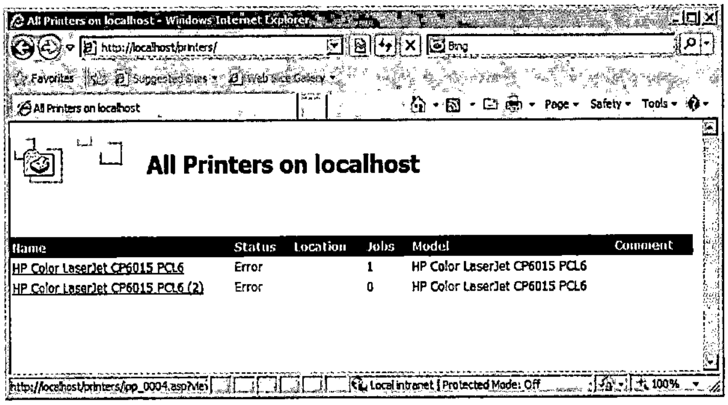

FIGURE 11.5 The Web-Based Printer Management page

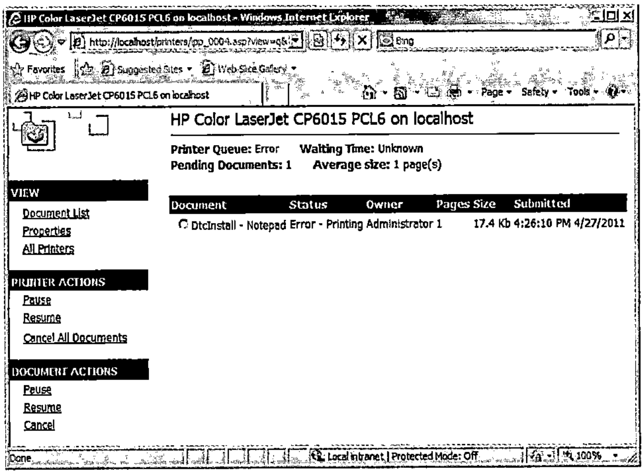

FIGURE 11.6 Managing print jobs in the web-based interface

THE ESSENTIALS AND BEYOND

Windows servers can act as both file servers and print servers. As a file server administrator, you must understand share permissions and NTFS permissions. Three share permissions are available, including Read, Change, and Full Control. NTFS offers more robust and granular permissions, allowing you to set permissions down to the file level. When a user accesses a file through a shared folder on the network, the combined share and NTFS permissions granted to the user impact the resulting permissions the user will have. Using NTFS permissions, you cannot give the user greater permissions than the share allows; however, you can restrict permissions with NTFS to be less than the share allows. The Distributed File System (DFS) is another excellent component of Windows file servers that allows you to provide file replication (DFS replication) and simpler distributed data access (DFS namespaces).

As a print server, Windows Server allows you to share physically attached printers and printers connected via TCP/IP ports. You cannot share a printer that the server accesses through another Windows machine on the network. As a print server administrator, you should know how to provide additional drivers for different client operating systems and how to manage print jobs. Windows Server also supports web-based printing and web-based print server management through the Internet Printing role service of the Print and Document Services server role.

ADDITIONAL EXERCISES

▶ Create a folder on a server and share the folder on the network, allowing Everyone to have Read access and Administrators to have Full Control.

▶ Create a folder in the folder that was shared in the preceding exercise, and set NTFS permissions on it to allow Administrators to have Full Control, but Everyone to have no access.

▶ Install a printer on the server. Configure it to use LPT1 even though the physical printer is not connected.

To compare your answers to the author's, please visit:

www.sybex.com/go/winadminessentials

REVIEW QUESTIONS

1. A user just printed a very important print job. You want to ensure that this new print job prints immediately after the one currently printing. What action should you take? (Choose the single best answer.)

A. Pause all other print jobs

B. Cancel all other print jobs

C. Restart all other print jobs

D. Change the priority on the new print job

(Continues)

THE ESSENTIALS AND BEYOND *(Continued)*

2. True or false: When you explicitly deny a permission, that permission cannot be granted to the user through any other group membership.

3. You have installed a printer on a Windows Server 2008 R2 server and shared it on the network and performed no other actions. Users on Windows 7 x86 clients cannot print to the printer. What must you do?

   A. Add 32-bit drivers   **C.** Reinstall the printer

   B. Add 64-bit drivers   **D.** Reinstall the Windows 7 client
                                          operating systems

4. What must be enabled to allow a Windows server to distribute print jobs to multiple printers from a single print queue?

5. What NTFS permission allows users to view the items in a folder, but not to read the contents of those items?

   A. Read   **C.** Write

   B. Modify   **D.** List Folder Contents

6. Define print job.

7. Define a DFS namespace.

8. A folder named Test in a share named Data has the NTFS permission of Everyone Read. The share has the permission of Everyone Change. The share also has the permission of Domain Admins Full Control. When Lisa, who is not an administrator, accesses the Test folder, what permission will she have on that folder?

   A. Full Control   **C.** Read

   B. Change   **D.** None

9. What is the proper default URL used to access the web-based printer management interface on a Windows server named SRV5 that has web-based management installed and enabled?

   A. `http://printers`   **C.** `http://printers/SRV5`

   B. `http://SRV5/printers`   **D.** `http://SRV5`

10. True or false: The Distributed File System can be used to centralize distributed data.

CHAPTER 12

Remote Access Technologies

As the modern workforce becomes more mobile, more and more administrators are finding it necessary to support remote servers in their computer networks. Remote access technologies allow end users to connect to an organization's network from their homes, hotel rooms, coffee shops, and a wide variety of other locations. This chapter covers the remote access technologies used to remotely manage servers; however, many of the same technologies are used to allow remote access to users. These servers may be installed in a different building on the same campus, in a different city, or even in a different country. Remote access technologies are a very important component of our modern global society. These technologies include virtual private networks, Remote Desktop Services for remote access to Windows machines, and Remote Assistance for requested help from Microsoft. In this chapter, these technologies will be covered in the following topics:

▷ **Planning for Remote Administration Tools**

▷ **Understanding Remote Desktop Services**

Planning for Remote Administration Tools

Windows servers and clients support two types of remote desktop control without the use of third-party applications:

- ► Remote Assistance
- ► Remote Desktop Services

Both are addressed in this section briefly, and Remote Desktop Services is covered in greater detail in the section of this chapter titled "Understanding Remote Desktop Services." This section also addresses virtual private networks and the roles they play in remote access.

Understanding Remote Access Solutions

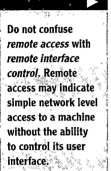

Do not confuse *remote access* with *remote interface control.* Remote access may indicate simple network level access to a machine without the ability to control its user interface.

Remote access to computers is an important part of network administration. The need for remote control of client computers goes all the way back to MS-DOS and a program called Tiny that is still being updated today.

Remote interface control or, on modern computers, remote desktop control allows the administrator to work with the users' computers or with the servers as if they were sitting in front of the machine. Remote desktop control can be used for many administrative actions, including:

▶ Installing new software with administrative credentials

▶ Adding device drivers to the computer

▶ Configuring services that can be configured only through graphical interfaces on the local machine

▶ Performing actions that the local administrator is unable to perform due to lack of permissions, knowledge, or skill

In modern Windows systems, the Remote Desktop Services (RDS) feature provides remote access to the Windows Desktop. RDS is comprised of a set of server services and a client application. The server services provide the infrastructure for remote access to server Desktops. The client application understands the communications protocol used to communicate with this infrastructure and allows users to view and interact with the server's Desktop within the client application. Screens are sent from the server to the client while mouse actions and keyboard keystrokes are sent to the server from the client. All application processing occurs on the server rather than the client. RDS is covered in more detail in the section of this chapter titled "Understanding Remote Desktop Services."

The protocol used by RDS is the Remote Desktop Protocol (RDP).

Remote Assistance (RA) is different from RDS. RA provides a solution for users or administrators to receive help from someone else using a request and response engine. The user with access to the local desktop interface must request help from another individual before that individual can connect. In a client computing RA scenario, the requesting user is known as the novice and the responding assistant is known as the expert. In a server RA scenario, the local administrator may request assistance from a consultant or a Microsoft support technician.

RA can be used to allow either remote viewing or remote control. When remote control is allowed, the RA assistant can interact with the requesting user's Desktop. When it is disabled, the assistant can only view the user's actions. Remote viewing is useful when you need someone to see your actions and correct errors in those actions, but you do not have the required trust to allow that individual access to control your machine.

By default, the RA feature is not installed on Windows Server 2008 or R2. You can add the feature using Server Manager and then use the following procedure to place a request for remote assistance:

1. Log on to the server as an administrator.

2. Select Start ➤ All Programs ➤ Maintenance ➤ Windows Remote Assistance.

3. In the Windows Remote Assistance dialog, select Invite Someone You Trust To Help You.

4. Select to Save This Invitation As A File.

5. Provide a filename and location in the Save As dialog, and click Save.
   The Windows Remote Assistance application window will appear and display a password the remote assistant will need to access your machine, as shown in the following image.

> Before the feature is added, the System Properties dialog will simply show the Remote Assistance section as a grayed-out listing and the administrator won't be able to interact with it.

After generating the invitation file using this procedure, you must send it to the remote assistant. You can attach it to an email for delivery or place it on a shared network location that the remote assistant can access. On servers with Microsoft Outlook installed, you can even select to send the invitation as an email in step 4 of the preceding procedure.

When the assistant receives the invitation, the following procedure is performed:

1. He initiates a connection and enters the password provided.
   To initiate the connection from a supporting Windows client machine, the assistant simply double-clicks on the invitation file and then enters the appropriate password as provided by the requestor.

2. The requestor must respond by clicking Yes in the dialog box that appears when the assistant connects.

3. If the assistant wants to control the Desktop, he must request control and the requestor must grant this control.

Figure 12.1 shows the RA client connected to a Windows Server 2008 R2 machine from a Windows 7 client computer.

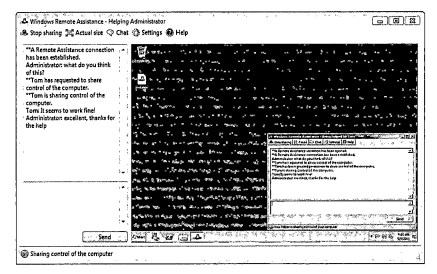

FIGURE 12.1 Connecting to a Windows Server 2008 R2 machine from a Windows 7 client with RA

Virtual Private Networks (VPNs)

While RDS and RA can be used to access servers and clients from remote locations and control their Desktops, it can be dangerous to open such connections across the Internet. If you want to communicate across the Internet for remote control or even to access the organization's data, you should encrypt the connection. While the protocol used by RDS may encrypt the communications, network-level remote access may be encrypted or unencrypted. Virtual private networks (VPNs) provide tunneled communications across networks and can encrypt the communications as well. Most VPNs implemented across public networks like the Internet use encryption.

The process of converting data from its normal state to an unreadable state is known as *encryption*. The unreadable state is known as *ciphertext* (or *cipher data*) and the readable state is plaintext (or plain data). The normal way to encrypt data is to pass it through an algorithm using a key for variable results. For example, let's say you want to protect or encrypt the number 108. Here is a very basic algorithm for encrypting numeric data:

original data / crypto key + (3 × crypto key)

Using this algorithm with a key of 4, produces this calculation:

$$108 / 4 + (3 \times 4) = 39$$

In order to recover the original data, both the algorithm and the key must be known. Modern crypto algorithms are much more complex than this and keys are usually much longer, but this simple example illustrates the concept of encryption. Figure 12.2 illustrates the components involved in the encryption process.

Actual encryption algorithms used to create VPN connections are so complex that PHD-level knowledge is usually required to understand them.

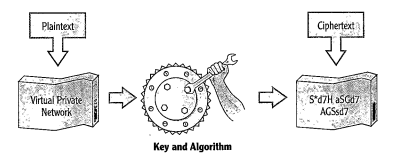

FIGURE 12.2 The components in the encryption process

VPNs use encryption algorithms to secure the communications through the tunnel. The tunnel is simply the encapsulation of network data. For example, that which would normally be communicated directly on the network is encapsulated within additional protocols (the VPN protocols) and then sent across the network. This tunneling allows for communications across different network types and for the authentication and encryption of the communications channel.

VPNs and encryption are covered in more detail in *Microsoft Windows Security Essentials* (Sybex, 2011), another book in this series.

Several VPN protocols exist, but some are more secure than others. Due to its wide implementation base, the Layer 2 Tunneling Protocol (L2TP) with IP Security (IPSec) is by far the most common secure-VPN solution in use. However, the following VPN protocols may be used in Windows Server 2008 R2 installations without requiring additional software from third-party vendors:

IPSec may be implemented with authentication only. If a VPN is created using only authentication, no encryption is used.

PPTP The Point-to-Point Tunneling Protocol (PPTP) has been in Windows for several versions. It does provide security, but it not as secure as L2TP/IPSec. However, it is very easy to configure and is often still used when security is not the most important aspect of the VPN connection. PPTP uses TCP port 1723.

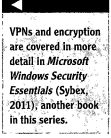

L2TP/IPSec The L2TP/IPSec VPN solution is very common and can be very secure when configured with the appropriate authentication and encryption. Because IPSec is used to provide the encryption, if the VPN is not configured properly, it is possible to create the connection in an insecure manner and leave it vulnerable to eavesdropping. Always be careful to implement the proper authentication and encryption with an L2TP/IPSec VPN. L2TP uses UDP port 1701.

SSTP   The Secure Socket Tunneling Protocol (SSTP) was first added to Windows in Windows Server 2008 and Windows 7. SSTP is simple to implement, like PPTP, but provides the security equivalent of L2TP/IPSec VPNs. SSTP uses TCP port 443 for communications because it is SSL-based.

When selecting a VPN protocol, you must ensure that both the client and the server support the protocol. It is important to remember that, while SSTP is easier to implement than L2TP/IPSec, it is only supported by Windows 7 clients and Windows Server 2008 out-of-the box. Windows Vista with SP1 also supports SSTP. Windows XP does not support SSTP at the time of this writing.

Because L2TP/IPSec is the most commonly used VPN solution, it will be covered in more detail here. IPSec is short for IP Security, and it is actually a security solution that involves three potential provisions:

Confidentiality   Confidentiality is provided by encrypting the payload or data that is transmitted.

Integrity   Integrity is ensured through hashing algorithms such as MD5 or the more secure SHA-1.

Nonrepudiation   Nonrepudiation, which is the inability of a sender to deny sending the communication, is ensured in that the message digest (the result of the hashing algorithm) is encrypted with the secret key or some credential that only the sender would know but the receiver can access. This may be a public/private key pair where the sender encrypts the data with her private key and the receiver decrypts it with the public key. If the message digest can be successfully decrypted, the sender cannot deny sending the initial packet and, therefore, cannot repudiate (deny origination of) the data.

IPSec has often been said to be an unnecessarily complex VPN protocol, but in reality it doesn't have to be that complicated. You simply have to ensure that you enable the same encryption and hashing settings on both ends of the VPN connection. You will usually want to use the strongest form that is supported by both devices. The reality is that some vendor's implementation of IPSec will simply not connect to other vendor's implementations. For this reason, some have chosen to purchase dedicated VPN devices (sometimes called VPN concentrators or routers) to place on either side of the connection being secured.

> ▶
> Hashing algorithms are one-way processes. A variable amount of data can be input to the algorithm, but it always generates a fixed-length number that is considered unique to that input data.

Understanding Remote Desktop Services

Remote Desktop Services (RDS) is the new version of Terminal Services. Terminal Services was initially released as a special version of Windows NT 4.0 Server in the 1990s. It remained as a feature of Windows Server through Windows Server 2003 R2. With the release of Windows Server 2008, the technology was renamed to Remote Desktop Services even though the core usage and functionality did not change. RDS provides the service that allows administrators to access Desktops from remote locations and allows users to access virtual desktops and virtual applications in the enterprise. This section explains important topics you should understand in order to plan for the use of RDS in an organization.

Remote Desktop versus Remote Desktop Services

The first thing you should understand is the difference between what Microsoft calls Remote Desktop and Remote Desktop Services. Remote Desktop is a feature built-into Windows servers and clients that allows administrators to connect to a machine and manage it from a remote client using the Remote Desktop Client software. Remote Desktop is not intended for users to gain access to applications on servers. Remote Desktop does not require additional licensing because it is intended to be used only for support purposes and not for running applications from remote computers. It uses the same RDP protocol as Remote Desktop Services, but it is much simpler to enable and configure.

Remote Desktop Services enables hundreds of users to access applications running on Windows servers. For example, with Remote Desktop Services, users can run Microsoft Office from the server. However, Remote Desktop Services can also be used to allow administrators to access various administration tools from remote locations. In summary, Remote Desktop Services allows everything Remote Desktop allows and it allows multiple users to access it simultaneously.

To enable Remote Desktop on a Windows Server 2008 or R2 server, follow this procedure:

1. Click the Start menu, right-click on Computer, and select Properties.

2. Click the Advanced System Settings link on the left menu of the System screen.

3. Select the Remote tab in the System Properties dialog box.

4. Choose either of the following:

  ▶ Allow Connections From Computers Running Any Version Of Remote Desktop

  ▶ Allow Connections Only From Computers Running Remote Desktop With Network Level Authentication

5. Click OK.

You can also click the Select Users button to add users who can access the desktop remotely. By default, only Administrators may access the remote desktop.

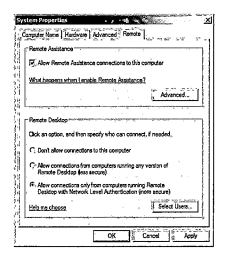

After enabling Remote Desktop on the server, you can connect to it from a Windows client using the Remote Desktop Connection application and the following procedure:

1. From a Windows 7 or Vista Desktop, select Start ➢ Accessories ➢ Remote Desktop Connection.

2. In the Remote Desktop Connection dialog, enter the server name or IP address of the server to which you want to connect.

3. Click the Options drop-down arrow to customize the display, access to local resources, programs to execute upon connection, and the experience within the connection, such as the graphical richness of the connection.

4. On the General tab, enter the username with which you want to connect and then click Connect.

[Image: Remote Desktop Connection dialog box — General tab with Logon settings: Computer: 192.168.10.80, User name: administrator, "You will be asked for credentials when you connect." checkbox "Allow me to save credentials"; Connection settings with Save, Save As, Open buttons; Options, Connect, Help]

5. When prompted for credentials, enter the password for the username you entered in step 4.

 If you see a prompt like the one in the following image, do not be alarmed. This indicates that the server is using a self-signed certificate.

The username you enter must have the rights to connect using Remote Desktop.

[Image: Remote Desktop Connection warning dialog — "The identity of the remote computer cannot be verified. Do you want to connect anyway?" The remote computer could not be authenticated due to problems with its security certificate. It may be unsafe to proceed. Certificate name: Name in the certificate from the remote computer: SRV1.training.local. Certificate errors: The following errors were encountered while validating the remote computer's certificate: The certificate is not from a trusted certifying authority. Do you want to connect despite these certificate errors? "Don't ask me again for connections to this computer" View certificate, Yes, No]

6. If you know you can trust the server, click Yes to connect.

After completing this procedure, you will be connected to the server's Desktop and can interact with it as if you were sitting in front of the machine with a monitor, keyboard, and mouse. Figure 12.3 shows the remote connection to a Windows Server 2008 R2 server from a Windows 7 client. You can see that Server Manager is running, as well as a Command Prompt window. The remote connection will allow full utilization of the system.

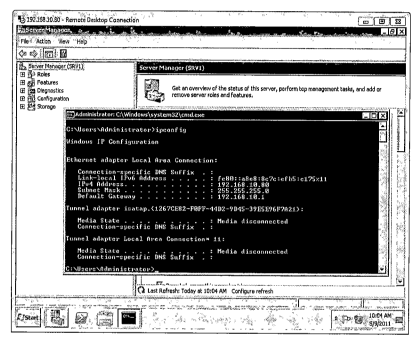

FIGURE 12.3 A remote connection to a Windows Server 2008 R2 machine with Remote Desktop enabled

RDS Licensing

Unlike Remote Desktop, RDS requires licenses for use. You can install it and use it in a testing mode for 120 days, but if you want to use it on a permanent basis, you must install an RD Licensing server. An RD Licensing server is simply a server that runs the Remote Desktop Licensing role service. The RD Licensing server must be activated with Microsoft to allow for RD client access licenses to be deployed. The reason for this licensing requirement is simple: RDS allows client computers to run a virtual desktop or a virtual application on the server but control the mouse and keyboard from the client. The client can be a full-blown installation of Windows 7 or a special thin network client designed just for use with RDS.

Remote Desktop Role Services

The preceding section referenced the Remote Desktop Licensing role service of the RDS server role. Six role services are available with RDS on Windows Server 2008 R2. The following descriptions explain the purpose of these role services:

Remote Desktop Session Host RD Session Host is the core of RDS. It allows the server to host applications or a complete desktop for user utilization. The users actually connect to a RD Session Host server to run the programs, access the virtual desktop, and use the other resources of the server.

Remote Desktop Virtualization Host The RD Virtualization Host is used when you want to provide users with a complete virtual machine. This is different from a virtual desktop, where the user has a desktop on the server, but many other users do as well. With RD Virtualization Host, the user actually has a virtual machine running in Hyper-V just for them. They can install applications (if permitted by the administrator) and work with that virtual machine as if they were running their own dedicated computer.

Remote Desktop Licensing As previously described, the RD Licensing service role is used to provide client access licenses to the RDS clients. These licenses are required to connect to an RD Session Host server.

Remote Desktop Connection Broker RD Connection Broker is used to allow session load balancing when RDS is implemented in a server farm instead of being implemented as a single server. The RD Connection Broker selects the appropriate server in the farm for a new session request and also maintains sessions to allow for session reconnects.

Remote Desktop Gateway When you want to allow users to connect to RD Session Host servers over the Internet, you can use the RD Gateway role service. The RD Gateway role service requires that IIS be installed on the server as well as the Network Policy and Access Services role. When connections are made through an RD Gateway, they are secured using HTTPS with encryption and authentication.

Remote Desktop Web Access RD Web Access should not be confused with RD Gateway. While RD Gateway provides access across the Internet, RD Web Access actually provides access to remote desktops or remote applications inside of the web browser. Windows 7 clients may also access RD Web Access applications directly from their Start menu.

Clearly, RDS is comprised of many components and can become quite complex, depending on the implementation. To learn more about RDS, see the following Microsoft TechNet page:

http://technet.microsoft.com/en-us/library/dd647502(WS.10).aspx.

APPLICATION VIRTUALIZATION

One of the key features in RDS is the ability to perform application virtualization. Starting the RDP version 6.0, which was first available in Windows Vista and Server 2008, administrators can configure applications to run on the server but appear as local applications on the users' desktops. The users click on a Start menu icon to launch the application, and it appears on their local desktop just as a locally installed application would.

The feature that allows for application virtualization is called RemoteApp. RemoteApp can be implemented through direct Start menu icons for connectivity or through RD Web Access for Internet browser-based connectivity. Because the applications are installed and managed from a central server, updates to the application are much easier and less time-consuming. There is no need to update dozens or hundreds of clients. Instead, the single server is updated and all clients will automatically use that new application installation.

THE ESSENTIALS AND BEYOND

Remote access to server Desktops is important for both administrative usages and end-user support purposes. From an administrative standpoint, Remote Desktop can be used to access servers, manage their desktops, and run installed applications across the network. From an end-user standpoint, Remote Desktop Services (RDS) can be deployed so that users can run applications on servers, access personal desktops on servers, or even access entire virtual machines based on Hyper-V.

The protocol used by both Remote Desktop and RDS is the Remote Display Protocol (RDP). When planning for access to remote desktops across the Internet, security is an important consideration. You should use a Virtual Private Network (VPN) connection, such as PPTP, L2TP/IPSec, or SSTP to secure the link. Alternatively, you can use RD Gateway to access RDS servers, which will utilize HTTPS to encrypt data communications. An enhancement to the RDP protocol with the release of version 6.0 was application virtualization. This version of the protocol allows applications to run on the server but appear to run on the local desktop to the accessing user.

(Continues)

THE ESSENTIALS AND BEYOND _(Continued)_

ADDITIONAL EXERCISES

▶ Enable Remote Desktop on the server.

▶ Connect to the server using the Remote Desktop Connection client in Windows 7.

▶ Create a Remote Assistance request.

To compare your answers to the author's, please visit:

www.sybex.com/go/winadminessentials

REVIEW QUESTIONS

1. Which VPN protocol is supported by the most Windows systems, but provides less security?

   A. PPTP

   B. SSTP

   C. L2TP/IPSec

   D. RDP

2. True or false: By default Remote Assistance is enabled on Windows Server 2008 and Windows Server 2008 R2.

3. What VPN protocol uses SSL?

   A. PPTP

   B. SSTP

   C. L2TP/IPSec

   D. RDP

4. What protocol is used for communications with the RD Session Host server from the Remote Desktop Connection client?

5. What dialog box is used to enable Remote Desktop on Windows Server 2008?

   A. Computer Properties

   B. Server Properties

   C. System Properties

   D. Remote PropertiesDP

6. Define Remote Desktop Services.

7. Define encryption.

8. Which one of the following RDS role services allows users to run applications within a web browser?

   A. RD Virtualization Host

   B. RD Session Host

   C. RD Licensing

   D. RD Web Access

(Continues)

THE ESSENTIALS AND BEYOND *(Continued)*

9. Which one of the following RDS role services actually provides the desktop experience or application experience to the connecting users?

   A. RD Gateway

   B. RD Session Host

   C. RD Licensing

   D. RD Web Access

10. True or false: Without IPSec, L2TP is a tunnel-only protocol.

CHAPTER 13

Server Troubleshooting

Troubleshooting skills are very important for server administrators. Resolving problems in modern operating systems requires an understanding of common troubleshooting processes and tools. Users often measure their satisfaction with the services administrators provide based on the time it takes to fix their problems.

The master troubleshooter understands the tools and techniques available to her. Habile administrators understand the two primary topics of this chapter:

▷ **Troubleshooting Processes and Procedures**

▷ **Troubleshooting Tools**

Introducing Troubleshooting Processes and Procedures

Troubleshooting processes and procedures are used to resolve problems as quickly as possible. Frequently, they are established and defined by the hardware and software vendors who supply them. A lot of administrators develop their own troubleshooting processes over time. You can group troubleshooting processes, procedures, and best practices together as a methodology. A troubleshooting methodology does the following:

▶ Defines the processes used to troubleshoot a problem

▶ Defines the procedures to be performed at each step in the process

► Recommends best practices for documentation and procedural actions, such as the best physical environment in which to perform hardware maintenance or the proper way to install or remove hardware

Troubleshooting may require a systematic approach or a specific approach. A systematic approach considers the entire system and is sometimes called *systems thinking.* A specific approach is used for each troubleshooting category. For example, when troubleshooting network adapter problems, you can follow a specific process, which may look something like this:

Each hardware component in a server may require a different troubleshooting approach.

1. Verify that the physical network adapter is installed properly.

2. Verify that the operating system has detected the network adapter.

3. Verify that the driver has been installed appropriately.

4. Verify that the network protocols, such as TCP/IP, are configured properly.

Notice that each step works up in the order required for the adapter to work. This is a bottom-up approach to a specific problem because it begins at the hardware layer and ends at the software configuration layer. Alternatively, you could start at the top (with the network protocols or software configuration) and work down to the bottom (the physical installation of the adapter). Either way, this is a specific process for a categorical problem: a nonfunctioning network adapter.

To help you fully understand troubleshooting methodologies, several are explained in the following sections, including:

► REACT

► OSI model

► Hardware/software model

► Symptom, diagnosis, and solution

► Systems thinking

REACTing

REACT is the troubleshooting methodology used at SysEdCo. It is presented here as an example of a methodology you may develop for yourself after working in the IT industry for some time.

DEVELOPING REACT

Early in my IT career, I worked as a help desk analyst and a telephone troubleshooter. Frequently, I would forget to do something important in the troubleshooting process that would cost me minutes or even hours of time—not to mention the added stress. This is why I developed an acronym to remind me of the stages I should go through when troubleshooting a problem. I work through the acronym until I reach a solution. I always reach a solution by the end of the process represented by the REACT acronym. Sometimes the solution is a complete reload of a device's firmware and settings, and sometimes it is a complete reload of a client computer's operating system; however, more often than not, I find a simpler solution.

The REACT acronym stands for the following five stages of troubleshooting:

▶ Research

▶ Engage

▶ Adjust

▶ Configure

▶ Take note

The methodology is represented in Figure 13.1 with the common tasks performed in each stage. I'll cover each one briefly in the following sections so that you can understand how they fit together and why I go through these stages.

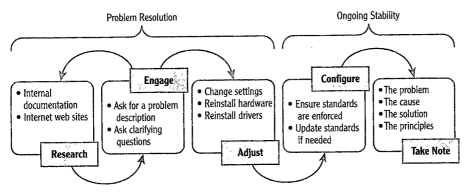

FIGURE 13.1 The REACT methodology

Research

It was probably 1997 when I was trying to resolve a problem with a Microsoft Access 95 database. Every time the user tried to open the database, she received an error that read, "A device attached to the system is not functioning." When I see an error about a device, the first thing I think of is hardware. I spent more than two hours trying to verify that all the hardware was functioning properly, and of course, it was. At the end of the day, I went home tormented by my failure to resolve the problem.

The next day, I decided to do some research, so I opened the MSDN CD. I searched for the error message and found that the error could be generated if VBRUN300.DLL was corrupt. VBRUN300.DLL was used by all Visual Basic 3.0 applications. The problem was that Microsoft Access and this database did not rely on Visual Basic 3.0's runtime for anything; however, my mind was racing. The jungle of my mind suddenly became clear and I realized the implications: If the corruption of VBRUN300.DLL could cause the error, maybe any corrupt DLL could cause the error. I reinstalled Microsoft Access and the error went away.

You are probably wondering what the moral is of this intriguing story. The moral is that I could have saved the first two hours of work with a few minutes of research. My new standard is, research at least fifteen minutes before moving to the Adjust stage with any new problem that requires troubleshooting. Not all problems require troubleshooting, although there is some misunderstanding of what troubleshooting really is. Here is my favorite definition:

> *Troubleshooting* is the process of discovering the unknown cause and solution for a known problem.

If you know the solution to a problem, you don't need to troubleshoot. You only need to fix the problem. In other words, you only need to research problems in real troubleshooting scenarios according to this definition. By researching for just fifteen minutes, I can often ascertain the cause and solution to a problem without spending any time adjusting various settings and parameters. For example, if a server is displaying a specific error message, I will search for that error message at Google.com to see what I can discover. I may also search the vendor's website. If I can't find the specific cause or solution, I can usually get some sort of direction so that I can focus on the right area as I engage or adjust stages.

During the Research stage, you can use both internal documentation and Internet websites. Your internal documentation will become more and more valuable as you use this methodology because the last stage is all about

> A wealth of free troubleshooting information is provided at the Microsoft TechNet website, as well as at the MSDN website.

documenting what you've learned. Several Internet websites are useful when troubleshooting Windows servers, including the following:

TechNet   The Microsoft TechNet site is located at technet.microsoft.com. Here you can find a wealth of technical knowledge related to Microsoft products.

MSDN   The MSDN site is located at msdn.microsoft.com and includes very specific information for programmers, but it also includes useful troubleshooting information.

EventID.net   The site at www.eventid.net is very useful for tracking down the causes of event log entries.

The EventID.net website provides a search engine for locating event ID information. Entries from other administrators who have analyzed the same event IDs are very helpful.

Engage

Although you may be eager to move from research to adjusting, you should engage any users involved in the problem. During the Engage stage, you should ask for a problem description and then ask questions to clarify the situation.

Ask questions such as "Do you know if anything about your system has changed in the past few days?" Notice I didn't say, "Did you change anything?" The latter question will usually cause people to become defensive and fail to get you any valuable information. The users do not usually have any knowledge of what caused the problem, but when they do, they can save you hours or even days of trouble. Always engage the user. Other questions that might be provide beneficial information include:

User interaction is very important when you are analyzing user-related problems.

> ► When did the problem start happening?

> ► Is this the first time this problem has occurred or has it happened in the past as well?

> ► Are you aware of any others experiencing similar difficulties?

> ► When was the last time it worked?

> ► Is it turned on? (Seriously.)

You may wonder how engaging users will help you troubleshoot server problems. The answer lies in the fact that users use the servers. Many times, the first report of a server problem comes from a user. That user may receive an error message that is different from the problems logged in the event logs on the server, and the user's perspective can greatly enhance your understanding of the problem. Engaging the user could simply be listed as a subtask of the Research stage, but it is so important that the REACT methodology separates it so that it is never forgotten.

You may need to you loop back-and-forth between the Research and Engage stages a few times before moving on to the Adjust stage. This is represented in Figure 13.1 with the left-pointing arrow above the stages. For example, you may discover new information while engaging the user that causes you to perform more research on the Internet.

> The amount of time spent in the Research and Engage stages will vary depending on the complexity of the problem.

Adjust

Interestingly, we've just arrived at the stage where many techs, server administrators, and network administrators begin. This is the stage where you try different things to see if you can track down the cause of your problem or you make the changes you discovered should be made in the Research and Engage stages. You might try updating the software on a server or installing new device drivers. You could change settings or disable features to see if the problem goes away. The point is that this is where you begin the "technical" side of troubleshooting.

Once you've completed these first three stages, you always come to a solution. Again, the solution sometimes entails reinstalling the application or operating system, but the solution gets things working again. You may have your solution after the Research stage, or you may have it after the Engage stage. Whether you made it all the way to the Adjust stage or you solved the problem earlier in the process, once you've made your adjustments you are ready to move to what I call the ongoing stability stages: Configure and Take Note.

Configure

This is the first of the two ongoing stability stages. In the Configure stage, you ensure that the systems and devices are configured and operating according to your standards before leaving the physical area (or exiting the Remote Management tool). This allows you to maintain a standardized environment, and a standardized environment is usually more stable. Of course, with a reinstallation, you will need to reinstall according to the original specifications for the installation and then apply any configuration changes that have been approved or processed since that time.

> Standardized environments are easier to manage and support. They are easier to troubleshoot because they provide a consistent set of configurations.

In some cases, your configuration standards may be insufficient and require changes. If you see the same problem repeatedly occurring, it could indicate that a change should be made to your base configuration standards. The configuration manager should be notified so that she can make the appropriate changes. In some environments, a dedicated configuration manager may not exist, but the person responsible for defining the basic configuration for systems should be notified. In such scenarios, you may be required to revisit the problem system at a later time after the configuration standards have been updated to ensure the new standards are properly enforced on the machine.

Take Note

This final stage completes the Troubleshooting process and ensures that you get the greatest benefit out of this methodology going forward. (The Take Note stage is the second ongoing stability stage.) By documenting your findings, what I call *take note*, you provide a searchable resource for future troubleshooting. For example, the situation I shared earlier (where the device error was generated) should be documented, and I suggest documenting the following at a minimum:

▶ The problem with any error messages if they existed

▶ The cause concisely explained

▶ The solution with any necessary step-by-steps

▶ Any learned principles

While it takes time to document a problem and solution, doing so can save much more time in the future when you need the information again.

   If your organization does not provide a centralized trouble-ticket-tracking system or help-desk solution, I encourage you to consider creating your own database. You can use any desktop database application, such as Microsoft Access or FileMaker. Just be sure you can document the needed information and can query it easily.

Stepping Through the OSI Model

The OSI model can also be used for troubleshooting when you experience networking problems. The OSI model provides a seven-layer architecture for network modeling and analysis (Figure 13.2):

▶ Layer 7: Application

▶ Layer 6: Presentation

▶ Layer 5: Session

▶ Layer 4: Transport

▶ Layer 3: Network

▶ Layer 2: Data Link

▶ Layer 1: Physical

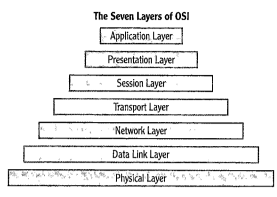

FIGURE 13.2 An illustration of the OSI model

The concept here is to walk up or down the OSI model and analyze the system at each layer. This allows you to break the problem into logical sections and then verify that the system is operating properly in each of these sections (OSI layers). You may choose to analyze only Layers 1 through 3, or you may choose to evaluate all seven (or even eight layers if you're considering the user layer, which is sometimes called Layer 8) layers.

Layer 1

Layer 1 is the physical layer. Analyzing it would entail evaluating the server's network adapters, client devices, or infrastructure devices to ensure that they are working properly at the hardware level. For example, is the radio in a wireless adapter still functioning appropriately or not? With client devices, this can be tested quickly by removing the wireless LAN client device (assuming it's a USB, CardBus, or another kind of removable device) and installing it in another computer that is using the same model device and is working. If the new computer stops working too, the wireless LAN device is most likely at fault at the hardware level or the software level (firmware). If it is an access point (AP) and you have a spare, you could load the identical configuration on the spare and place it in the same location to see if the problem persists. If the problem does not persist, again, the radio—or some other hardware/firmware issue—may be failing.

An additional key is to evaluate the hardware used by Layer 1 (sometimes called Layer 0 by industry professionals, although an actual Layer 0 is not in the OSI model). On the wired network, you may evaluate patch panels, connectors, and cabling at this point.

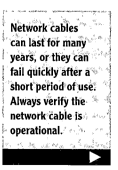

Network cables can last for many years, or they can fail quickly after a short period of use. Always verify the network cable is operational.

Layer 2

Layer 2 is where the network switches live. Make sure the switch ports are still working properly, that VLANs are configured appropriately, and that port security settings are set accurately on your switches. Switches evaluate incoming frames and forward them based on information in the frame, so make sure the switching rules or filters are set up appropriately. Of course, the problem could be at the cable and connector level, but you should have checked that at Layer 1. Within the server, ensure that the network adapter is installed and configured with the appropriate drivers. The adapter provides the Layer 2 address (known as a MAC address) for the network.

Layer 3

If you still haven't found a solution after evaluating the wireless radios, cabling, and connectors at Layer 1 and after checking the switches and network adapters at Layer 2, you might need to move on to Layer 3. Here, you'll need to check the IP routing tables to ensure proper configuration and make sure any filters applied are accurate. Using common operating system tools such as `ipconfig`, `ping`, and `arp`, you can ensure that you can route data from one location on the network to another and that networking is functioning at Layer 3 (the Network layer of the OSI model).

The `ipconfig` command is used to view the IP configuration on a client or server. It is also used to request a new IP address when DHCP is used; however, DHCP is rarely used to acquire an IP version 4 address for a server. Instead, static addresses are used to provide consistency in the networked environment. To use `ipconfig` to view all available IP addressing information, execute the `ipconfig /all` command at a Windows Command Prompt.

Listing 13.1 shows a portion of the command's output. This portion lists the basic IP configuration settings on the server and the specific settings for the Ethernet adapter.

◄

IP version 4 addresses look like four numbers separated by periods (for example, 192.168.12.18). IP version 4 addresses are usually *static* (manually configured) on servers.

Listing 13.1: The `ipconfing/all` Output

```
Windows IP Configuration

    Host Name . . . . . . . . . . . . : SRV1
    Primary Dns Suffix  . . . . . . . : training.local
    Node Type . . . . . . . . . . . . : Hybrid
    IP Routing Enabled. . . . . . . . : No
    WINS Proxy Enabled. . . . . . . . : No
    DNS Suffix Search List. . . . . . : training.local
```

```
Ethernet adapter Local Area Connection:

   Connection-specific DNS Suffix  . :
   Description . . . . . . . . . . . : Intel(R) PRO/1000 MT Network Connection
   Physical Address. . . . . . . . . : 00-0C-29-AF-52-45
   DHCP Enabled. . . . . . . . . . . : No
   Autoconfiguration Enabled . . . . : Yes
   Link-local IPv6 Address . . . . . : fe80::a8e8:8c7c:efb5:c175%11(Preferred)
   IPv4 Address. . . . . . . . . . . : 192.168.10.80(Preferred)
   Subnet Mask . . . . . . . . . . . : 255.255.255.0
   Default Gateway . . . . . . . . . : 192.168.10.1
   DHCPv6 IAID . . . . . . . . . . . : 234884137
   DHCPv6 Client DUID. . . . . . . . : 00-01-00-01-15-0C-16-82-00-0C-29-80-BC-23
   DNS Servers . . . . . . . . . . . : ::1
                                       127.0.0.1
   NetBIOS over Tcpip. . . . . . . . : Enabled
```

The ping command is used to test connectivity to a remote node on the network. It is useful when you are testing different scenarios. For example, if a service is not responding, you may want to ping the server to see if the server is still up and running even though the service has failed. The ping command is used as follows:

```
ping ip_address | host_name
```

For example, to ping the IP address of 192.168.10.1, you should execute the following command:

```
ping 192.168.10.1
```

The output of this command is shown in Listing 13.2. Notice that the results are successful in this case.

Listing 13.2: The ping 192.168.10.1 Output

```
Pinging 192.168.10.1 with 32 bytes of data:
Reply from 192.168.10.1: bytes=32 time<1ms TTL=64
Reply from 192.168.10.1: bytes=32 time<1ms TTL=64
Reply from 192.168.10.1: bytes=32 time<1ms TTL=64
Reply from 192.168.10.1: bytes=32 time<1ms TTL=64

Ping statistics for 192.168.10.1:
    Packets: Sent = 4, Received = 4, Lost = 0 (0% loss),
Approximate round trip times in milli-seconds:
    Minimum = 0ms, Maximum = 0ms, Average = 0ms
```

When the ping fails, you will see output similar to that in Listing 13.3. This time, the IP address 192.168.10.113 is tested and is unresponsive.

Listing 13.3: The ping 192.168.10.113 Output

```
Pinging 192.168.10.113 with 32 bytes of data:
Reply from 192.168.10.80: Destination host unreachable.
Reply from 192.168.10.80: Destination host unreachable.
Reply from 192.168.10.80: Destination host unreachable.
Reply from 192.168.10.80: Destination host unreachable.
```

By default, the ping command sends four ping requests. You can adjust this default with the -n switch. For example, the command ping 192.168.10.1 -n 25 would send 25 ping requests to the target IP address. Figure 13.3 show the command-line switch options available for customization of the ping command.

FIGURE 13.3 Viewing the help for the ping command

The arp command is used to view the Address Resolution Protocol (ARP) cache on the local machine. If you are unable to communicate with a device on the local network segment (usually within the same IP network address), you can use the arp command to view the local cache and verify that the proper MAC address is listed for the target machine. For example, Listing 13.4 shows the output of the arp -a command on a Windows Server machine.

ARP resolves IP addresses (Layer 3 addresses) to MAC addresses (Layer 2 addresses). IP addresses are used to communicate across the routed network; MAC addresses are used on local network segments.

Listing 13.4: The Output of the arp -a Command

```
Interface: 192.168.10.80 --- 0xb
  Internet Address      Physical Address      Type
  192.168.10.1          00-24-b2-5a-2d-76     dynamic
  192.168.10.252        00-0d-0b-95-8b-b1     dynamic
  192.168.10.255        ff-ff-ff-ff-ff-ff     static
  224.0.0.22            01-00-5e-00-00-16     static
  224.0.0.252           01-00-5e-00-00-fc     static
```

Upper Layers

Finally, if you've tested the first three layers and can't find a problem there, the network infrastructure is probably working fine. It's time to move to the upper layers. Look at the configuration settings in your server applications and services. Verify that the authentication mechanisms are installed and configured correctly. Try using different tools and software that provide the same basic functionality. Do they work? If so, there may be a compatibility problem with the specific application you're using and the hardware on which it is operating.

As you can see, the OSI model method of troubleshooting can help you both focus and move through a sequence of testing procedures until you find the actual source of the networking problem. I've only touched on the concept here, but you can take it further by learning more about what happens at each layer and the tools that can be used to test at that layer. For example, you can use a spectrum analyzer to test and troubleshoot the physical layer of a wireless network and a protocol analyzer to inspect the data-link layer of wired and wireless networks.

> ▶
>
> For more information on the OSI Model, see *Microsoft Windows Networking Essentials* book by Darril Gibson (Sybex, 2011).

Troubleshooting with the Hardware/ Software Model

The hardware/software model is a troubleshooting methodology that is used in an attempt to narrow the problem to either hardware or software. There are certain problems that are commonly hardware problems, and there are others that tend to be software problems. Many administrators will try to troubleshoot software first and then hardware. Others will do the opposite. In most cases, the situation itself will help you to determine which should be your first point of attack. If everything is working in a system except one application, that is often a good sign that the software is the problem. If multiple applications that use the same hardware are experiencing the same problem, that is often a good sign that the hardware is the problem. These are not absolute rules, but they are good general guidelines.

Hardware Problems

When troubleshooting servers, specific hardware problems tend to generate common symptoms. While I cannot provide you with a comprehensive list of symptoms mapped to every problem, the list in Table 13.1 is a good place to start.

TABLE 13.1   Common Hardware Problems and Symptoms

Hardware Problem	Symptoms
Memory failure	Random application crashes, random operating system crashes, and system lockups
Insufficient processing capabilities	Poor performance, inability to launch applications, and temporary system lockups
Disk failure	Corrupted data, inability to boot, and system crashes
Network adapter failure	Intermittent loss of connectivity and complete loss of connectivity
Video adapter failure	Corrupted display and system crashes
System board failure	Any of the previously listed symptoms

Software Problems

Software problems are related to the software running on the server and can cause many symptoms similar to hardware failures. Table 13.2 lists common software problems and their symptoms.

TABLE 13.2   Common Software Problems and Symptoms

Software Problem	Symptom
Corrupted files	System crashes, inability to boot, and application crashes
Poorly written drivers	System crashes and nonfunctioning hardware
Unsupported bit-level software	On 64-bit operating systems, error messages indicating that 16-bit software is not supported and on 32-bit operating systems, error messages indicating that 64-bit software is not supported
Improperly configured software	Application crashes, error messages, and lack of functionality
Poorly written software	Corrupted data, application crashes, and error messages

Symptom, Diagnosis, and Solution

Because certain symptoms usually surface with specific problems, many issues can be resolved in a similar way to human health issues:

1. Look at the symptom.

2. Identify the most likely cause (diagnosis).

3. Treat it (solution).

Repeat this process until the problem is resolved. The following explains each of the three stages:

Symptom Defining the symptoms means gathering information about the problem. What is happening? Where is it happening? What technology is involved? Which users, if any, are involved? Has it always been this way? Answering questions like these will help you determine the various details about the problem. Good questions are at the core of effective problem definition.

Diagnosis Based on the information gathered from your symptoms analysis, what is the most likely cause or what are the most likely causes?

Solution The solution is the potential fix for the problem. Based on your diagnosis, you can treat one or all, but you will most likely learn more by treating one cause at a time. Try one solution based on your diagnosis first and evaluate the results. This gives you expert knowledge over time.

ADJUST STAGE IN REACT

The diagnosis and solution process is what I call the Adjust stage in my REACT methodology. You make changes and try different tactics until something solves the problem. You document the solution for future reference, but you also mentally document it. This is called *experience*. As you gain more and more of it, you eventually approach the level of expertise that helps you solve problems more quickly. This is why I look at problems as stepping stones to a better future; solving this network or computer problem today will make me more capable of solving other problems tomorrow.

Here's an example that demonstrates how the symptom-diagnosis-solution procedure works. A computer system is no longer able to communicate on the network, and the LEDs are not illuminated. You may try replacing a hardware adapter because you determine that, based on the symptoms, the most likely cause is a failed card. After replacing the card, you note that you still have the same problem. Next, you decide to try using the adapter in another machine that is currently using the same adapter model and is working. When you do this, the adapter works in the other computer. Next, you attempt to reload the drivers in the malfunctioning computer, but this doesn't help either. In the end, you discover that the expansion port is experiencing intermittent failures in the malfunctioning computer. You send it to the vendor for repairs.

Systems Thinking

Systems thinking is the process of analyzing all interdependent components that comprise a system. In other words, it is the opposite of being narrow-minded in the troubleshooting process. I've seen administrators blame everything from network connectivity to application errors on an operating system or a particular brand of PC instead of looking for the actual problem. While some operating systems and some PC brands may seem more prone to problems than others, the reality is that there are probably thousands of individuals out there who have had the opposite experience as you. In other words, if you like the computers from company A because they are very stable and you don't like the computers from company B because of your experience with them, there is likely someone (or thousands) out there who feels exactly the opposite because of his or her experience.

The point is simple: rather than focusing on a vendor that I do not like, I focus on the actual problem and seek a solution. When I do this, I'm less likely to just reinstall every time a problem comes up. I want to ask questions like:

- ▶ What are the systems or devices between this device and the network or device with which it is attempting to communicate?

- ▶ What other devices are attempting to communicate with the same system at this time?

- ▶ What has changed in the environment within which the system operates?

- ▶ Has the system been physically moved recently?

Asking these kinds of questions causes you to evaluate factors that are more related to the actual system you have in place and less related to the vendors that have provided the components. Indeed, if a vendor has provided you with bad components over a period of time, you will likely discontinue partnering with that vendor; however, automatically blaming a problem on a vendor does not help you solve the problems you are facing right now. For that, you need systems thinking and a good methodology.

Whether you adopt one or more of these methodologies, pursue another methodology, or create one of your own, you should consider how to troubleshoot problems and then make sure you use an efficient and effective process.

ITIL AND TROUBLESHOOTING

The Information Technology Infrastructure Library (ITIL) is a set of documents that define best practices for technology management. ITIL was initially created by the United Kingdom Office of Government Commerce, but it has found widespread acceptance in IT departments around the world.

The ITIL includes seven publications that describe best practices, including:

- ▶ Service Support
- ▶ Service Delivery
- ▶ Infrastructure Management
- ▶ Security Management
- ▶ The Business Perspective
- ▶ Application Management
- ▶ Software Asset Management

Within Service Support are the concepts of incident and problem management. According to ITIL, an *incident* is an event that is not part of standard operations and that may cause an interruption or a reduction in the quality of a service. The *problem* is the underlying cause of the incident. ITIL suggests that you first resolve the incident (get things back up and running) and then discover the root cause so that it can be prevented in the future. For more information on ITIL, see:

    http://www.itil-officialsite.com

Troubleshooting Tools

Windows servers include dozens of troubleshooting tools when you include all of the Command Prompt commands and PowerShell cmdlets that can be used for problem analysis. The beginning administrator should be aware of four very useful tools available in Windows servers and clients. These tools are

- ▶ Task Manager
- ▶ Performance Monitor
- ▶ Resource Monitor
- ▶ Event Viewer

The following sections introduce you to these four tools.

Task Manager

When it comes to troubleshooting, the Task Manager is one of the most frequently used applications in Windows. It lists the running processes on your system and allows you perform several actions against these processes, including:

- ▶ Raising the priority
- ▶ Lowering the priority
- ▶ Shutting down or killing the task
- ▶ Viewing information about the processes

To launch the Task Manager, follow this procedure:

1. Right-click on the taskbar (the area where your application buttons are displayed).

2. Select Start Task Manager.

Figure 13.4 shows the Task Manager running with the Processes tab selected. The Processes tab is the primary tab used for the actions listed. For example, this is the tab you would use to view information about processes running on your server.

◄ You can also press Ctrl+Shift+Esc as a shortcut key to launch the Task Manager.

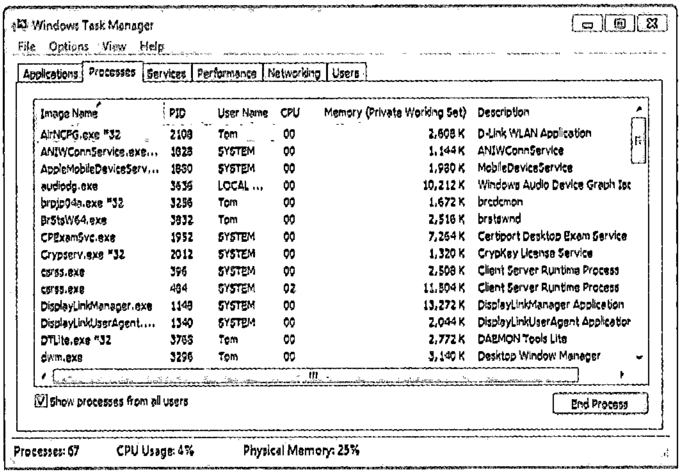

FIGURE 13.4 The Windows Task Manager with the Processes tab selected

If you want a process to get more processor time, you can raise its priority. Six priorities are supported, including Low, Below Normal, Normal, Above Normal, High, and Realtime (listed from low to high). By default most processes run at the Normal priority. You can right-click on a process in the Task Manager, and select the priority you want to assign to it.

Sometimes an application or service will lock up and become unresponsive. In such scenarios, you may have to *kill* the process associated with the application or service so that you can restart it. When you kill a process, you simply force its removal from memory on the system. You can right-click on a process and select End Process to kill it.

In many cases, you simply want to view information about the processes. The Task Manager displays the process name (it calls this the image name), the Process ID (PID), the username under which the process runs, the CPU time percentage consumed, the memory used for the private working set, and a description. While these are the default displayed columns, several other columns may be added to the display using the View Select Columns menu option. Figure 13.5 shows the Select Process Page Columns dialog.

The Processes tab is certainly the tab most commonly used by administrators in the Task Manager. However, the other tabs are also useful. The Application tab lists the user applications currently running on the server. The Services tab lists the background services running. Depending on the version of Windows Server you are running, you may have a Networking tab, which provides performance information related to the network adapters in your system. You may also have a Users tab, which shows the users currently logged on to the system.

> You can also use the taskkill command at the Command Prompt to kill a task.

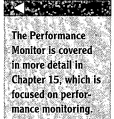

FIGURE 13.5 Adding new columns to the Process tab in Task Manager

All Windows operating systems include a Performance tab in the Task Manager. This tab shows the current CPU usage and the recent history of CPU usage for each processor in the server. It also shows memory consumption and provides a button that links to the Resource Monitor, which is discussed in a later section of this chapter.

Performance Monitor

The Performance Monitor is known as the Reliability and Performance Monitor on Windows Server 2008 and Vista. On Windows Server 2008 R2 and Windows 7, it is simply called the Performance Monitor. It is used to capture information about the performance of your server or computer.

Performance Monitor works by capturing values from performance counters. The performance counters are arranged into groups. For example, the Processor group includes the % Processor Time counter and the % User Time counter. Both counters are related to the processor.

The Performance Monitor is covered in more detail in Chapter 15, which is focused on performance monitoring.

▷ The % Processor Time counter tracks the amount of time the processor is busy performing active tasks.

▷ The % User Time tracks the amount of time the processor is focused on User mode tasks, as opposed to Privileged mode (Kernel mode) tasks.

User mode and *Kernel mode* are the two primary operating modes in the Windows operating systems.

User Mode   The mode in which your applications run

Kernel Mode   The mode in which the operating system and device drivers run

User mode has limited access to hardware and software. Kernel mode has full access to hardware and software. Sometimes it is useful to know which mode is consuming more processor time.

From a troubleshooting perspective, the Performance Monitor is mostly used to determine what is causing a performance problem. You can discover whether the core problem is related to the processor, memory, networking, or disks. You can even narrow the monitoring down to individual services and how they are working. For example, you can track how SQL Server is using memory, if you are using it as your DBMS.

To access the Performance Monitor, perform the following procedure:

1. Select Start ➤ All Programs ➤ Administrative Tools ➤ Performance Monitor.

2. In the console tree on the left, click on the Performance Monitor node.

Another method you can use to access the Performance Monitor is to use the *Start and Type procedure*: click on the Start menu and type what you're trying to find. For example, if you click Start, type **perfmon**, and press Enter, you will launch the Performance Monitor application. Figure 13.6 shows the Performance Monitor running and displaying information about the % Processor Time counter.

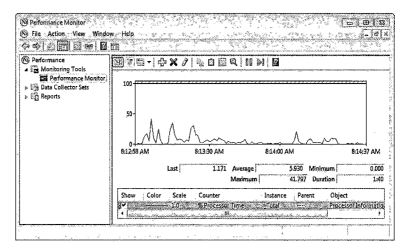

FIGURE 13.6 Viewing % Processor Time counter data in Performance Monitor

Resource Monitor

The Resource Monitor is new to Windows Server 2008 and still exists in Windows Server 2008 R2. In both systems, you access the Resource Monitor from within the Task Manager or by searching for **resmon** on the Start menu. The Resource Monitor is like the Task Manager all grown up. It is more powerful and provides more valuable information than the Task Manager ever has.

To launch the Resource Monitor and view the information it provides, follow this procedure:

Chapter 15 provides information on using the Resource Monitor for performance analysis.

1. Press the Windows key on your keyboard (if you do not have a keyboard with the Windows key, press Ctrl+Esc to get the same results).

2. You will default to the Search field on the Start menu.

3. Type **perfmon /res** in the Search field.

4. Press Enter.

At this point, you should see a screen similar to the one in Figure 13.7 As you can see, the Resource Monitor shows information related to four areas of the system: the CPU, disk, network, and memory.

FIGURE 13.7 Viewing the Resource Monitor on Windows Server 2008

To see another interesting feature of the Resource Monitor, execute the `perfmon /report` command.

You'll see a screen indicating that the performance analysis will run for approximately 60 seconds. When the analysis is complete, you will see a report like the one in Figure 13.8. The Resource Monitor is one of the components of the Reliability and Performance Monitor on Windows Server 2008 and Vista or the Performance Monitor on Windows Server 2008 R2 and Windows 7. Now you know how to access it directly.

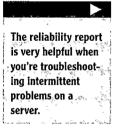

FIGURE 13.8 Viewing the Resource Monitor report

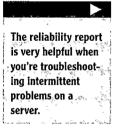

You can also view the reliability report for a Windows Vista, Windows 7, or Windows Server 2008 and 2008 R2 machine with the perfmon /rel command.

The reliability report was obvious and easy to find in Windows Vista, but it's a bit more buried in Windows 7 and Windows Server 2008 R2. The reliability report shows the history of updates, errors, and alerts on the system. For example, if a new driver was installed recently, it will be logged in the reliability report. If an application or service crashes, that will be logged in the report as well. This type of information can provide very important clues during the troubleshooting process.

Event Viewer

The Event Viewer is used to inspect the event logs on a Windows computer. Windows Server 2008 added important features to the Event Viewer, which allow it to support central logging. You can access the Event Viewer in the Administrative Tools group of the Start menu, or you can simply click Start, search for Event Viewer, and press Enter. Figure 13.9 shows the Event Viewer interface on Windows Server 2008 R2.

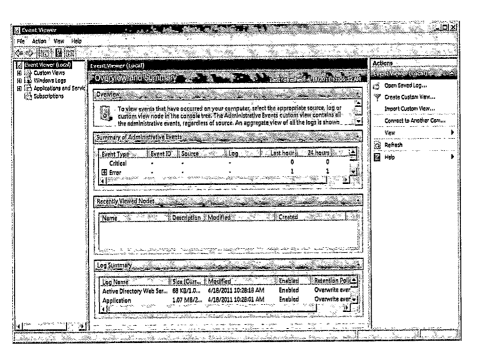

FIGURE 13.9 The Event Viewer application on Windows Server 2008 R2

Four event log entry levels may be shown in an event log. These levels include:

Critical   A failure has occurred and the application or components could not automatically recover.

Warning   An issue has occurred that may impact a service or component and may require action by the administrator to prevent more severe problems.

Error   A problem has occurred, and it may impact functionality within the triggering service or component.

Information   A change has occurred in a service or component, which was not an error, but it was logged for documentation purposes.

An event log entry includes several items of information that are useful for troubleshooting problems. These information elements are called *properties*, and each event log entry has one or more of these properties. The properties include:

- ► Source
- ► Event ID
- ► Level

> Additional properties are available, but they are not displayed by default. For more information on these additional properties, see http://technet .microsoft.com/ en-us/library/ cc765981(WS.10) .aspx.

▶ User

▶ Operational Code

▶ Log

▶ Task category

▶ Keywords

▶ Computer

▶ Date and Time

The Event Viewer supports filtering logs so that you can see only the information you want. As an example, you may want to view only log entries with a level of critical, warning, or error. The vast majority of log entries are informational. By filtering to only the three levels mentioned, you enable a view with less information, making it easier to browse through and locate potential problems. Figure 13.10 shows the Filter Current Log dialog with the mentioned filtering configured. You access this dialog by right-clicking on a log and selecting Filter Current Log.

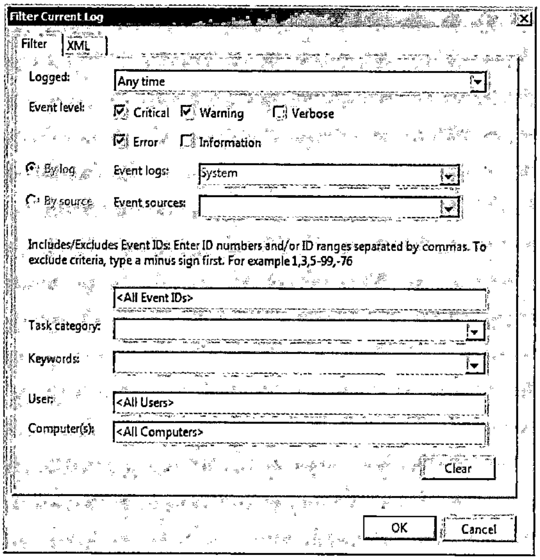

FIGURE 13.10 Configuring a log filter in Event Viewer

You should be aware of the four primary event logs and the information they contain:

Application   The Application log includes events generated by applications or services running on the server. This is where you might find errors generated by services such as SQL Server or Exchange Server.

Security   The Security log includes events generated based on audited security events. Failed logon attempts, failed file access, successful logon attempts, and successful file access are all representative of what you might find here. The actual events generated for this log will depend on the auditing configuration on your server.

Setup   The Setup log contains events generated by installation programs. Most modern installation programs use the Microsoft Software Installer (MSI) format and will add entries to this log.

System   The System log includes events generated by the Windows operating system components. As an example, a failed driver would cause a log entry to be added to this log.

In most cases, the Event Viewer is used when a problem occurs and you are performing research to identify the cause of the problem. You may locate a suspect entry in the log and want to learn more about it. You can search for the Event ID value at EventID.net and find useful information.

In other scenarios, you may want to centralize the log files. Windows Server 2008 and later versions support this option through event subscriptions. One server acts as the subscriber to the other servers and pulls the events into its local log databases. To use event subscriptions, the Windows Remote Management (WinRM) service must be enabled and configured on each server. You do not usually subscribe to all events on a remote server, but you typically subscribe only to important events that you want to centralize. For a more detailed explanation of the steps required to enable event subscriptions, see:

```
http://technet.microsoft.com/en-us/library/cc749183%28WS.10%29.aspx
```

THE ESSENTIALS AND BEYOND

Troubleshooting requires technical skills and an understanding of processes and procedures. Processes and procedures are often documented as *troubleshooting methodologies*. You may develop your own methodology over time, or you can use existing methodologies that have been tested and proven by other organizations. The Information Technology Infrastructure Library (ITIL) provides documents that include troubleshooting best practices. Windows Server includes several tools that can be used for troubleshooting, including the Task Manager, Performance Monitor, Resource Monitor, and Event Viewer.

ADDITIONAL EXERCISES

▶ Using the Event Viewer, filter the Application log to show only Critical-level and Error-level events.

▶ Use the Performance Monitor to view the live statistics for the Bytes Total/sec counter in the Network Interface group.

▶ Launch the Notepad application, and then use the Task Manager to kill its process.

▶ Use the `ping` command to test connectivity to `www.sysedco.com`.

To compare your answers to the author's, please visit:

`www.sybex.com/go/winadminessentials`

REVIEW QUESTIONS

1. What shortcut key combination is used to open the Task Manager?

   A. Ctrl+Esc

   B. Ctrl+T

   C. Ctrl+Shift+Esc

   D. Alt+T

2. True or false: The ITIL defines an incident and a problem differently.

3. You experience the following symptoms: corrupted display and system crashes. Which one of the following hardware items has most likely failed?

   A. Disk

   B. CPU

   C. Memory

   D. Display adapter

4. Name an OSI model layer that may be evaluated during the troubleshooting process for network problems?

5. What event log severity level includes entries always indicating an unrecoverable problem?

   A. Errors

   B. Warning

   C. Critical

   D. Information

(Continues)

6. Define ITIL.

7. Define Event Viewer.

8. What can be used to limit the event log entries displayed in the Event Viewer?

   A. Performance counters   C. Event filtering

   B. Event subscriptions   D. Task Manager

9. Which one of the following is used to kill tasks running on a Windows machine?

   A. Task Manager   C. Event Viewer

   B. Performance Monitor   D. ARP

10. True or false: Networking problems are always constrained to the server machine.

CHAPTER 14

Performance Tuning

Performance tuning is the process used to improve the way a system performs, and it is a twofold task. As an administrator, you must find ways to improve the performance of an underperforming server. To help you analyze and improve server performance, Windows Server includes multiple tools, including the Command Prompt tools, Resource Monitor, and Performance Monitor. These tools, which are available on Windows clients as well, will help you analyze performance so that you can adjust settings; remove services or applications; install improved services, applications, or drivers; or take other actions to improve system performance.

Yet, not all performance problems are related to underperforming servers. In modern server environments, it is not uncommon to have servers that are under-utilized. Newer technology, called virtualization, can help administrators use more of the resources in each of their servers. Gaining performance results is the primary focus of this chapter and is explored through these topics:

▷ **Performance Myths**

▷ **Performance Tuning Tools**

▷ **Virtualization and Performance**

Performance Myths and Truths

Before you investigate the specific tools used for performance monitoring and analysis, it's important that you understand the realities of performance tuning and server implementation. To do this, you need to avoid falling into the traps caused by some of the myths surrounding performance analysis and improvement. The following myths seem to propagate through the server administration world:

Myth　If processor utilization is high, a faster processor is needed.

Truth　One system component is seldom the culprit.

Myth　Eighty percent of the performance is determined by the application code.

Truth　Better code is better, but better design is best.

Myth   An optimized server is the only key to database performance.

Truth   It still has to travel the network.

The truths behind these myths are discussed and explained in the following sections. Although some myths have their origins in facts, they represent rare scenarios that prove to be the exceptions and not the rule.

One System Component Is Seldom the Culprit

When Microsoft introduced Windows 2000 Server, they changed the System Monitor tool (which was called the Performance Monitor in Windows NT) so that it started with three default counters (% Processor Utilization, Avg. Disk Queue Length, and Pages/sec). This change provided a tremendous help in overcoming the myth that a "faster processor is needed," but such beliefs still lurk in the shadows. Sadly, Windows 7 and Windows Server 2008 R2 reverted back so that only the % Processor Utilization counter shows; hopefully, most administrators now know that they must monitor more than this one counter. Undeniably, there are scenarios where a faster processor is needed. However, it's also true that a faster processor, typically, is not going to provide the greatest performance gain. In fact, the culprit is seldom one component but is more likely to be a combination of two or more things that need to be addressed.

> The Performance Monitor tool is used to capture information related to the performance of the server components, including the hardware and software. It is covered later in this chapter.

For example, assume you've monitored the CPU utilization on your server, the virtual memory pages per second, and the length of the hard drive queue. The CPU utilization is at an average of 82 percent. This reading would be rather high as an average, although it is not necessarily high as a single reading. You could double the processor speed and only reduce the utilization to 80 percent. Why would doubling the processor speed produce only a 2 percent change in utilization? It could happen if the pages-per-second reading was really high. A high pages-per-second reading would indicate that you do not have sufficient physical memory in the server. In a scenario like this, you might be able to cut CPU utilization as much as 20 to 40 percent by simply doubling the memory. If the pages-per-second reading is very high, not having enough memory in the system is a likely culprit. If the hard drive queue length is high, you should also explore getting faster hard drives or using a RAID 0 array to store the virtual memory file. This configuration change would allow for faster reads and writes to virtual memory and could also reduce CPU utilization.

As this example shows, if you look at one counter and make your performance judgment based on that single counter alone, you may well make an errant decision. It is usually best to monitor multiple counters and then consider them as an integrated whole before making your performance improvement decisions.

Better Code Is Better, But Better Design Is Best

It is very true that poorly written code modules can reduce the performance of any server deployment. However, the common thinking that 80 percent of a system's performance comes from the code is frequently untrue. You can have the best written code in history and still have a poorly performing database if the physical and logical designs are poorly constructed and implemented.

By controlling what software is installed on a given server, you can greatly improve the performance of that server. Additionally, by using the right technology, you can improve the server's performance. For example, placing data files on a stripe set RAID array can improve physical writes and reads to and from storage. Adding more memory can reduce the required virtual memory (paging file access) and improve performance. The point is that many things can be done in the physical design of a system to improve its performance, which will in turn improve the performance of the applications on the system.

In this context, *virtual memory* refers to the use of hard drive space for temporary storage of data so that more information can be stored in RAM.

It Still Has to Travel the Network

Finally, you can do everything to optimize the server, code, and physical design and still have a poorly performing server solution if the network between the server and the clients is overloaded. Performance is both a measurable fact and a perceptive reality. Stated differently, you can measure the server's potential and ensure that it is fast enough, but still receive communications from users who feel that the "server is slow" because the network cannot handle the throughput demanded. Even with a well-performing server, the data still has to travel across the network. Therefore, you will need to ensure that the network throughput is sufficient for your purposes. If you do not have control of the physical network, be sure to check with your infrastructure network administrators before you implement a server solution that is data-transfer intensive.

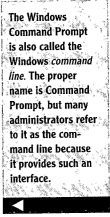

The Windows Command Prompt is also called the Windows *command line*. The proper name is Command Prompt, but many administrators refer to it as the command line because it provides such an interface.

Command Prompt Tools

The Windows Command Prompt provides several commands that can be used to analyze the performance of a server. The `tasklist` command is used to view the tasks running on the server. The `sc` command is used to configure, start, and stop services at the Command Prompt as an alternative to the `net start` and `net stop` commands. The `taskkill` command is used to remove an application from memory. The `openfiles` command shows the files open on the computer by running processes. The `shutdown` command is used to shut down the server or shut down and restart it. The `systeminfo` command is used to display system software and hardware summary information at the Command Prompt. The typeperf command is used to display performance counter values.

Clearly, the Command Prompt provides many commands that can assist in performance analysis and improvement. The following sections briefly explain the most commonly used of the listed commands.

Using the *TaskList* Command

The tasklist command is used to list the tasks or processes running on a Windows machine. The command can be executed without any parameters to list all running tasks. However, it also provides powerful parameters that modify its operations and output. The following parameters are available (italicized items represent variable placeholders that should be replaced with the defined object):

/S *system*   Specifies the remote system to which to connect.

/U *[domain\]user*   Specifies the user context under which the command should execute.

/P *[password]*   Specifies the password for the given user context. Prompts for input if omitted.

/M *[module]*   Lists all tasks currently using the given exe/dll name. If the module name is not specified, all loaded modules are displayed.

/SVC   Displays services hosted in each process.

/V   Displays verbose task information.

/FI *filter*   Displays a set of tasks that match a given criteria specified by the filter.

/FO *format*   Specifies the output format. Valid values include: TABLE, LIST, and CSV.

/NH   Specifies that the "Column Header" should not be displayed in the output. Valid only for TABLE and CSV formats.

/?   Displays the help information.

For example, to show all processes consuming 15,000 KB of memory or more, execute the following command:

```
tasklist /fi "memusage ge 15000"
```

The output of this command is shown in Figure 14.1. Note that the Mem Usage column shows only values greater than or equal to 15,000. This command can help you locate processes consuming large amounts of memory. You could alternatively

---

> Command parameters are also called command-line switches. They often switch command features on or off.

filter by the CPUTIME to locate processes consuming large amount of processor time. For example, you may want to see any processes that have consumed more than 1 minute of CPU time. This command would look like the following:

```
tasklist /fi "cputime ge 00:01:00"
```

```
Administrator: C:\Windows\system32\cmd.exe
C:\Users\Administrator>tasklist /fi "memusage gt 15000"

Image Name                     PID Session Name     Session#    Mem Usage
========================= ======== ================ =========== ============
lsass.exe                      536 Services                  0     30,820 K
svchost.exe                    888 Services                  0     15,548 K
svchost.exe                    940 Services                  0     31,976 K
svchost.exe                    284 Services                  0     17,340 K
Microsoft.ActiveDirectory     1408 Services                  0     38,032 K
dfsrs.exe                     1480 Services                  0     17,880 K
dns.exe                       1536 Services                  0    161,236 K
inetinfo.exe                  1584 Services                  0     31,392 K
MsDtsSrvr.exe                 1672 Services                  0     21,852 K
sqlservr.exe                  1980 Services                  0     98,192 K
SMSvcHost.exe                 2044 Services                  0     24,548 K
WSSADMIN.EXE                  2120 Services                  0     17,800 K
OWSTIMER.EXE                  2364 Services                  0    167,512 K
svchost.exe                   2720 Services                  0     16,884 K
WebAnalyticsService.exe       2844 Services                  0    140,548 K
SMSvcHost.exe                 2980 Services                  0     18,420 K
svchost.exe                   3576 Services                  0     20,312 K
mssearch.exe                  2360 Services                  0     46,712 K
w3wp.exe                      3068 Services                  0    165,560 K
w3wp.exe                      4180 Services                  0    242,104 K
explorer.exe                  4644 Console                   1     36,464 K

C:\Users\Administrator>
```

FIGURE 14.1 Viewing processes using more than 15,000 KB of memory

Using the *SC* Command

The sc command is used for service configuration and control. You can use it to perform several tasks, including:

You may remember from Chapter 2 that the net start and net stop commands can be used to start and stop services as well.

▶ Start and stop services with the start and stop parameters.

▶ View the status or extended status of a service with the query and queryex parameters.

▶ Modify the Windows accessible configuration settings for a service with the config parameter.

The Windows accessible configuration settings include things like the startup type (Automatic, Delayed, Manual, and Disabled), the binary or executable path name, and the type of service (kernel mode service, file system service, etc.).

▶ Configure settings for service failure, such as reset, reboot or run a command, with the failure parameter.

Several additional parameters are available for the sc command. To see them, simply execute the sc /? command.

As an example of usage, the following command sets the startup type to Automatic for the Windows Remote Management (WinRM) service:

```
sc config winrm start= demand
```

Using the *TaskKill* Command

The space between the start= parameter and the auto keyword is required.

The taskkill command is a very simple command. Administrators use it to end processes from the Command Prompt. It supports many of the same parameters as the tasklist command. In fact, its greatest power lies in the ability to kill multiple tasks at once using filters. In most cases, however, it is used to end a single task or process. For example, to kill the notepad.exe process, if it is running, execute the following command:

```
taskkill /im notepad.exe
```

The /im parameter indicates that the image name or executable name is to follow. You can also kill tasks with the process ID of the task using the /pid parameter. Adding the /f parameter will force the process to close. For example, if Notepad is open and you have changed the contents of the active text file, the process will not willingly close. With the /f parameter, the process will close and the changes will be lost.

Using the *Shutdown* Command

In many cases, you will want to shut down or restart a server. You may shut down the server to replace hardware or add hardware with the intention of improving performance. You may restart the server after making changes so that the new changes can take effect. Either way, the shutdown command is used to either shut down or restart the server.

The shutdown command supports many command-line parameters; however, the most frequently used are /r, /s, /m, /t, and /f. These parameters are defined in the following list:

/r   Shut down and restart the computer.

/s   Shut down the computer.

/m \\\computer   Specify the target computer.

/t xxx   Set the time-out period before shutdown to *xxx* seconds. The valid range is 0 to 315360000 (10 years), with a default of 30. If the timeout period is greater than 0, the /f parameter is implied.

/f   Force running applications to close without forewarning users. The
/f parameter is implied when a value greater than 0 is specified for the /t
parameter.

For example, the following command will shut down and restart the server in
90 seconds and force the closure of any running processes:

```
shutdown /r /t 90 /f
```

Figure 14.2 shows the Command Prompt command after being executed in
the background with the popup dialog that displays the shutdown message. To
abort a shutdown, execute the shutdown /a command.

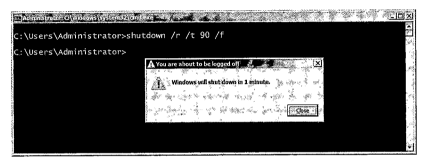

FIGURE 14.2 Executing a shutdown command on Windows Server

Using the *SystemInfo* Command

The systeminfo command is used to gather and display information about
the software and hardware in a Windows machine. When the /s *system_name*
parameter is used, it can display information about the local machine (which is
the default) or a remote machine.

Listing 14.1 shows the output of the systeminfo /fo list command. As you
can see, the command provides information about the machine name, operating system version, installation date, processor memory, hotfixes installed, and
network adapters.

Listing 14.1: The Output of the systeminfo Command

```
Host Name:              SERVER1
OS Name:                Microsoft Windows Server 2008 R2 Enterprise
OS Version:             6.1.7600 N/A Build 7600
OS Manufacturer:        Microsoft Corporation
OS Configuration:       Primary Domain Controller
```

```
OS Build Type:            Multiprocessor Free
Registered Owner:         Windows User
Registered Organization:
Product ID:               55041-507-0544026-84394
Original Install Date:    12/22/2010, 9:17:27 AM
System Boot Time:         4/20/2011, 5:55:12 AM
System Manufacturer:      VMware, Inc.
System Model:             VMware Virtual Platform
System Type:              x64-based PC
Processor(s):             4 Processor(s) Installed.
              [01]: Intel64 Family 6 Model 23 Stepping 7 GenuineIntel ~3570 Mhz
              [02]: Intel64 Family 6 Model 23 Stepping 7 GenuineIntel ~3570 Mhz
              [03]: Intel64 Family 6 Model 23 Stepping 7 GenuineIntel ~3570 Mhz
              [04]: Intel64 Family 6 Model 23 Stepping 7 GenuineIntel ~3570 Mhz
BIOS Version:             Phoenix Technologies LTD 6.00, 9/18/2009
Windows Directory:        C:\Windows
System Directory:         C:\Windows\system32
Boot Device:              \Device\HarddiskVolume1
System Locale:            en-us;English (United States)
Input Locale:             en-us;English (United States)
Time Zone:                (UTC-05:00) Eastern Time (US & Canada)
Total Physical Memory:    4,095 MB
Available Physical Memory: 2,033 MB
Virtual Memory: Max Size: 8,189 MB
Virtual Memory: Available: 4,949 MB
Virtual Memory: In Use:   3,240 MB
Page File Location(s):    C:\pagefile.sys
Domain:                   SharePoint.local
Logon Server:             \\SERVER1
Hotfix(s):                6 Hotfix(s) Installed.
                          [01]: KB974405
                          [02]: KB2032276
                          [03]: KB2079403
                          [04]: KB2207559
                          [05]: KB2207566
                          [06]: KB2286198
Network Card(s):          1 NIC(s) Installed.
                          [01]: Intel(R) PRO/1000 MT Network Connection
                                Connection Name: Local Area Connection
                                DHCP Enabled:     No
                                IP address(es)
                                [01]: 192.168.10.99
                                [02]: fe80::196c:b3da:a400:a9e3
```

Using the *TypePerf* Command

The final Command Prompt command related to performance is the typeperf command. This command allows you to view the values of performance counters at the Command Prompt. To use TypePerf, you must know the name of the performance counter you want to view. Dozens of counters are available on every Windows system, and when you install additional services such as SQL Server or SharePoint, they may add additional counters.

The good news is that you can output a list of available counters with their descriptions using the typeperf -q command. You may want to redirect the output of the command to a file by executing the following command:

```
typeperf -q > counters.txt
```

The preceding command will create a text file named counters.txt containing all of the counters and descriptions.

> Performance counters are defined and described in the section titled "Understanding Performance Counters."

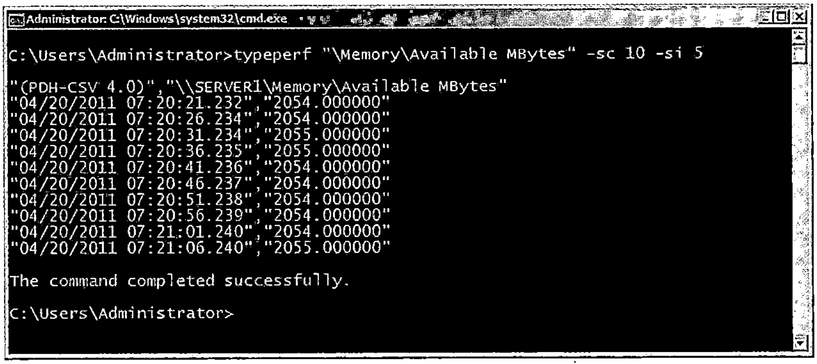

FIGURE 14.3 Using the typeperf command to view the Available Mbytes performance counter

Now that you have a list of the counters, you can view any counter you want. For example, the following command will show the values in the \Processor Information(*)\%Processor Time counter.

```
typeperf "\Processor Information(*)\% Processor Time"
```

By default, the typeperf command continuously lists the counter value every second until you press Ctrl+C to interrupt the output. You can use the -si switch to specify the frequency of the output and the -sc switch to specify the number of samples to take. For example, the following command will check the value of the \Memory\Available Mbytes counter every 5 seconds and will output the value ten times:

```
typeperf "\Memory\Available MBytes" -sc 10 -si 5
```

Figure 14.3 shows the output of the preceding command. The default output uses the comma-separated value (CSV) format, but you can change this format with the -f parameter, if you like.

Resource Monitor

The Resource Monitor, also called resmon, is used to view data related to the current performance of a Windows system. It includes five tabs, as shown in Figure 14.4. The tabs are described as follows:

Overview   The Overview tab shows summary information for the core performance-related components in a computer system: CPU, Disk, Network, and Memory. Additionally, you can see a line graph of utilization for each component on the right side.

CPU   The CPU tab includes performance information specific to the CPU, including processes, services handles, and modules. *Handles* are pointers that refer to system objects like files, Registry keys, and folders. *Modules* are helper files and programs, which are usually installed as dynamic link libraries (DLLs). Additionally, the sidebar line graphs are all changed to show information related to CPU usage.

Memory   The Memory tab shows the processes running and the memory they have consumed. Additionally, a graphical display of memory assignment is presented. The sidebar line graphs are changed to show information related to memory performance.

Disk   The Disk tab shows disk access activity and available storage space. You can view the activity by process so that you can locate processes performing heavy disk operations. The sidebar graphs are changed to reflect disk performance information.

Network   The Network tab is the right-most tab in the interface, and it shows information related to networking communications. You can view network traffic by process and also see the active TCP connections. The Listening Ports section shows the processes running on your computer system and the TCP or UDP ports on which they are listening. The sidebar line graphs are changed to show information related to network performance.

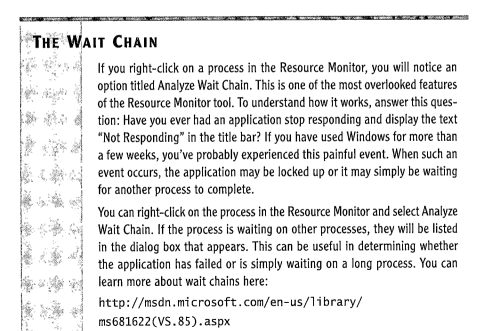

FIGURE 14.4 The Resource Monitor on Windows Server 2008 R2

THE WAIT CHAIN

If you right-click on a process in the Resource Monitor, you will notice an option titled Analyze Wait Chain. This is one of the most overlooked features of the Resource Monitor tool. To understand how it works, answer this question: Have you ever had an application stop responding and display the text "Not Responding" in the title bar? If you have used Windows for more than a few weeks, you've probably experienced this painful event. When such an event occurs, the application may be locked up or it may simply be waiting for another process to complete.

You can right-click on the process in the Resource Monitor and select Analyze Wait Chain. If the process is waiting on other processes, they will be listed in the dialog box that appears. This can be useful in determining whether the application has failed or is simply waiting on a long process. You can learn more about wait chains here:

http://msdn.microsoft.com/en-us/library/
ms681622(VS.85).aspx

Performance Monitor

The Performance Monitor is really just a prebuilt console that uses the System Monitor, which is an ActiveX control that ships with all Windows systems. ActiveX controls can be added to other applications to provide enhanced functionality. The System Monitor tool is used to analyze live performance data, log performance data over time, log performance data when events occur, and fire alerts when performance counters report outside of specified thresholds.

> You can launch the Performance Monitor using several methods. One of the simplest methods is to click Start, type perfmon, and press Enter.

WHAT'S IT CALLED?

Over the years, Microsoft has changed the name used to refer to the System Monitor shortcut. For example, in Windows NT it was known as the Performance Monitor and it was a standalone application. In Windows 2000 and Server 2003, it was simply called Performance, and the shortcut named Performance was actually a link to an MMC that loaded the System Monitor ActiveX control among other snap-ins. In Windows Server 2008, it was called the Reliability and Performance Monitor and the System Monitor was a very small subset of the default snap-ins in the console. Now, in Windows Server 2008 R2, it is known as Performance Monitor once again, so we've now gone full circle. Isn't life with software vendors wonderful?

> An ActiveX control is a programmer's dream. It allows the programmer to insert functionality into his application without having to write all the code himself.

The ActiveX control can be used from within applications as well as the Microsoft Management Console (MMC) that exists by default after installation. Additionally, you can snap it into a custom console that you use with other snap-ins to build a performance and troubleshooting environment that meets your needs.

Configuring the System Monitor will vary depending on your objectives. When you want to monitor live activity, you will use it in one way; and when you want to log activity to be analyzed at a later time, you will use it in another way. Newer Windows systems use Data Collector Sets instead of individual performance logs, but the old performance logs are still buried in there. I'll show you how to get to them in the section titled "Capturing and Logging Performance Data" later in this chapter.

When you want to include the System Monitor in a customized Microsoft Management Console (MMC), you will add it as a snap-in. The process is not as intuitive as you might first think, but it becomes clearer when you remember

that the System Monitor is really just an ActiveX control. To create a custom
MMC with the System Monitor loaded, follow this procedure:

1. Open an existing MMC by double-clicking it. You can also create a new
   MMC by selecting Start ➢ Run and then running MMC.EXE from the
   Run dialog.

2. Click the File menu, and select Add/Remove Snap-in.

3. Click the Add button.

4. Select ActiveX Control in the Available Stand-alone Snap-ins area, and
   click the Add button to launch the Insert ActiveX Control Wizard.

5. Click Next in the Insert ActiveX Control Wizard.

6. In the Control Type area, scroll down and select the System Monitor
   Control, and then click the Next button.

7. Type a name for the System Monitor, or accept the default of System
   Monitor Control, and click Finish.

8. Click Close in the Add Stand-alone Snap-In dialog.

9. Click OK in the Add/Remove Snap-in dialog.

After completing the steps in this procedure, you can click on the System
Monitor control in the left pane and then use it in the right pane. You will need
to add the performance counters you want to view. In this mode, you can't log
data; you can only view live results as shown in Figure 14.5.

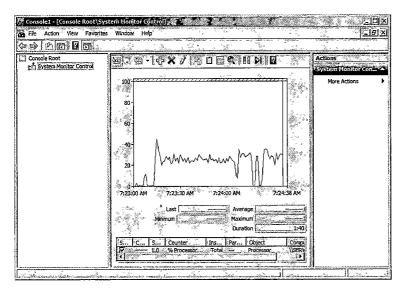

FIGURE 14.5 Using the custom MMC with the System Monitor Control to view live data

Understanding Performance Counters

Remember that additional performance counters can be added to the server when you install additional roles or services such as IIS, Exchange Server, SharePoint, SQL Server, or Active Directory Domain Services.

The Performance Monitor is used to gather the values of *performance counters,* which are memory resident values for different system metrics. Performance counters exist for the network adapters, CPUs, memory, hard disks, and services on your server. The counters include descriptions within the Performance Monitor and, as you saw earlier in this chapter, these descriptions can also be displayed using the `typeperf` command at the Command Prompt.

Because the CPU, memory, hard disks, and network adapters have the greatest impact on server performance, these counters are the most important. Table 14.1 lists some of the available counters for each of these categories with their descriptions. These counters are useful when analyzing each of these components.

TABLE 14.1 Performance Counters and Descriptions

Object	Counter	Description
CPU (Processor)	Processor/ % Processor Time	The percentage of elapsed time the processor spends to execute a non-idle thread. It is calculated by measuring the percentage of time the processor spends executing the system idle thread and then subtracting that value from 100%. (Each processor has an idle thread that consumes cycles when no other threads are ready to run). If this value is greater than 75–85%, it is an indicator of CPU over utilization.
CPU (Processor)	Processor/ % User Time	The percentage of elapsed time the processor spends in the user mode. User mode is a restricted processing mode designed for applications, environment subsystems, and integral subsystems. The alternative, privileged mode or kernel mode, is designed for operating system components and allows direct access to hardware and all memory. If this value is high (more than 30–40%), then one or more applications is consuming excessive processor time.
CPU (Processor)	Processor/ % Interrupt Time	The time the processor spends receiving and servicing hardware interrupts during sample intervals. This value is an indirect indicator of the activity of devices that generate interrupts, such as the system clock, the mouse, disk drivers, data communication lines, network interface cards, and other peripheral devices. These devices normally interrupt the processor when they have completed a task or require attention. If this value is greater than 15%, it may indicate a hardware failure.

(Continues)

TABLE 14.1: *(Continued)*

Object	Counter	Description
CPU (Processor)	System/ Processor Queue Length	The number of threads in the processor queue. There is a single queue for processor time even on computers with multiple processors. Therefore, if a computer has multiple processors, you need to divide this value by the number of processors servicing the workload. If this value is greater than two times the number of CPUs for more than a short period of time, it indicates CPU overutilization.
Memory	Memory/ % Committed Bytes in Use	The ratio of Committed Bytes to the Commit Limit. Committed memory is the physical memory in use for which space has been reserved in the virtual memory paging file should it need to be written to disk. The commit limit is determined by the size of the paging file. The result is the amount of virtual memory in active use. If this value is greater than 75–80%, it indicates that the server has insufficient memory.
Memory	Memory/ Available Mbytes	The amount of physical memory, in megabytes, immediately available for allocation to a process or for system use. If this value is less than 5% of total physical RAM, it indicates that the server has insufficient memory.
Memory	Memory/ Pages/sec	The rate at which pages are read from or written to the virtual memory paging file on disk to resolve hard page faults. A hard page fault occurs when a requested page of memory (a 4 KB chunk of memory) is not found in RAM and must be retrieved from the virtual memory on disk. If this value is greater than 1000, it may indicate a memory leak.
Memory	Memory/Free System Page Table Entries	The number of page table entries not currently in used by the system. This counter displays the last observed value only; it is not an average. If this value is less than 5000, it may indicate a memory leak.
Disk	LogicalDisk/ % Free Space	The percentage of total usable space on the selected logical disk drive that was free. If this value is below 10–15%, you are at risk of running out of free space.

(Continues)

TABLE 14.1: *(Continued)*

Object	Counter	Description
Disk	PhysicalDisk/ Avg. Disk Queue Length	The average number of both read and write requests that were queued for the selected disk during the sample interval. If this value is greater than two times the number of spindles, it means the disk may be a bottleneck.
Network Adapter	Network Interface/Bytes Total/Sec	The rate at which bytes are sent and received over each network adapter. If more than 70% of the interface data rate is consumed, the network is considered saturated.
Network Adapter	Network Interface/ Output Queue Length	The length of the output packet queue (in packets). If this is longer than two, there are delays and the bottleneck should be found and eliminated, if possible.

> Don't be alarmed by the lack of emphasis on display or video performance. In most cases, servers are not dependent on video performance to serve their clients.

Defining a Baseline

A *performance baseline* is a collection of performance statistics taken at a time when the system is performing optimally. This baseline can be created using the Performance Monitor by collecting relevant performance counter values related to the disk, CPU, memory, and network. In fact, you could collect the twelve counters listed in Table 14.1 and use that as your baseline.

The baseline is used to analyze performance in the future. You can create a new collection of performance counters and then compare it against the baseline to locate variances. For example, did the CPU % Processor Time average 43 percent during the baseline, but it now averages 76 percent? A variance like this indicates significant changes in the CPU utilization on the server. If you have not added more users or processes to the server, look for suspect processes running on the server. A well-meaning administrator may have added a new process to the server without realizing the impact it would have.

The baseline can also be used to identify high and low utilization times. If you need to schedule a batch job, such as a backup, it is best to schedule it during a low-utilization time window. For example, if you create the performance baseline by monitoring for an entire day, you may notice that CPU utilization averages only 8 percent during the hours from 11 P.M. and 7 A.M. This time window would be a good time to schedule tasks that will impact the performance of the server.

> *Malware* is software that is installed on your system with ill intent, such as a virus or spyware. Malware often causes increased CPU utilization and memory consumption.

Developing Monitoring Points

When you use the Performance Monitor, you want to ensure that you use it with the proper methods and processes. This means that you must select the right monitoring point. As an example, this section uses a SharePoint 2010 installation to illustrate the importance of developing the right monitoring points.

SharePoint 2010 uses three server types to provide the services it offers. These three SharePoint server types are:

Web Front End (WFE)   The WFE server is the one that is accessed by the users. It runs IIS as the web server and serves the web pages to the clients. It interacts with the application and database servers to access services and data they provide. For example, the WFE will provide the search page to the user; however, when the user sends a search request to the WFE server, the WFE server forwards the request to the proper application server that is running the search service.

Application Server   The application server is the server that runs the services for SharePoint 2010. For example, it runs the search service to perform searches and indexes on data sources such as web pages, shared folders, and databases. It also runs Excel Services to perform Excel calculation in the web browser. In other words, the application server is the real work horse in SharePoint 2010.

Database Server   The database server, which is always SQL Server in SharePoint 2010, is the storage location for the SharePoint sites content and configuration settings. One or more content databases store the content for the SharePoint sites. Additional databases are used to store search-related information.

Developing or determining monitoring points is all about defining where you should do performance analysis in order to resolve performance problems. For example, if searches are slow, what server should be analyzed to improve the performance of the search engine? If typical page views are slow, what server should be analyzed to improve the performance of standard page views? To answer these questions, you'll need to answer the following questions:

- ▶ What database server is used for the SharePoint site in question?

- ▶ What server acts as the search server for the SharePoint site in question?

- ▶ What server manages the SharePoint site in question?

The database server must be known because many performance problems that occur in SharePoint farms originate in the backend database. If the database is

> SharePoint 2010 is Microsoft's content management and business collaboration solution that runs on Windows Server operating systems.

Although not covered in detail in this book, the SQL Server Profiler is an important tool that ships with SQL Server. It is used to monitor the actual queries executed against the server.

slow, nearly everything about the SharePoint farm will be slow. To see this, use the SQL Server Profiler and monitor the requests made of the SQL Server during active use of the SharePoint site. You'll see that nearly every click requires one or more database reads. When database access is slow, you need to monitor the SQL Server database servers.

The search server is also important. This is the server running the search service and crawling the SharePoint sites and other content sources. In many cases, a single server will be configured to crawl content sources spanning multiple servers. If the performance is not sufficient, you may need to distribute the search functions across multiple servers. When search performance is slow, you need to monitor the application servers running the search service.

Of course, the server managing or hosting the problematic SharePoint site (meaning the IIS server running the application and site) could be the performance bottleneck. In such a scenario, you should establish the site server as the monitoring point.

Ultimately, the monitoring point selection is a simple task. Determine which server most directly impacts the performance or stability of the issue in question and then monitor that server. To do this, you must understand the applications and services running on each server and how they are utilized by users and other servers on the network.

Viewing Live Performance Data

You can view live performance data in the Performance Monitor on Windows Server machines. The live data shows the values of monitored counters moment-by-moment. Live monitoring is useful when you know something is about to happen and you want to see the value of various counters as it happens. For example, if searches are slow, you may want to watch live counter values while searches are performed. This can help you locate potential sources of the search performance problem.

To view live performance counters, follow this procedure:

1. Select Start ➢ Administrative Tools ➢ Performance Monitor.

2. Expand Monitoring Tools ➢ Performance Monitor.

3. Click the green plus sign (+) icon to add a counter.

4. In the Add Counters dialog, scroll down through the Available counters list, and click the plus sign (+) beside the Processor entry to expand the list of counters within the Processor collection.

5. Choose the % Interrupt Time counter and ensure that _Total is selected in the Instances of Selected Object section, and then click the Add button.

6. Choose the % User Time counter and ensure that _Total is selected in the Instances of Selected Object section, and then click the Add button.

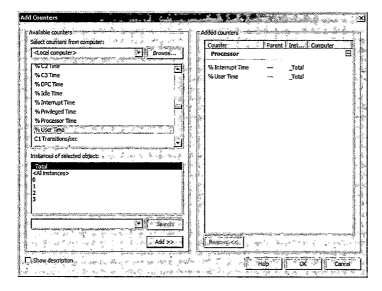

7. Click OK to close the Add Counters dialog.

8. Monitor the values for the counter by clicking on the counter in the list at the bottom of the Performance Monitor screen.

Capturing and Logging Performance Data

In addition to monitoring live performance data, you can log the performance statistics by creating a Data Collector Set (DCS). A DCS is a collection of performance counter values and possible trace values from lower-level operating system actions. The Performance Monitor always includes two DCSs out-of-the-box and may include more depending on the components installed on the server. For example, an AD domain controller will include a DCS named Active Directory Diagnostics.

The two built-in DCSs that are always included are the System Diagnostics and System Performance DCSs. You cannot alter either DCS, but you can run them in order to generate reports.

You can also create a custom DCS to log the performance data of interest to you. For example, when you want to log SharePoint statistics over time, you will need to create a custom DCS. To create a DCS, following this procedure:

Versions of Windows prior to Windows Vista and Windows Server 2008 used performance logs instead of Data Collector Sets.

When creating a DCS in a production environment, you can use any name you choose; however, the later procedures in this chapter use the name MyCustomDCS.

1. Launch the Performance Monitor.

2. Expand Data Collector Sets ➤ User Defined.

3. Right-click on the User Defined node, and select New ➤ Data Collector Set.

4. On the Create New Data Collector Set screen, name the DCS MyCustomDCS.

5. Select Create from a template, and click Next.

6. Choose the System Performance template, and click Next.

7. Accept the default data root directory, and click Next.

8. Accept the default Run As option, and click Finish.

The preceding procedure simply created a DCS. Now you can customize it to your liking with this procedure:

1. If necessary, open the Performance Monitor and expand Data Collector Sets ➤ User Defined ➤ MyCustomDCS.

2. Double-click on the Performance Counter object in the MyCustomDCS DCS to open the Performance Counter Properties dialog.

3. Click the \UDPv4* Performance Counter item, and click Remove to remove it from the list.

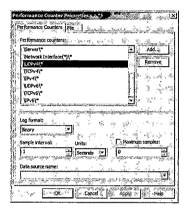

4. Repeat step 3 for the \TCPv4*, \IPv4*, \UDPv6*, \TCPv6*, and \IPv6* items.

5. Still in the Performance Counter Properties dialog, change the Log Format to Comma Separated.

   This change will allow many different applications to parse and process the log data, such as Excel or Crystal Reports.

6. Click OK.

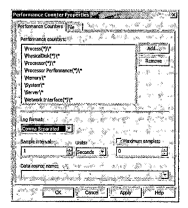

7. Right-click on the MyCustomDCS DCS node, and select Properties.

8. In the MyCustomDCS Properties dialog, select the Stop Condition tab.

9. Change the Overall Duration value to 60 Minutes, and click OK. This will allow the DCS to run for one hour.

10. Right-click on the MyCustomDCS DCS node, and select Start

After completing this procedure, you will have a new DCS. When you run the DCS, it will run for 60 minutes before you can view the report.

Viewing DCS Reports

The Performance Monitor is also the tool used to view the reports. In addition to the graphical view of reports, you can open the performance counter log in tools like Microsoft Excel in order to generate graphs and analyze the data in detail. To view a report created from a DCS, follow this procedure:

1. If necessary, open the Performance Monitor and expand Reports ≻ User Defined ≻ MyCustomDCS.

2. Select the report with the newest data by double-clicking on it.

3. View the graphical report that is displayed.

Sixty minutes is a good starting point for evaluating performance on a server. It typically provides a good sample of performance data. In some instances, you may choose to monitor for more than one hour.

Virtualization and Performance

Why cover virtualization in a chapter on performance tuning? This question is important, and to answer it you need to understand how virtualization relates to performance. Most of this chapter has focused on what to do when your servers are overburdened, but another problem has surfaced in the past few years and that is that many servers are underutilized. Administrators may install a quad core multiprocessor server with 16 GB of RAM and then find that they are using only 15 to 20 percent of the available resources. Using virtualization, you can use these resources for productive services and tasks.

To help you understand virtualization, this section provides the following information topics:

- ▶ Exploring virtualization modes
- ▶ Understanding Microsoft virtualization solutions
- ▶ Migrating from physical to virtual and vice versa

Exploring Virtualization Modes

Virtualization is the technology used to allow multiple operating systems to run on the same physical server concurrently. While dual-booting allows you to reboot a server into different operating systems, virtualization allows you to run these operating systems at the same time. Figure 14.6 shows the concept of virtualization. Notice that a single host (physical server), running Hyper-V in this case, actually runs multiple virtual machines with Linux, Windows Server 2008 with Exchange Server, Windows Server 2008 with IIS, Windows Server 2008 Active Directory and even a client test machine. The machine that runs the virtualization software is referred to as the *host*. The virtual machines run as *guest* operating systems on the host.

> Virtualization should never be confused with multi-booting or dual-booting. The latter technologies require a reboot to enter different operating systems. The former allows multiple systems to run simultaneously.

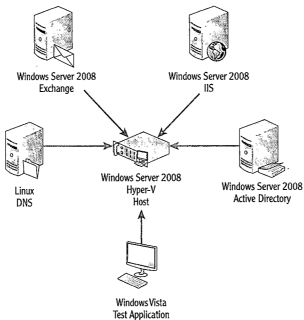

Windows Server 2008
Exchange

Windows Server 2008
IIS

Linux
DNS

Windows Server 2008
Hyper-V
Host

Windows Server 2008
Active Directory

Windows Vista
Test Application

FIGURE 14.6 Virtualization conceptualized

Several virtualization technologies exist. Microsoft provides virtualization solutions, but other vendors provide solutions as well. Microsoft solutions are discussed in the next section. Other virtualization solutions include:

- ▶ VMware ESX
- ▶ VMware Workstation, Fusion, and Player

► Parallels (Mac-only virtualization software)

► VirtualBox

If you want to learn more about the VMware solutions, visit www.vmware.com. To learn more about Parallels for the Mac, visit www.parallels.com. More information about VirtualBox can be found at www.virtualbox.org.

Administrators can implement virtualization in different ways depending on the software they use to create the host server. The two primary options are hypervisor-based solutions and OS-layered solutions. Virtualization software that runs in hypervisor mode typically performs much better than OS-layered solutions. Figure 14.7 shows the difference between the two and illustrates why one is better than the other.

VirtualBox is an excellent open-source virtualization solution. It runs on Windows, Linux, and Mac computers and supports running guest operating systems, including multiple Windows and Linux versions.

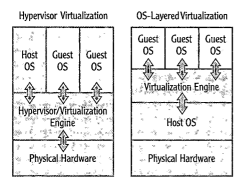

FIGURE 14.7 Hypervisor-based virtualization compared with OS-layered virtualization

The characteristics of hyper-visor-based virtualization mode and OS-layered virtualization mode are addressed in the following list:

OS-Layered Virtualization Mode   When OS-layering is used, the OS is the foundation layer running on the hardware. On top of this layer, you run a virtualization engine; and in the virtualization engine, you run virtual machines. Because of the extra layers, this mode does not perform as well as hypervisor-based virtualization mode. Examples of OS-layered virtualization solutions include Windows Virtual PC, Virtual PC 2007, Virtual Server 2005, and VMware Workstation.

Hypervisor-Based Virtualization Mode   Hypervisor-based virtualization places the virtualization engine directly on the hardware. It is the layer between the hardware and the host OS. The performance of hypervisor-based virtualization solutions is much better than OS-layered solutions. Examples of hypervisor-based virtualization include Hyper-V and VMware ESX servers.

Hypervisor-based virtualization solutions are often called *bare metal virtualization* because the virtual management layer runs directly on the hardware.

Understanding Microsoft Virtualization Solutions

Microsoft offers two new virtualization products starting with Windows Server 2008 and Windows 7. They also offer older virtualization software for previous version of Windows. The following current product offerings make up the core of Microsoft's virtualization solutions:

Hyper-V   Hyper-V is a hypervisor-based virtualization solution from Microsoft. It runs on Windows Server 2008 and Windows Server 2008 R2. It supports virtual networks, virtual hard drives, snapshots, and saved states. If you utilize the System Center Virtual Machine Manager (SCVMM) for administration of the Hyper-V environment, you can centrally manage your virtualization infrastructure and support features like the quick migration of virtual machine from one host to another and self-provisioning of virtual machines so that users can create their own virtual servers as needed.

Windows Virtual PC   Windows Virtual PC is the new version of Virtual PC for use on Windows 7. An important use of Windows Virtual PC is for the provisioning of XP mode. XP mode allows older applications that may not otherwise work to run on Windows 7 in an XP virtual machine while appearing to run locally on the Windows 7 Desktop. Windows Virtual PC can also be used to run many different operating systems as virtual machines.

The following older products still provide virtualization functionality on older Windows operating systems:

Virtual Server   Virtual Server 2005 and Virtual Server 2005 R2 are the predecessors to Hyper-V. They are OS-based virtualization solutions and do not perform as well as Hyper-V; however, they are the only options available from Microsoft for Windows Server 2003 R2 and earlier.

Virtual PC   Virtual PC 2007 is a desktop virtualization solution like Windows Virtual PC, but it runs on earlier versions of Windows such as Vista and XP. It can run many different operating systems in virtual machines.

When creating virtual machines, you must consider the following components:

Virtual Hard Drives   Virtual Hard Drives (VHDs) are files on the physical disk that represent hard drives to the virtual machines. For example, if you need a 10 GB hard drive in a virtual machine, you can create a 10 GB VHD file and use it as the virtual hard drive for the virtual machine. When creating VHDs, you

> Hyper-V R2 is the version of Hyper-V in Windows Server 2008 R2. It adds new features including live migration for moving running VMs from host to host and dynamic storage for hot swappable storage.

> XP mode is supported only on Windows 7. It is not supported on Windows Vista installations.

> When creating a virtual machine, you decide whether the VHD is *dynamic* and grows as needed to a maximum size or is *static* and consumes the full specified maximum size from the start.

can either indicate that they consume all space defined at the time of creation or that they consume only the space required based on the data in the VHD at that time. The VHD file can grow over time to the maximum size specified when it is configured for dynamic growth.

Virtual Memory   Virtual memory must be considered from two perspectives: memory assigned to the virtual machine and OS virtual memory. When creating a virtual machine, you can assign memory to it. This memory is sometimes called virtual memory, but the memory you assign to the virtual machine will be allocated from physical memory when the machine starts.

Be aware that if the OS virtual machine uses excessive virtual memory stored on the VHD files, just as an operating system running on a physical machine uses virtual memory, it can degrade the disk performance significantly. It is usually even more important to reduce the use of OS virtual memory within virtual machines than it is in physical machines.

OS virtual memory refers to the use of hard drive space for temporary storage of data to allow your system to use more memory than is available in physical RAM.

Virtual Networks   Virtual machines can access the network just like physical machines. In fact, virtual machines appear just like physical machines when you connect to them across the network. Microsoft Hyper-V supports three different virtual network types.

>**External Network**   Binds to the physical network adapter card and allows communications on the real network to which the host is connected.

>**Internal Network**   Allows communications only between the virtual machines and the parent partition (host OS) on the host server.

>**Private Network**   Allows only communications between the virtual machines; the parent partition is not accessible.

In addition to these three common network types, you can configure a *dedicated network*. In this case, you assign a single network adapter to a single guest virtual machine. No other virtual machine can use that adapter. If you have several adapters in the server, this method can be used to improve server performance.

Recoverability   Recoverability can be achieved in simple Hyper-V deployments using *snapshots* and *saved states*:

>**Snapshot**   A snapshot is a point-in-time capture of a virtual machine. You can create a snapshot and then revert to it later if a new driver or configuration setting causes problems within the virtual machine.

Saved States   Saved states are different than snapshots. You can shut off a virtual machine and indicate that you want to save its state. This is similar to placing a laptop in the hibernation state. When you power the virtual machine back on at a later time, it will restore the saved state rather than going through the normal boot process.

Migrating Between Physical and Virtual

The final topic you must consider when planning for virtualization is the conversion of physical machines to virtual machines or virtual machines to physical machines. Physical-to-virtual (referenced as P-to-V or P2V) is the process used to take existing physical server or client installations and convert them into virtual machines. The basic process involved requires these steps:

1. Strip out all unique hardware drivers and security identifiers.

2. Convert the drive to a VHD.

3. Load the VHD as the drive for a new virtual machine.

4. Boot the OS and load the Hyper-V-specific hardware drivers.

The SCVMM tool can perform these actions for you automatically. You can select a server on the network and have it converted to a virtual machine automatically.

The reverse process is virtual-to-physical (referenced as V-to-P or V2P). The process is very similar, except it requires imaging tools. The process looks like this:

1. Strip out all unique hardware drivers and security identifiers.

2. Convert the VHD to a drive image.

3. Load the image onto a physical machine.

4. Boot the OS and load the physical machine-specific hardware drivers.

An additional tool that is helpful when planning virtualization is the Microsoft Assessment and Planning (MAP) Toolkit. The MAP Toolkit can inventory the servers on your network and even recommend servers that are good candidates for conversion to virtual machines. The tool is a free download from Microsoft located at:

    http://technet.microsoft.com/en-us/library/bb977556.aspx

Every Windows installation has a unique identifier associated with it that identifies it on the network. This identifier must be changed when it loaded onto a new computer—physical or virtual.

You can use Microsoft's imaging tools to create a Windows Image (WIM) file, or you can use third-party tools, such as Ghost or Drive Image.

As you can see, virtualization is an important part of performance management. To get the best performance out of your servers, you will often use virtualization solutions to fully utilize them. Ultimately, it is one of the most important developments in recent decades in the area of server utilization and performance management.

THE ESSENTIALS AND BEYOND

Performance tuning requires an understanding of the entire system. Administrators should not try to tweak settings or add/remove software until they know the real cause of a performance problem. Several performance analysis tools are included in Windows, including the Resource Monitor, Performance Monitor, and even some Command Prompt utilities. The Resource Monitor is a useful tool that provides a quick reference to current performance conditions on a Windows machine. The Performance Monitor can also be used to view current performance conditions, but one of its greatest capabilities is in monitoring performance for a period of time and then analyzing the reports related to that monitoring period.

While performance tuning is often about reducing the load on servers, many newer servers are very powerful and are actually underutilized. In such scenarios, virtualization can be used to more fully utilize the servers' capacities. Virtualization allows you to run multiple operating systems concurrently on a single host computer. Hyper-V is Microsoft's server-based virtualization solution for Windows Server 2008 and Windows Server 2008 R2. Windows Virtual PC is available for Windows 7 clients.

ADDITIONAL EXERCISES

▶ Use the Resource Monitor to view network activity while downloading a large file from the Internet.

▶ Use the `tasklist` command to view the running processes consuming more than 20,000 KB of RAM.

▶ Use the Performance Monitor to view the values of the \Processor\% Privileged Time counter.

To compare your answers to the author's, please visit:

www.sybex.com/go/winadminessentials

(Continues)

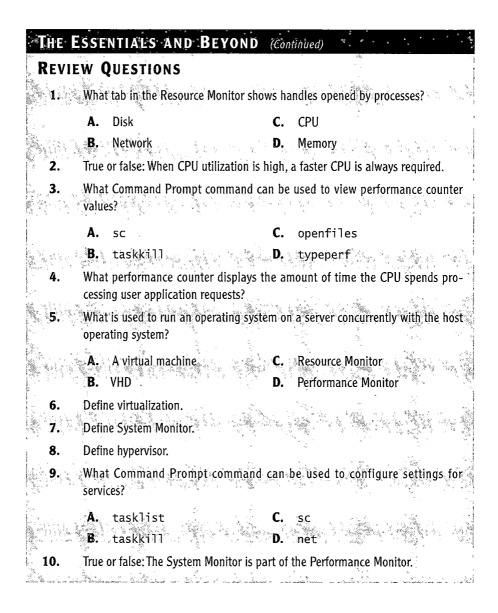

THE ESSENTIALS AND BEYOND *(Continued)*

REVIEW QUESTIONS

1. What tab in the Resource Monitor shows handles opened by processes?

   A. Disk

   B. Network

   C. CPU

   D. Memory

2. True or false: When CPU utilization is high, a faster CPU is always required.

3. What Command Prompt command can be used to view performance counter values?

   A. sc

   B. taskkill

   C. openfiles

   D. typeperf

4. What performance counter displays the amount of time the CPU spends processing user application requests?

5. What is used to run an operating system on a server concurrently with the host operating system?

   A. A virtual machine

   B. VHD

   C. Resource Monitor

   D. Performance Monitor

6. Define virtualization.

7. Define System Monitor.

8. Define hypervisor.

9. What Command Prompt command can be used to configure settings for services?

   A. tasklist

   B. taskkill

   C. sc

   D. net

10. True or false: The System Monitor is part of the Performance Monitor.

CHAPTER 15

Server Maintenance

Server maintenance is an important part of the server administrator's job. Maintenance includes both hardware and software tasks. In this chapter, you will learn about the maintenance responsibilities of a server administrator. These responsibilities include:

▷ **Maintaining the Hardware**

▷ **Planning for Server Downtime**

▷ **Understanding Windows Update**

▷ **Automating with Logs and Alerts**

▷ **Planning for Continuity**

Maintaining the Hardware

The first thing you must consider when maintaining a server is the hardware itself. Different hardware components demand different maintenance tasks. Additionally, you must ensure that the environment accommodates the hardware you are using. The following hardware items should be considered:

Memory   Like all hardware components, you should ensure that the memory chips in the server remain dust free. When dust builds up on the memory chips, they become hot and may even be damaged. For this reason, you should use compressed air to blow out the server cases periodically. In clean environments, this may only be required annually. In manufacturing environments, it may be required much more frequently. An additional memory maintenance task is more of a proactive task and that is to have extra memory on hand in case a memory chip fails.

Disk   The hard drives should be maintained in at least two ways. The first is to periodically defragment the hard drives. This will ensure that the drives perform optimally. The second task, which is not performed in all organizations, is to plan for the replacement of drives. Hard drives have ratings called Mean

Time Between Failure (MTBF), and this rating defines the expected average life of the drive. By planning to replace the drive shortly before this time, you will reduce surprise drive failure occurrences and increase uptime during important business hours.

Removable Drives   Removable drives such as USB, FireWire, and external SATA (eSATA) drives should be maintained in a similar manner to internal hard drives. They are still hard drives and still have MTBF ratings. Additionally, they should be defragmented periodically. Due to the portable nature of these drives, it is not uncommon for them to fail before the MTBF period. If important data is stored on removable drives, it should be duplicated elsewhere.

> If you need to store important data on removable drives, consider an external enclosure that supports RAID.

Processor   Like memory chips, the processor should be kept clean of dust. Additionally, you must ensure that it is properly cooled. This may require upgrading the cooling solution when you upgrade the processor. Vendors typically install a fan or other cooling solution that is ideal for the processor that comes with the server. If you install a faster processor, it may require an improved cooling solution.

Network   Other than dust removal, network adapters require very little maintenance at the hardware level. However, at the software level, it is important to ensure that you are running the best device driver available at the time. Vendors often release three or more new device driver versions after a hardware product is released. These newer drivers often improve performance and fix bugs in the software.

Graphic Cards   Because servers are mostly used for background services, they do not typically require high-end graphics adapters. However, with the advent of desktop virtualization and the desire to perform more graphically intensive tasks in virtual desktops, this is beginning to change. If your server has a powerful video card installed, cleaning and cooling will be an important factor for this device. Additionally, like the network adapter, you should ensure you're running the most stable device drivers available for the graphics card.

Ports   Server ports, including USB, FireWire, eSATA, video, serial, and other ports, should be cleaned of dust periodically. Other than this, maintenance of ports involves the replacement of ports when they fail. Many servers have the ports integrated into the system board and may not have expansion slots for adding new ports. If ports fail in such a server, you will have to replace the system board to recover the failed ports.

Power Usage   One of the most important and often overlooked aspects of running a server room or network operations center is power provisioning. You have probably experienced a problem with insufficient power at home when the breaker box flips a breaker or a power strip is overloaded. These events happen in business installations as well, and it is important to monitor power usage and ensure sufficient power provisioning for day-to-day operations.

Uninterruptible Power Supply (UPS)   UPS units are used to provide power to servers if the power from the electric provider should fail. They are not intended to run the servers for long periods and often provide only sufficient time to shut the servers down cleanly. Organizations that require continued uptime during power failures often install their own power generators in addition to utilizing UPS units. Most modern UPS units connect to servers via the USB port and allow the servers to monitor power failures and take action (such as shutting down the server) if the power fails for more than some defined period of time.

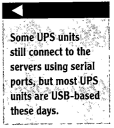

A UPS is also an excellent method of protection against power spikes and sags.

Cooling System   The final component and one that is very important to continued server operations is cooling. Cooling must be considered from two perspectives:

Some UPS units still connect to the servers using serial ports, but most UPS units are USB-based these days.

▶ The first is the proper cooling of the area in which the server's operate.

▶ The second is the cooling of the server internals.

Traditional internal cooling systems use heat sinks and fans to provide airflow. Modern cooling techniques include the use of liquid cooling procedures.

Whatever cooling solution you use, monitoring the temperature of server hardware is important. Regardless of the cooling system, should the environmental cooling solution fail, the servers can overheat. Overheating could potentially damage the servers permanently. So you should ensure that a proper temperature monitoring solution is implemented for the server room and for the servers themselves.

As you can see, many things must be considered when it comes to the server maintenance. If you want to learn more about server hardware maintenance in detail, consider reading *CompTIA Security+ Deluxe Study Guide: SY0-201* by Emmett Dulaney (Sybex, 2008).

32-BIT VERSUS 64-BIT COMPUTING

The landscape of computer processors is changing quickly over to 64-bit computing. It is difficult to purchase a new standard laptop or desktop today that does not include a 64-bit processor. Of course, you can still get 32-bit processors in Netbooks and you can build custom PCs and servers with 32-bit processors, but even that will become more difficult in the coming years. Most recent Microsoft software releases require a 64-bit system or support running on one. Because Windows Server 2008 R2 is 64-bit-only, all future releases will indeed be 64-bit.

Sixty-four-bit computing provides several advantages over 32-bit computing:

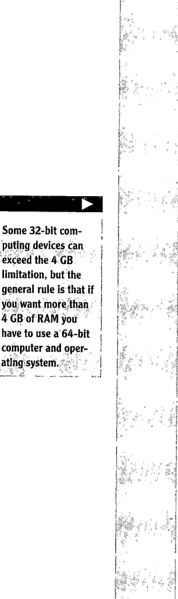

Some 32-bit computing devices can exceed the 4 GB limitation, but the general rule is that if you want more than 4 GB of RAM you have to use a 64-bit computer and operating system.

► You can use more than 4 GB of RAM in the system. This extended RAM support is a very important feature for high-performing application servers—for instance, database servers that access multi-gigabyte or even multi-terabyte databases. Sixty-four-bit processors can theoretically address hundreds of terabytes of RAM; however, the actual amount varies depending on processor design.

► The processor can work with larger chunks of data at a time, which can improve performance for applications that are optimized and compiled for 64-bit computing.

► Because of the preceding two benefits, intensive applications perform much better. As an example, encryption algorithms tested on 64-bit systems have demonstrated performance increases of 3 to 5 times their previous rates. Of course, the typical user running Microsoft Word is not likely to notice any difference in performance.

So what does it mean to move from 32-bit computing to 64-bit computing? The good news is that the interface is no different and the applications work just the same. The only people who really have to worry about the differences are the software developers and administrators. As an administrator, you only have to ensure you are using 64-bit drivers and 64-bit versions of your applications when they are available. Most 64-bit operating systems can still run 32-bit applications, and Windows Server 2008 or Windows Server 2008 R2 running a 64-bit edition is no different.

Planning for Server Downtime

It's time for a reality check. You simply can't keep a server running forever. Eventually, it will have to be taken offline for repair or replacement. As the server administrator, you must be prepared for server downtime. After a server is down for repair or updates, you'll need to reboot it to put it back in service. To be effective, you'll need to understand the boot process so you can trouble-shoot problems that may occur during boot up. In this section, you will review important actions required when you're planning for server down time and you'll learn about the server boot process for Windows servers.

Executing the Planning Actions for Downtime

It is essential that server administrators carefully plan server downtime. Unexpected downtime is very frustrating to users and can cost more in time and money than properly planned downtime. Anytime you must temporarily remove a server from the network, you should perform the following actions:

1. Determine the best time to take the server offline. This is typically a time when fewer users are accessing the services the server offers. It may be late at night or on the weekend, so be prepare to schedule your time at work.

2. Announce the server downtime with as much advanced notice as possible. At least a week is usually suggested. If you announce the downtime more than a week before the scheduled procedure, be sure to remind everyone one week before and again one day before the event.

Many organizations also announce server downtime an hour before the event via email or another method of message delivery in the organization.

3. Inform the appropriate technical support staff ahead of time of their responsibilities during the downtime. These individuals may include help desk personnel who must communicate with users who may call to report issues because they did not receive the advanced notifications. They may also include the administrators who will perform the procedure during the downtime.

4. Make sure to spend time evaluating and estimating the amount of time the procedure will require. You do not want to schedule an event only to have insufficient time to complete the process.

Of course, your specific situation may call for more steps than these, but make sure you follow these steps at a minimum. You might consider developing a roll-back strategy just in case the server upgrade or replacement fails. If you abide by these recommendations and any other internal policies your organization may have, you will experience fewer problems during planned downtime.

Understanding the Windows Server Boot Process

When a Windows server boots, it goes through a standard boot process every time it starts. This process involves testing the system, loading the operating system bootloader, and loading the operating system itself. The first thing that occurs is the loading of the system Basic Input/Output System (BIOS). The BIOS loads the stored configuration for the hardware in the system board of the server. It includes settings that determine whether the system boots from the internal hard drive, the CD/DVD drive, the floppy drive, or external drives. It also configures items such as hardware-assisted virtualization, which is required for Hyper-V, and memory and CPU settings. The BIOS is responsible for configuring or enabling the following items:

Vendors use different BIOS software solutions, and the screens may differ from one server to another. Check your server documentation for specifics on how to use your BIOS.

▶ Storage

▶ Memory

▶ Cache

▶ Ports

▶ Integrated devices such as audio, network, and video adapters

▶ Date and time settings

▶ Power management settings

▶ Hardware-assisted virtualization settings

After the BIOS loads, Power On Self Test (POST) is executed. The POST is responsible for testing the health or operational status of various system components. One of the key actions performed by many POST processes is the testing of memory. You can configure many systems to perform rigorous testing of memory during startup. This is useful when you suspect memory problems, but it should not typically be enabled on production servers. The extended tests simply delay the boot process when everything is working well.

The next action is the loading of the boot sector from the boot device. The boot sector (or bootsector) is configured to load the proper bootloader for the operating system that is installed. The simple role of the boot sector, then, is to load the operating system boot loader.

One kind of boot sector (or boot record) is the Master Boot Record (MBR). The MBR has a partition table that defines the partitions on the drive. The MBR defines the active partition so that the boot process may begin from that partition. Only one partition can be marked active at a single time and that partition is used to boot the operating system.

The Windows bootloader (OSLOADER in Windows Server 2008 and later) uses either the BOOT.INI file or the Boot Configuration Database (BCD) to determine the operating systems installed on the machine and select the default operating system for booting. The BOOT.INI file is used by Windows Server 2003 R2 and earlier. The BCD is used by Windows Server 2008 and later. The BDC is edited using the BCDEDIT Windows application, which is launched from the Command Prompt. BOOT.INI is a simple text file that can be edited with Notepad and other text editors.

Once the appropriate operating system is selected, the bootloader loads the operating system kernel and hands control over to the kernel to boot the operating system.

To configure startup options from within Windows Server 2008 or R2, follow this procedure:

1. Click Start, right-click on Computer, and select Properties.

2. Click the Advanced System Settings link in the left side of the System window that opens.

3. On the Advanced tab, click the Settings button within the Startup And Recovery section.

4. In the Startup And Recovery dialog, configure the settings as required.

From the Startup And Recovery dialog, you can configure any of the following items:

▶ Default operating system

▶ Delay time for the operating system selection menu on a multi-boot system

Seen infrequently today, boot sector viruses target this boot sector. Cleaning the system with the operating system running is difficult, and you must boot from another drive to clean the boot sector.

You can use Safe mode to boot the system with a minimal set of configuration settings. Simply press F8 when you first power on the system to load the boot menu and select Safe Mode.

▶ Delay time for the recovery options menu, when required

▶ System failure actions—such as automatically restarting and performing a *memory dump* (saving debug information into a specified file for troubleshooting)

Understanding Windows Update

The Windows Server operating system must be maintained just like a desktop operating system. Software must be updated for several reasons, including security, stability, and error resolution. If a security vulnerability is discovered in an operating system, device driver, or application, that vulnerability must be corrected through a software update, often referred to as a *patch*. Software is typically installed as compiled executables. As such, most commercial software can't be edited or fixed by users or other programmers while maintaining the support of the vendor. The software vendor must provide a new executable or an update program must be used to modify the existing executable at a binary level. The same type of updates must be used to resolve stability issues and errors.

Window Server can be updated through individual updates or through service packs that continue a compilation of changes. An update may fix a single problem or a small number of problems. A service pack typically includes all patches up to the time of the service pack release and may also include new updates or even new product features.

As you plan your patch management for Windows Servers, you must remember to include all applicable software components—including applications such as Exchange Server, SQL Server, IIS, SharePoint, and any number of additional third-party products. There are three basic options for the patch management.

Manual Patches   Manual patches can be applied to the Windows Server operating system or to other software on the server, such as SharePoint, IIS, SQL Server, or Exchange Server. This method may be useful if you do not use Windows Software Update Services and you need to apply a small number of updates in order to resolve a security or stability problem. In a small environment, manual updates may be an option. In large-scale deployments with dozens of servers, manual patching is simply not feasible due to the administrative interaction required to perform all the other tasks to maintain any given

A memory dump can be analyzed by trained engineers, but most administrators rely on Microsoft support to analyze a memory dump and inform them of the area of problem on their systems.

A system or application can be unstable without generating an error. For example, the system may simply stop responding. These are considered stability issues and are often repaired through software updates.

deployment. However, it is important to know that some patches must be applied manually. For example, SharePoint servers require the administrator to apply the patches manually, although they can be installed automatically.

Windows Update The next viable approach to system updates is through the use of Windows Update. Through Windows Update, you can manually or automatically check for updates. You also can indicate whether the updates will be installed automatically once downloaded. This is a feasible process for medium-sized deployments, but it will not likely serve large-scale deployments well. Windows Update defaults to receiving updates only for the Windows Server components and will not typically cover any auxiliary software that may be installed. In the section titled "Updating with Windows Update," you will see how to run Windows Update and enable updates for additional Microsoft products.

Many server software applications support installing updates or patches that are not applied until the administrator manually applies them.

Windows Server Update Services Windows Server Update Services (WSUS) is used to centrally manage updates and specify the ones you want to deploy to client computers. WSUS supports clients ranging from Windows 2000 Professional to Windows Server 2008 R2. You may install all updates or choose only those you want to install. Figure 15.1 shows the deployment architecture for WSUS. In the section titled "Using Windows Server Update Service," you will learn how to enable WSUS on a Windows Server 2008 R2 server machine. WSUS is an excellent solution for large-scale deployments and can even be used in small deployments with just a few servers and clients.

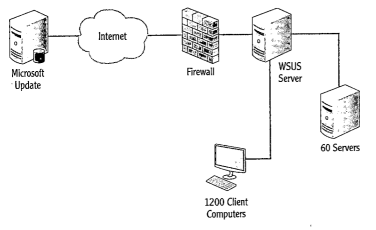

Microsoft Update

Internet

Firewall

WSUS Server

60 Servers

1200 Client Computers

FIGURE 15.1 WSUS implementation architecture

Updating with Windows Update

Windows Update can be used to update Windows server and client computer systems. If you want to receive updates for more than just Windows, you can enable Microsoft Update, which will provide updates for Microsoft Office and many other Microsoft products. The following procedure is used to enable Microsoft Update:

1. Open the Start menu and select All Programs ➤ Windows Update.

2. In the Windows Update screen, click the Find Out More link in the text pane that reads "Get updates for other Microsoft products."

Windows Update

Check for updates for your computer
Always install the latest updates to enhance your computer's security and performance.

Check for updates

Most recent check for updates: 9/16/2010 at 8:08 PM
Updates were installed: 9/16/2010 at 8:09 PM. View update history
You receive updates: For Windows only.

Get updates for other Microsoft products. Find out more

3. When the new Microsoft Update web browser is displayed, click the More Supported link to see the supported products.

4. In the new browser window, read through the list of products that receive updates from Windows Update and then close that window to return to the Microsoft Update window.

5. In the Microsoft Update window, check the "I agree to the Terms of Use for Microsoft Update" check box and click Next.

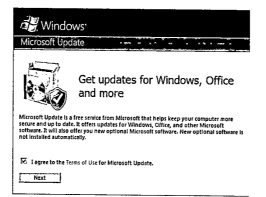

Windows·
Microsoft Update

Get updates for Windows, Office and more

Microsoft Update is a free service from Microsoft that helps keep your computer more secure and up to date. It offers updates for Windows, Office, and other Microsoft software. It will also offer you new optional Microsoft software. New optional software is not installed automatically.

☑ I agree to the Terms of Use for Microsoft Update.

Next

6. Select Use Recommended Settings and click Install. If a screen appears asking you to allow the program to make changes to the computer, click Yes.

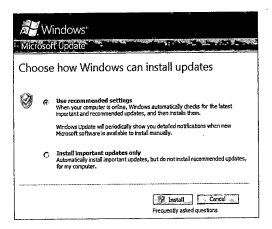

7. The Windows Update screen will reappear and the check for updates will begin automatically.

   You may close all windows because Windows Update is now configured to download updates automatically.

In some cases, you will want to disable automatic updates and configure Windows Update so that it never checks for updates. You would do this if you want to check for updates manually. For example, some organizations assign this responsibility to an administrator. The administrator is required to check for updates at a specific time each week and apply the ones that are important. This is often performed in environments that require high levels of uptime and, therefore, the need the newest stability and security patches, but where they do not want to implement WSUS.

To configure Windows Update for manual updates, you must set it to Never Check For Updates. To do this and then check for updates manually, follow this procedure:

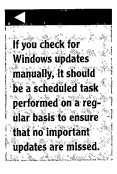

If you check for Windows updates manually, it should be a scheduled task performed on a regular basis to ensure that no important updates are missed.

1. Click Start and select All Programs ➤ Windows Update.

2. From the options list on the left, select Change Settings.

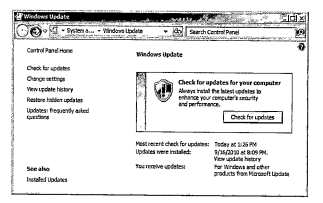

3. From the Important Updates drop-down list, choose Never Check For Updates (Not Recommended), and then click OK.

4. Click the Check For Updates button and wait patiently while the system looks for available updates.

5. On the results screen, click the Important Updates link.

6. Choose the updates you want to install from the listed updates, and then click OK.

7. Click Install Updates to install the selected updates.

Using Windows Server Update Service

WSUS is a service that runs on a set of Windows servers and acts as an infrastructure that provides an internal source of updates to the other servers and clients on your Microsoft network. The benefits of WSUS over manual patches or direct use of Windows Update are twofold:

▶ You have the power to choose the updates globally. You will not have to select from a list of updates again and again on dozens or hundreds of computers.

▶ Your Internet bandwidth is more efficiently used. The updates are downloaded once to the internal server. All internal machines then download the updates from that internal server, which reduces the required Internet bandwidth. You can even schedule the WSUS server to download all of the updates in the middle of the night when fewer employees are accessing the Internet in most organizations.

Figure 15.1 shows the deployment model for a typical WSUS deployment. The WSUS server sits between the internal servers and clients and acts as the update server to those internal clients. The WSUS server becomes a client of the Microsoft Update servers. All updates are downloaded to the WSUS server; the clients and other servers download and apply the updates from the WSUS server. Because the WSUS server acts as an intermediary, you have the opportunity to choose the updates you want to deploy before they are applied.

To use WSUS on a Windows Server installation, you must add the WSUS role. Early versions of Windows Server require that you download and install WSUS. Windows Server 2008 R2 has the WSUS server role on the distribution DVD so you can add it like any other server role. The following procedure is used to install the WSUS server role on Windows Server 2008 R2.

1. Open the Start menu, and select Administrative Tools ➢ Server Manager.

2. In the left page, expand the Roles node, and then right-click on Roles and select Add Roles.

3. If the Before You Begin screen appears, click Next.

4. Select the Windows Server Update Services role, and click Next.

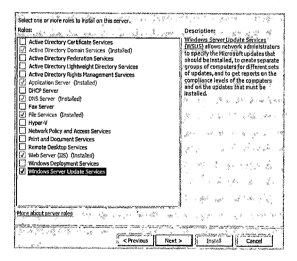

5. On the Introduction to Windows Server Update Services screen, read the information and then click Next.

6. On the Confirm Installation Selections screen, click Install.
   If a newer version is available online, the process will download that version and install it on your Windows Server 2008 R2 machine.

7. The WSUS installation screen appears. Click Next.

8. Accept the terms of the License agreement, and click Next.

9. If any missing-component notifications appear, document the component names so you can download them and install them later, and then click Next.

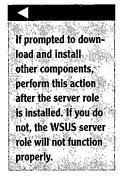

If prompted to download and install other components, perform this action after the server role is installed. If you do not, the WSUS server role will not function properly.

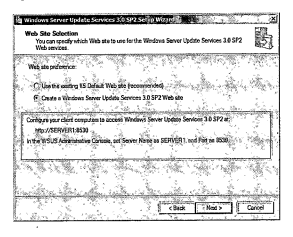

10. Specify the location for local update storage, and click Next.

11. Accept the defaults on the Database Options screen, which indicates the use of the Windows Internal Database, and click Next.

12. On the Web Site Selection screen, choose Create A Windows Server Update Services 3.0 SP2 Web Site, and click Next.

13. On the Ready to Install screen, click Next. The installation will begin.

After performing the steps in this procedure, you will need to configure the WSUS service according to your needs. Complete configuration is beyond the scope of this book; however, you will need to use the WSUS Configuration Wizard to configure the following items:

▶ Participation in the Microsoft Update Improvement Program.

▶ The upstream server, which indicates whether updates are received from Microsoft Update or another internal WSUS server. (A layered hierarchy of WSUS servers is often used in large organizations to better control update management and optimize the delivery of updates to various network segments and locations.)

▶ Whether a proxy server is required for Internet access.

▶ The languages for which you want to download updates (you can greatly reduce downloads by selecting only needed languages).

▶ The products for which you want to receive updates.

▶ The types of updates to receive, such as Security, Tools, Critical, etc.

▶ The synchronization schedule, which determines when the WSUS server will acquire updates from the Microsoft Update server on the Web.

Figure 15.2 shows the Choose Products screen of the Windows Server Update Services Configuration Wizard with the Office and SQL Server selections in view.

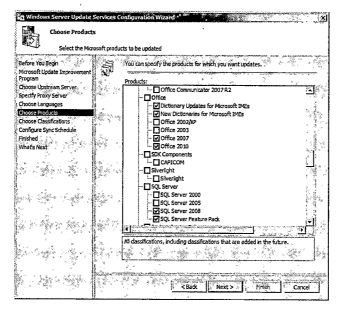

FIGURE 15.2 The WSUS Configuration Wizard's product-selection screen

Although WSUS and the other update methods discussed in this section can be used for the Windows Server, SQL Server, IIS, Exchange Server, SharePoint, and many other programs, special consideration must be made for each product. One often overlooked factor in performing updates is the impact the update will have on custom code. For example, if your organization has implemented custom code on top of the existing default code in SharePoint Server 2010, an update could cause the custom code to fail. You can usually avoid this by encouraging programmers to follow Microsoft's best practices when writing code and by testing the updates in lab environments before applying updates to an active production server.

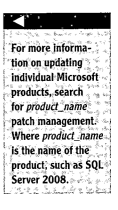

For more information on updating individual Microsoft products, search for *product_name* patch management. Where *product_name* is the name of the product, such as SQL Server 2008.

A SMALL BUSINESS CHOOSES AN UPDATE SOLUTION

Widgets America, a small business, wanted to implement SharePoint Server 2010, which requires a SQL Server installation. They did not have a SQL server in their environment, so the SharePoint Server 2010 project demanded more than simply installing a web server application (which is what SharePoint Server itself actually is). The project entailed a SQL Server deployment, the IIS server deployment, and the SharePoint services deployment.

The company had been performing all updates manually. This was not a huge problem for a small business; however, they were about to install three additional servers. Two servers would run both SharePoint and IIS, and the third server would be a dedicated SQL Server for the backend database. The business already had four other servers, and they also had more than 40 client computers. During the project planning process, the administrator realized it was time to move beyond manual updates.

The good news for Widgets America was that WSUS is not processor or memory intensive. With some analysis, it became clear that one of the servers running SharePoint and IIS would be underutilized. WSUS was installed on this server and scheduled to download updates between 1 A.M. and 5 A.M. This small business did not have a second or third shift, so the heaviest Internet downloads could happen in the middle of the night when no other users needed Internet access.

In the end, the Widgets America was able to implement an automated update solution with absolutely no extra cost to the project. The administrator set up the WSUS service on the server so no consulting fees were required. Even small businesses can benefit from and easily implement WSUS in their environments.

Automating with Logs and Alerts

The Event Viewer is a primary tool for working with server logs. (See Chapte 13, "Server Troubleshooting," to review the Event Viewer if needed.) You can create scheduled tasks that run whenever a particular event log entry is added to a log. Another method, which uses performance logs and alerts, can be used to notify you of performance factors on a server. In earlier versions of Windows Server, the Performance Monitor allows you to directly create alerts as individual objects. In Windows Server 2008 and R2, you must create a Data Collector Set (which you learned about in Chapter 14, "Performance Tuning") and then create a performance counter alert object within the Data Collector Set.

> A *performance alert* is triggered when the performance counter reads above or below a threshold you define. For example, you could indicate that an alert should trigger when free memory is below 2 megabytes.

When you create a performance alert, you can configure two alert actions and an alert task. The two available alert actions are as follows:

Log An Entry In The Application Event Log   This alert action can be enabled by checking a single check box in the Alert Action tab of the Data Collector Properties dialog. When checked, an entry will be added to the Event Viewer Application log each time the alert is triggered.

Start A Data Collector Set   You can select from a list of Data Collector Sets that you have previously created on the Alert Action tab of the Data Collector Properties dialog. This enables you to gather performance statistics at the time the alert is triggered.

For the alert task, you can define an application to run when the performance alert is triggered. If the application requires command-line arguments, you can also provide those. The alert task is a useful parameter because you can use it to notify an administrator of a problem by executing a script that sends an email.

To create a Data Collector Set (DCS) and a Performance Counter Alert object, follow this procedure:

1. Click Start, search for **Performance Monitor**, and press Enter.

2. Expand Data Collector Sets and User Defined in the console tree.

3. Right-click on the User Defined node, and select New ➤ Data Collector Set.

4. In the Create New Data Collector Set Wizard, enter a name for the new DCS, choose to Create Manually (Advanced), and then click Next.

5. When asked what type of data you want to include, choose Performance Counter Alert, and click Next.

6. Accept the default root directory, and click Next.

7. On the final page of the wizard, select Save and Close, and then click Finish.

    You now have an empty DCS.

8. Right-click on the DCS you just created, and select New ➤ Data Collector.

9. Name the new data collector as desired.

10. Select the Performance Counter Alert option, and click Next.

11. On the next screen of the Create New Data Collector Wizard, add each performance counter for which you want to configure alerts.

12. Set the alert threshold to above or below the appropriate value, and click Next.

13. Click Finish to complete the creation process.

14. Right-click on the newly created Data Collector, and select Properties.

15. Configure the Alert Action and Alert Task tabs as desired, and then click OK.

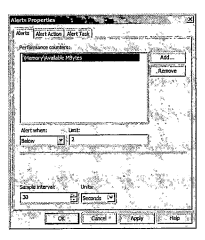

Planning for Continuity

Business continuity is the collection of planning, administration, and disaster recovery tasks that allow your networks and systems to remain in operation or be recovered quickly in the event of a failure. Failures in server systems can be caused by many events, including:

▶ Hardware failure

▶ Software failure

▶ User actions

▶ Security incidents

▶ Fires, floods, and other natural disasters

▶ Electrical provisioning issues

▶ Telecommunications problems

Regardless of the cause of the failure, a server administrator must plan for business continuity in such scenarios. For beginning administrators, these tasks include disaster recovery procedures, such as data backup and restoration and data redundancy. Administrators also need to understand clustering so they can decide whether or not to utilize it when a situation requires high availability.

Disaster Recovery

Disaster recovery planning involves establishing the tasks that need to be taken to allow an organization to continue operations when a major problem occurs. These major problems include fires, floods, and other natural disasters as well as man-made disasters. Four key factors impact the availability of your systems. These four factors are security, stability, life expectancy, and redundancy.

Security   Security must be considered as an availability issue because a security incident can indeed make a resource unavailable. For example, a denial of service (DoS) attack against a SQL server can make it unavailable to the SharePoint servers regardless of clustering or other availability technologies utilized.

Stability   Stability is a factor of hardware and software quality. Quality hardware should not overheat and should operate effectively for long periods of uninterrupted time. Poorly designed systems often suffer from heat problems and shut themselves off or damage hardware components resulting in down time. For this reason, Microsoft recommends using only certified hardware for clustered installations.

Life Expectancy   Hard drives have a value called Mean Time Between Failures (MTBF). MTBF indicates the life expectancy of the drive. While it is important to purchase drives that will last a long time, it is more important to know when drives are expected to fail. Many organizations plan for drive replacements just before the MTBF is reached. In RAID systems with dynamic data regeneration, the drives can be replaced one-by-one with no down time at all. For other hardware, check with the vendor to determine life expectancy.

Redundancy   The key to high availability is redundancy. This is true in every area of life. If you are designing an application and the application is due in thirty days and you are the only programmer working on the application, you carry great risk. If you are sick and unable to work for a week, the deadline is sure to be missed; however, if you have other programmers who can take up the work when you are unavailable, the work of the project continues. In the same way, redundant hardware helps keep systems running and available for user access. Redundancy also applies to data. Redundant data is data that is stored in more than one place or it is stored with recovery data, such as the parity bits used in RAID 5 storage.

As a server administrator, you must plan for all four components in both your server availability plan and your disaster recovery plan. The server availability plan will document the technologies and configurations used to ensure the server is available when needed.

An important component of disaster recovery is a backup and restore plan for your data. The plan should define the following at a minimum:

- ▶ The frequency of backups

- ▶ The type of backups

- ▶ The storage locations for backup media

- ▶ The security requirements for the backups

Three common backup types are used: full backup, incremental backup, and copy backup:

Full Backup   In this case, all data is backed up. The full backup takes the longest, but it includes everything in a single backup.

Incremental Backup   This backup type backs up only the data that has changed. When you restore an incremental backup, you must first restore the most recent full backup and then restore each incremental backup in sequence.

Copy Backup   Windows Server 2008 and R2 also support a backup type called copy. A copy backup will back up all the files specified, but it will not truncate transaction logs for applications such as Exchange Server and SQL Server. If you use a third-party tool for your backups and you want to use Windows Server Backup for a specific backup task, you should always perform copy backups to avoid creating problems for the third-party backup application.

Starting with Windows Server 2008, all backups using built-in tools are created using the Volume Shadow Service (VSS). This allows for easier implementation of background backup processes.

Windows Server Backup is not installed by default on Windows Server 2008 or R2, but it can be added as a feature using the following procedure:

1. Click Start ≻ Administrative Tools ≻ Server Manager.

2. Expand Features in the left navigation pane.

3. Click the Add Features link to launch the Add Features Wizard.

4. On the Select Features screen, scroll down the features list until you see Windows Server Backup Features.

5. Select both the Windows Server Backup and Command-Line Tools items, and click Next.

6. Click Install on the Confirm Installation Selections screen to begin the installation.

7. When the installation completes, click Close to complete the installation.

After installing the Windows Server Backup feature, you can use the following procedure to perform a full server backup:

1. Click Start ≻ Administrative Tools ≻ Windows Server Backup.

2. Select Action ≻ Backup Once from the application's main menus.

3. Accept the default setting on the Backup Options screen of the Backup Once Wizard, and click Next.

4. On the Select Backup Configuration screen, choose Full Server (Recommended), and click Next.

5. On the Specify a Destination Type screen, choose a storage location and click Next.

6. On the next screen, specify the exact location for the backup, accept the defaults for Access Control, and click Next.

7. On the confirmation screen, verify that your settings will meet your needs, and click Backup to back up the entire server.

8. Observe the Backup Progress.

9. When the backup Status field is equal to Completed, click Close.
   The backup will be listed in the Windows Server Backup screen and can be used for restoration in the future.

In addition to one-time backups like the one explained in the preceding procedure, you can also schedule backups. In fact, most organizations schedule backups so that they occur automatically and regularly. The administrator typically receives a notification regarding backup success or failure.

When planning server backup strategy, you also need to consider how to back up user data. User data includes word processor documents, spreadsheets, presentations, graphics files, project plans, and myriad other data types. Most modern organizations configure their users' computers so that data is saved to the server by default. This allows centralization of the user data backups. To accomplish this, you must configure folder redirection. Folder redirection is a configuration option in Group Policy that allows you to redirect the users' documents and other folders to a networked location. With this configuration, the users can simply save their data in what appears to be local \documents folder and it will be placed on the server automatically. Additionally, the administrators can back up the data from the central location.

It is very important to test your backups by performing a trial restoration in a lab environment. Do not wait for a disaster to attempt a restoration.

ACTIVE DIRECTORY DOMAIN SERVICES AND BACKUPS

The AD DS domain database is essential to Windows network operations. If you do not back up the domain database and then you lose it because of drive failure or corruption of data on all of your domain controllers, you will be in a very bad situation. To back up the domain database, you should back up something called the system state on the domain controllers. The system state data can be backed up on any Windows server, but on domain controllers it includes the domain database as well. The system state includes the following items:

▶ Boot files

▶ Certificate services

▶ Cluster database

▶ Registry

▶ IIS metabase

▶ Performance counter configurations

▶ COM+ registration database

▶ AD domain database file

▶ AD SYSVOL folder

As you can see, two important items related to AD are backed up with the system state: the domain database file and the SYSVOL folder. The Windows Server Backup utility is used to back up the system state and restore it in the event of data loss.

Clustering

Clustering can be used for the many server technologies. It allows more than one server to provide the same services to the network while appearing as a single server to the clients. The Windows Failover Clustering service provides server clustering for Windows-based servers.

A *cluster* is a collection of servers that work together to provide services to the network. The unique thing about a cluster of servers, as opposed to separate servers performing independent functions, is that the collection of clustered servers is accessed as a single server from the client perspective. You may have two servers in a cluster, but they appear as one to the users and applications. For example, when using a SQL Server installation on a cluster, applications will still point to a single SQL Server database server even though you are using failover clustering for the SQL Server. *Failover clustering* is used when a cluster is configured to automatically redirect clients to another server in the cluster when one server fails.

Clusters nearly always share storage. If you have two physical servers that you want to use in a cluster and data storage is involved, both servers must have access to the shared storage. Each server is considered a *node* in the cluster. It is this shared storage that allows the servers to access the same data and the services to failover from one server to another rapidly. The shared storage should be a fault-tolerant storage solution to prevent downtime from storage failures. Fault-tolerant storage solutions include RAID cabinets, storage area networks (SANs), and distributed storage. RAID cabinets are storage devices that support various implementations of RAID, such as RAID 0 (striping), RAID 1 (mirroring), and RAID 5 (striping with parity).

It is important to remember the following rule of high availability: Your system is only as available as its weakest link.

What does this rule mean? It means that you have to look at the cluster nodes, the network between these nodes, the shared storage, and the stability of hardware components and identify the weakest link. The weakest link is the lowest performing or least available link. This is why Microsoft recommends using the Failover Clustering service only with validated hardware. *Validated* hardware has been tested by Microsoft or service providers to ensure stability and compatibility with the Failover Clustering service.

Windows Server offers another clustering feature called *network load balancing* (NLB) that should not be confused with *failover clustering*. NLB is used to distribute workloads across multiple servers on a session-by-session basis.

See Chapter 3 for details on SANs and RAID implementation.

THE WEAKEST LINK

As an example of the "weakest link" concept, consider the Windows Vista and Windows 7 feature called the Windows Experience Index (WEI). WEI rates various hardware components and uses these ratings to determine the performance expectations of the system. Microsoft knows that a system with a very fast processor, but a very slow hard drive would still have performance problems. In the same way, a system with a very fast hard drive and very fast memory, but a very slow processor will also have performance problems. For this reason, the WEI is actually based on the weakest link or the lowest performing component.

The same is true for your clusters. If you have expensive and stable servers but faulty storage, the cluster will not live up to your expectations. If the network is slow between the cluster and the clients accessing it, the performance will suffer. All components must be selected, installed, and configured in order to achieve the level of performance and reliability required.

THE ESSENTIALS AND BEYOND

Windows Server maintenance begins with hardware maintenance. You should ensure that your memory, CPU, drives, ports, and other hardware components are free from dust and in a healthy operational state. It is also important to plan for server downtime so that a server replacement or upgrade has as little impact on your users as possible. Next, you must consider how you will keep your server software up-to-date. Windows Update can be used manually, and you can enable Microsoft Update to receive updates for other Microsoft products such as the Microsoft Office suite. Windows Server Update Services (WSUS) may be used to implement an internal update server so that updates can be downloaded once from the Internet and then distributed to servers and clients within your internal network.

Another important tool you can use to manage your Windows Server environment is performance logs and alerts. These performance counter alerts are used to monitor a performance counter and take action should performance exceed or fall below a configured threshold. Finally, you must plan for business continuity. Problems will occur and when they do, you should be ready to respond. Having a well-planned backup and restoration procedure is where it starts. You can use Windows Server Backup to perform backups and restorations. If you must back up the AD domain database, be sure to back up the system state on the domain controllers. You can also use clustering to reduce the likelihood of a service failing on the network, because clustering uses multiple servers to act

(Continues)

as one on the network. If one server fails, another server in the cluster can take over the responsibilities of the failed server.

ADDITIONAL EXERCISES

▶ Use Windows Server Backup to make a one-time backup of the system state on a domain controller.

▶ Create a DCS with a performance counter alert that monitors the free space on drive C: and adds an event log entry when it falls below 500 MB free space.

▶ Use Windows Update to check for updates for a server and apply any important updates.

To compare your answers to the author's, please visit:

www.sybex.com/go/winadminessentials.

REVIEW QUESTIONS

1. What components could you configure for exclusion in WSUS to greatly reduce the size of the update downloads?

   A. Languages

   B. Proxy server

   C. The upstream server

   D. The synchronization schedule

2. True or false: Clustering usually requires shared storage.

3. Why is it important to blow dust out of your servers periodically?

   A. To keep them running cool

   B. To rid them of bacteria

   C. To rid them of that dirty feeling

   D. To ensure they are running warm

4. Name a primary benefit of 64-bit computing over 32-bit computing?

5. What is the most common interface used to connect a UPS unit to a server?

   A. USB

   B. FireWire

   C. eSATA

   D. PS/2

6. Define BIOS.

7. Define Microsoft Update.

8. Which one of the following options is not available in the configuration dialogs so that it could be executed automatically by a performance counter alert if triggered?

   A. Run a program

   B. Write an entry to the application log

   C. Start a DCS

   D. Shut down a service

(Continues)

THE ESSENTIALS AND BEYOND *(Continued)*

9. What kind of backup will back up only changed data?

   A. Full

   B. Copy

   C. Incremental

   D. None of the above

10. True or false: Multiple Windows servers can be configured to work together and can be presented as one server on the network.

Answers to Review Questions

Chapter 1

1. **B** A server is a network-connected device that provides services to the network, such as IP configuration and name resolution, and the devices on that network. Servers may provide for file storage, authentication and many other services.

2. **True** Because SQL Server is a database management system, it is used to store the information of value to an organization. It is also used to analyze and retrieve this information. Therefore, it is categorized as an information service.

3. **C** A client is defined as a computing device or application that consumes services. Servers provide the services that clients consume.

4. **ver.** The ver command shows the version number (not the name) of the operating system. For example, Windows Server 2008 R2 is the name of an operating system, but the version is 6.1.

5. **A** Blade servers are installed into docking stations called enclosures. Some companies use unique terms for the enclosures, such as the BladeCenter offered by IBM.

6. A collection of responsibilities provided to the network or networked devices

7. A software program that supports or augments the functionality of server roles

8. **D** The Print and Document Services role allows you to share printers and scanners on the network. You can centralize both printer and scanner management through this role.

9. **C** The CMD command is used to launch the Windows Command Prompt. Command.com is the older 16-bit command interpreter from Windows 3.1 and DOS.

10. **False** IPv4 and IPv6 are supported in Windows Server 2008 and Windows Server 2008 R2.

Chapter 2

1.   **B** Database servers are very I/O intensive. I/O intensive servers do not work as well in virtual environments.

2.   **True** Because multiple virtual servers run on a single physical server, total power consumption is reduced.

3.   **B** A dual-core processor must run at a minimum of 1.3 GHz or faster. A single-core processor must run at 1.4 GHz or faster.

4.   **512 MB.** The minimum requirement is 512 MB, but most organizations start with a baseline that doubles this to 1 GB.

5.   **C** Press **Shift+F10** to bring up a Command Prompt window during the installation process.

6.   A software module that communicates with the hardware device and the operating system.

7.   Preboot Execution Environment

8.   **D** Adding the AD DS role may be performed on some servers, but it is not required on all servers. Most of the initial configuration tasks must be performed on all server installations.

9.   **C** The Windows System Image manager (WinSIM) comes with the Windows Automated Installation Kit (WAIK) and provides a GUI interface for creating and managing unattend.xml files.

10.   **False** Signed drivers are validated to come from a trusted source. Unsigned drivers are not. It is up to you to ensure that the unsigned driver is safe based on your knowledge of its source.

Chapter 3

1.   **D** Only NTFS supports the Encrypting Files System (EFS), which allows for the encryption of data during storage.

2.   **True** Microsoft developed exFAT so that removable media could be formatted and used by multiple systems and so that large volumes could be created.

3.   **B** A storage area network (SAN) provides block-level access using either Fibre Channel or iSCSI. Network attached storage (NAS) may provide block-level access, but it often provides file-level access only.

4.   **RAID 1.** RAID 1 is mirroring. Mirroring creates a duplicate copy of all data on the mirror drive while using the primary drive as the active drive.

5. **B** Software-based RAID relies on the computer's CPU to perform RAID processing. For this reason, software-based RAID does not perform as well as hardware-based RAID in most implementations.

6. A dynamic disk

7. The Distributed File System (DFS)

8. **D** FAT volumes support a maximum of a 4 GB file size. The NTFS file system can support files that are multiple terabytes in size.

9. **B** Both Fibre Channel and iSCSI can use host bus adapters (HBAs) to connect to the SAN. An HBA is a very special kind of adapter that does far more than a standard network interface card (NIC).

10. **False** You can create primary and extended partitions on only basic disks. Dynamic disks contain volumes.

Chapter 4

1. **B** The Windows Update service allows users to check for updates at the Windows Update or Microsoft Update websites.

2. **False** Third-party vendors can and often do provide services that run on Windows servers.

3. **A** When a service is set to the Disabled startup type, you cannot even start the service manually. You must first change the startup type to Manual, Automatic, or Automatic (Delayed Start) and then you can start the service manually.

4. **Least privilege.** The principle of least privilege states that users and systems should have no greater access than is required to perform their intended duties. This definition means that systems can do what they need to do and nothing more. Other systems can access the secured system to perform their intended operations and can do nothing more. Least privilege is essential to secure network operations.

5. **A** The EFS service provides the functionality required to implement encryption on the NTFS files system. If the service is not running, users will be unable to access data encrypted with EFS.

6. An application or innate operating system component that runs on Windows and provides services to the local machine, the network, or both.

7. The services on which another service depends or the other services that depend on a specific service.

8.   **C** The old saying is true: you can never have too much memory in a Windows computer. You can certainly have more than the operating system can use, but you should always give a server as much memory as you can. The three common causes of service problems are service dependency issues, improper service configuration, and insufficient privileges.

9.   **A, C** The Remote Desktop Services service must be running to allow a user to control the Windows Server Desktop across the network. Through this service, a user can log on to the Windows Server Desktop using the Remote Desktop Connection client. The user can control the Desktop using her keyboard and mouse as if she were sitting at the server locally.

10.   **False** The Server service, as well as the Workstation service, is on both the Windows Server operating systems and the Windows clients, such as Windows 7 and Windows Vista.

Chapter 5

1.   **B** The very last thing that is checked for resolution is the Lmhosts file, which contains NetBIOS names to IP address mappings.

2.   **False** Built-in containers exist for storage of user accounts and groups. You can create organizational units for your own needs, but built-in containers do exist.

3.   **A** Replication, which can be intersite or intrasite replication, is the process that ensures consistency across all copies of the AD database on different AD servers (DCs).

4.   **The forest.** The forest is the trust boundary because all domains in a forest trust all other domains through some transitive trust path.

5.   **A, D** DNS is implemented to provide hostname resolution. DNS is required in AD implementations. DHCP is implemented to provide IP configuration settings to computers. Although DHCP is not required, it does make network management easier.

6.   A hierarchical group of domains sharing the same root namespace.

7.   A location defined by IP subnets for intersite AD replication and potential use of unique site-based Group Policies.

8.   **D** A shortcut or manual trust can be created directly between the two child domains so that the transitive trust path does not have to be traversed for authentication to occur.

9.   **A** A single domain can span multiple sites, so you are required to create only one domain in this scenario.

10.   **True** Windows Server 2008 R2 first introduced the AD Recycle Bin, and you must be at the Windows Server 2008 R2 functional level to take advantage of it. This also requires that all domains be at the Windows Server 2008 R2 functional level.

Chapter 6

1. **C** The first of the high-level planning steps is to determine the number of forests required. AD installations support a single forest and they support multiple forests.

2. **False** Only one schema can be shared across a forest. It is possible that two or more applications could conflict with each other when they attempt to modify the same schema. You can create application forests so that they can have a dedicated schema and eliminate such conflicts.

3. **C** An AD domain can handle many thousands of users. Having more than 1,200 users is not, by itself, a valid reason to create a separate domain.

4. **The first domain installed.** When you install the first domain controller for the first domain in the forest, you are creating the forest root domain.

5. **B, C** You can delegate administrative permissions to a user for an OU. You can link or apply different Group Policies to each OU.

6. A trust relationship between forests. A forest trust may be a one-way or two-way transitive trust. A two-way trust is required for both forests to fully trust the other forest's domains.

7. An Active Directory forest used to store and share centralized resources needed by all or many users on the network.

8. **B** As a best practice, always start with two DCs and add additional DCs as needed. Two DCs are considered the minimum number for fault-tolerant purposes. If you have only one DC and that DC fails, users will be unable to log on.

9. **B, D** Microsoft defines DC locations as hub locations and satellite locations. Hub locations are the centralized locations where DCs are located, and these DCs serve many users within the organization while often acting as replication partners to satellite locations. Satellite locations are those DC locations serving fewer users (typically, a branch office location) and are connected to a hub DC.

10. **False** The GC contains a partial replica of all objects in all of the forest domains. This subset of data is used to provide faster searches of the directory. The GC also contains the Universal Groups and their full memberships.

Chapter 7

1. **C** Every user is automatically a member of the Domain Users group. Additionally, every user is a member of the Everyone group.

2. **True** Local groups can contain accounts and groups from any domain in in the forest in which the local machine participates.

3.   **A** Global groups can contain only other global groups.

4.   **Remote Desktop Services.** The Sessions tab is relevant only to Remote Desktop Services connections. You can set properties for the connection (session) such as the delay timer for ending a disconnected session, the delay timer for ending an active or idle session, the setting for disconnecting or ending a session when the active or idle timer expires, and the setting for allowing reconnections to sessions from any client or from the original client only (called the originating client in the user Properties interface).

5.   **D** The Profile tab allows you to set the home directory path, the logon script, and the roaming profile path.

6.   A type of group that may not be assigned permissions and that is often used for email distribution lists.

7.   AGDLP stands for Accounts (A), Global groups (G), Domain local groups (DL) and permissions (P).

8.   **A** You can create queries in ADUC to display a subset of the information within the AD domain. You can export the queries as XML files to be imported into other administration machines.

9.   **D** ADUC can be used to delegate administrative control to users and groups who are not members of the Domain Admins group.

10.   **True** You can manage the Domain Naming Operations Master role using Active Directory Domains and Trusts. You can only move the Domain Naming Operations Master role to another DC within the same forest, and you must be logged on as a member of the Enterprise Admins group to perform this action.

Chapter 8

1.   **A** As long as the GPOs are created on a Windows 7 client, they will work with earlier versions of AD.

2.   **True** A single GPO can be linked to more than one container, such as a site, domain, or OU.

3.   **A** The Remote Server Administration Tools (RSAT) include the GPMC so that you can manage Group Policy from a client. The MMC, Remote Desktop Client, and GPEDIT.MSC solutions are all installed on Windows clients by default.

4.   A custom MMC with the Group Policy Object Editor loaded. The traditional GPEDIT.MSC console allows only the editing of local policies. To work with MLGPO, you must use a custom MMC.

5. **A and D** Three GUI tools are commonly used for Group Policy management. The first is the Group Policy Management Console (GPMC), which can be installed on client computers by installing RSAT. The second is the GPEDIT.MSC command for direct editing of local policy settings. The third is the custom MMC with the Group Policy Object Editor loaded for MLGPO support.

6. A Group Policy Object (GPO) is a collection of settings that can be applied to Windows computers by linking it to a container within the AD structure.

7. A simple method for configuring settings through GPOs with dialog boxes similar to those in the local Windows GUI interface. Unlike policies, preferences may be changed by users to override the preference settings.

8. **A** PowerShell supports Group Policy management through an add-on module. Use the Import-Module GroupPolicy command to enable Group Policy management.

9. **A** Centralized Group Policy is a feature of AD. You must have an AD network to take advantage of it.

10. **False** MLGPOs are applied in the order of local policy settings, Administrator/Non-Administrator settings and then specific user settings. Therefore, specific user settings override Administrative and Non-Administrative user settings because they are applied last.

Chapter 9

1. **B** By default, SMTP uses port 25 and POP3 uses port 110. FTP usually operates on port 21 and MAPI uses dynamic ports.

2. **True** The Developer Edition is exactly like the Enterprise Edition except that it is not licensed for production use.

3. **C** While POP3 and IMAP may be supported, the default protocol used is the MAPI protocol.

4. **SCOM, SCVMM, and DPM.** Each of these solutions is a monitoring solution for different purposes.

5. **C** An n-tier application-server plan includes more than one server, where *n* is the number of tiers in the model. For example, if a user opens a web browser to access a SharePoint site and then uses the search engine on that site, one server could provide the web frontend while another performs the search.

6. A server that can send and receive email messages on the behalf of users and store messages in user mailboxes.

7. A server that provides collaboration services such as instant messaging, calendar sharing, document sharing, and workflow processes.

8. **C** The Network inspection service (NIS) scans the network packets looking for malware and other attack types.

9. **C** SharePoint 2010 is a collaboration solution. It does not offer malware scanning.

10. **False** The database server or database management system (DBMS) is not the same thing as the database. The database server or DBMS provides access to the database for users or applications.

Chapter 10

1. **C** Digest authentication is based on secret keys. While Basic authentication sends the password across the network in an easily decodable form, digest authentication requires that the secret keys and passwords not be sent across the network in any form.

2. **False** IIS 7.0 shipped with Windows Vista and Server 2008. IIS 7.5 shipped with Windows 7 and Windows Server 2008 R2.

3. **D** Seven requests will be required: one request for each of the images and one request for the HTML code file.

4. Loosely coupled, extensible, or interoperable. Web services are interoperable in that they can communicate with other web services. They are extensible in that they can be improved upon by adding new code or modules. They are loosely coupled in that they are not required to be fully aware of the inner workings of the other web services. Any one of these three would be a valid response.

5. **A, D** You can create a website or an FTP site by right-clicking on the Sites container in the IIS Manager. SharePoint sites are created from within the specialized SharePoint administration interface called Central Administration. Joomla! sites can be created in IIS, but it requires installing the Joomla! software. Joomla! is an open source content management system.

6. A service that receives incoming requests and sends responses to those requests within Internet Information Services. The default protocol listener is HTTP.sys; it is used for standard website requests and responses.

7. A protocol that provides encryption for HTTP communications between a web client and a web server. Typically, it is identified by the HTTPS protocol designator in the URL of the website.

8. **C** FTP uses plaintext transfers, which means that the data is unencrypted. IIS supports the use of SSL with FTP to provide the encryption if desired.

9. **A** When you use a self-signed certificate, you have no way to force public users to install the certificate and trust your server. They will receive a warning that the certificate could not be validated.

10. **False** You can create a self-signed certificate from within the IIS Manager and use it for SSL services from the web server.

Chapter 11

1. **D** You only need to change the priority on the new print job. The default priority for all print jobs is 1. If you set the priority to anything higher, it will print next.

2. **True** Always remember that explicit denial of a permission always wins over any other permission settings.

3. **A** Windows Server 2008 R2 is a 64-bit operating system, so only the 64-bit drivers are installed by default. The x86 nomenclature indicates a 32-bit version of the operating system, so you must add the 32-bit drivers.

4. **Printer pooling.** Printer pooling allows print jobs to be sent from a single print queue to multiple printers. The printers show up as a single printer to the users.

5. **D** With the List Folder Contents permission, users can view the contents of a folder, but not read the contents of actual files.

6. A document waiting to be printed in the print queue

7. A simple namespace that is representative of a collection of shared folders, which may be distributed among multiple servers, grouped together into a single virtual shared folder on the server.

8. **C** The NTFS permission overrides the share permission because it is more restrictive. Lisa will have Read permissions on the Test folder in the share.

9. **B** By default, the printer management website is located in the printers virtual directory under the server name.

10. **True** You can configure each server to replicate its shared data to a central server, thereby centralizing the data.

Chapter 12

1. **A** PPTP has been supported in Windows since the 1990s, but it is the least secure of the supported protocols.

2. **False** Remote Assistance is a feature that must be added to the server. Remote Assistance is installed by default for the clients, but not for the servers.

3. **B** The Secure Sockets Tunneling Protocol (SSTP) uses SSL and, therefore, port 443 by default.

4. **Remote Desktop Protocol.** RDP has been used since Windows NT 4.0 Terminal Server Edition, and it is on version 6.1 in Windows 7 and Windows Server 2008 R2.

5. **C** The System Properties dialog box is used. The Remote tab allows for the configuration of Remote Assistance and Remote Desktop.

6. The server role in Windows Server 2008 and R2 that allows for remote Desktop control using the Remote Desktop Client software.

7. The process used to convert plaintext or readable text into ciphertext. Encryption can be used on any data because all data is represented by binary numbers within computer systems. The input to the encryption algorithm is one set of binary numbers and the output is another. The algorithm can both scramble and descramble the data.

8. **D** RD Web Access allows users to run applications or entire Desktops in a web browser using an ActiveX control.

9. **B** The RD Session Host is the component that actually allows servers to host applications or entire Desktops for remote control and access.

10. **True** IPSec provides the encryption and authentication for L2TP. L2TP is simply responsible for establishing the tunnel.

Chapter 13

1. **C** You can press Ctrl+Shift+Esc to open the Task Manager. This is much faster than the other methods available for accessing it.

2. **True** According to ITIL, an incident is an event that is not part of standard operations and that may cause an interruption or a reduction in the quality of a service. The problem is the underlying cause of the incident.

3. **D** Because display corruption is occurring, this is most likely the display adapter. It could also be the system board, which was not mentioned as an optional answer.

4. **Physical, Data Link, Network, Transport, Session, Presentation, Application.** Although the chapter focused on the lower three, any layer can be evaluated in the troubleshooting process.

5. **C** The Critical level indicates that a failure has occurred and the application or components could not automatically recover.

6. The Information Technology Infrastructure Library (ITIL) is a set of documents that define best practices for technology management.

7. An application used to view, search, filter, and manage event logs in Windows operating systems.

8. **C** Event filtering is used to limit the event log entries to those that come from a specific source, have a specific level of severity, or were created within a specified date range among other things.

9. **A** The Task Manager can be used to kill running tasks. You can also use the `task-kill` command form the Command Prompt.

10. **False** Networking problems can occur anywhere in the chain from the server to the accessing client. Switches can fail, routers can fail, and network cabling can fail.

Chapter 14

1. **C** The CPU tab shows both handles and modules.

2. **False** In many cases, insufficient memory or other system resources can cause CPU utilization to rise. Purchasing faster CPUs or more CPUs is not always the best method of dealing with high CPU utilization.

3. **D** The `typperf` command can be used to both list the available counters and the values of those counters.

4. **Processor\% User Time.** The Processor\% User Time performance counter shows user time. This is the time spent running user mode applications as opposed to privileged or kernel mode applications.

5. **A** A virtual machine is used to run the second operating system. The VHD may provide the hard drive, but a virtual machine is required to run the OS.

6. A method used to run multiple operating systems concurrently on a single physical machine. Each operating system runs in a virtual machine.

7. An ActiveX control that gathers information about performance counters and displays values as numeric information and line graphs.

8. The virtualization layer that sits between the hardware and the operating system in a bare metal virtual machine solution.

9. **C** The `sc` command can be used to configure service settings. The `net` command can only be used to start or stop a service.

10. **True** The System Monitor is an ActiveX control that is in Windows operating systems and may be loaded into other applications. The Performance Monitor loads the System Monitor to display performance data from a log or live analysis.

Chapter 15

1. **A** If you limit the languages that can be downloaded, you can greatly reduce the size of the total downloads.

2. **True** The shared storage can be a storage area network (SAN) or a RAID cabinet, among other solutions, but shared storage is required.

3. **A** Overheating can cause component failure. A primary cause of overheating is dust buildup around system components.

4. More memory may be installed that can then be addressed by the operating system, which in turn will allow the CPU to work with larger chunks of data.

    Increased memory support and larger data processing volumes will result in overall improved performance for many 64-bit applications.

5. **A** Most modern UPS units connect via USB cables.

6. The internal software (installed as firmware) of a computer or server that initiates the system and monitors the health of the hardware (the Basic Input/Output System, or BIOS).

7. The enhanced Microsoft updating solution that also supports updating Microsoft Office and other applications.

8. **D** You could create a custom script to shut down a service, but this is not a direct option in the dialogs.

9. **C** An incremental backup will back up only the changed data. A copy backup will back up all data, but it will not truncate log files because it will not flip the backup bit on the files that are backed up.

10. **True** Windows Clustering Service allows a group of Windows servers to appear as one server to the users, and it provides for fault tolerance in service provisioning.

Microsoft's Certification Program

Since the inception of its certification program, Microsoft has certified more than 2 million people. As the computer network industry continues to increase in both size and complexity, this number is sure to grow—and the need for *proven* ability will also increase. Certifications can help companies verify the skills of prospective employees and contractors.

Microsoft started with the Microsoft Certified Professional (MCP) program that validated individuals' knowledge and expertise on a wide variety of products. They have expanded these certifications into multiple different categories.

Microsoft Technology Associate (MTA)   The MTA certifications are entry-level certifications that are only available at academic institutions. They validate an individual's knowledge and basic understanding of key technology concepts. The three IT professional series certifications are Networking Fundamentals, Security Fundamentals, and Windows Server Administration Fundamentals. There are also several developer certifications. You must take and pass one exam to earn each MTA certification.

Microsoft Certified Technology Specialist (MCTS)   The MCTS is the next level of certification. For people who are not in an academic institution, these certifications can be the first certifications they earn. The MCTS certification program targets specific technologies instead of specific job roles. You must take and pass one to three exams to earn an MCTS certification in different technologies.

Microsoft Certified IT Professional (MCITP)   The MCITP certification is a Professional Series certification that tests network and system administrators on job roles rather than only on a specific technology. The MCITP certification program generally consists of one to three exams in addition to obtaining an MCTS-level certification.

Microsoft Certified Professional Developer (MCPD)   The MCPD certification is a Professional Series certification for application developers. Similar to the

MCITP, the MCPD is focused on a job role rather than on a single technology. The MCPD certification program generally consists of one to three exams in addition to obtaining an MCTS-level certification.

Microsoft Certified Master (MCM)   The MCM program is for experienced IT professionals who want to deepen and broaden their technical expertise on specific Microsoft server products. It includes three weeks of highly intensive classroom training, three computer-based tests, and one lab-based exam for each of the MCM certifications. There are five separate MCM certifications.

Microsoft Certified Architect (MCA)   The MCA is Microsoft's premier certification series. Obtaining the MCA requires a minimum of 10 years of experience and passing a review board consisting of peer architects.

Certification Objectives Map

Table A.1 provides objective mappings for the Microsoft Technology Associate (MTA) Windows Server Administration Fundamentals Exam (98-365). It identifies the chapters and sections where the 98-365 exam objectives are covered.

TABLE A.1   Exam 98-366 Objectives Map:
Identifying Causes of and Resolving Desktop Application Issues

Objectives	Chapter and section
Understanding Server Installation	**Chapters 1, 2, and 4**
Understand device drivers.	Chapter 2: Working with Device Drivers
▶ This objective may include but is not limited to: installation, removal, disabling, update/upgrade, rollback, troubleshooting, Plug & Play, IRQ, interrupts, and driver signing.	
Understand services.	Chapter 4
▶ This objective may include but is not limited to: what services are, which statuses a service can be in, startup types, recovery options, delayed startup, Run As settings for a service, stopping or pausing a service, service accounts, and dependencies.	

(Continues)

TABLE A.1 *(Continued)*

Objectives	Chapter and section
Understand server installation options.	Chapter 1 and
▶ This objective may include but is not limited to: choosing correct OS version, partitioning, F8 options, server core vs. full, interactive install, unattended install, automated install using WDS, upgrade vs. clean install, and firmware updates including BIOS.	Chapter 2
Understanding Server Roles	**Chapters 9, 10, 11, 12, 14, and 15**
Identify application servers.	Chapter 9
▶ This objective may include but is not limited to: mail servers, database servers, collaboration servers, monitoring servers, and threat management.	
Understand Web services.	Chapter 10
▶ This objective may include but is not limited to: IIS, WWW, and FTP; separate worker processes; adding components; sites; ports; SSL; and certificates.	
Understand remote access.	Chapter 12
▶ This objective may include but is not limited to: remote assistance, remote administration tools, Remote Desktop Services, licensing, RD Gateway, VPN, application virtualization, and multiple ports.	
Understand the file and print services.	Chapter 11
▶ This objective may include but is not limited to: local printers; network printers; printer pools; web printing; web management; driver deployment; file, folder, and share permissions vs. rights; auditing; and print job management.	
Understand server virtualization.	Chapter 14:
▶ This objective may include but is not limited to: virtualization modes, VHDs, virtual memory, virtual networks, snapshots and saved states, physical to virtual, and virtual to physical.	Virtualization and Performance

(Continues)

TABLE A.1 *(Continued)*

Objectives	Chapter and section
Understanding Active Directory	**Chapters 5, 6, 7, and 8**
Understand accounts and groups. ▶ This objective may include but is not limited to: domain accounts, local accounts, user profiles, group types, group scopes, group nesting, and AGDLP.	Chapter 7: Exploring AD Management Tools and Chapter 7: Working with Users and Groups
Understand organizational units and containers. ▶ This objective may include but is not limited to: purpose of organizational units, purpose of containers, delegation, and default.	Chapter 7: Understanding Organizational Units and Containers
Understand Active Directory infrastructure. ▶ This objective may include but is not limited to: domain controllers, forests, Operations Master roles, domain vs. workgroup, child domains, trusts, functional levels, namespace, sites, and replication.	Chapter 5 and Chapter 6
Understand group policy. ▶ This objective may include but is not limited to: group policy processing, Group Policy Management Console, computer policies, user policies, and local policies.	Chapter 8
Understanding Storage	**Chapters 3 and 11**
Identify storage technologies. ▶ This objective may include but is not limited to: advantages and disadvantages of different storage types; local (SATA, SCSI, IDE); NAS; SAN; fibre channel; iSCSI; NFS; FC HBA and FC switches; and iSCSI hardware.	Chapter 3: Identifying Storage Technologies and Chapter 3: Understanding Disk Types
Understand RAID. ▶ This objective may include but is not limited to: RAID 0, RAID 1, RAID 5, RAID 10 and combinations; and hardware and software RAID.	Chapter 3: Understanding RAID

(Continues)

TABLE A.1 *(Continued)*

Objectives	Chapter and section
Understand disk types. ▶ This objective may include but is not limited to: ATA, basic disk, dynamic disk, mount points, file systems, mounting a virtual hard disk, distributed file systems, and optical disks.	Chapter 11: Understanding DFS
Understanding Server Performance Management	**Chapters 14 and 15**
Identify major server hardware components. ▶ This objective may include but is not limited to: memory, disk, processor, network, 32 / 64 bits, removable drives, graphic cards, cooling, power usage, and ports.	Chapter 15: Maintaining the Hardware
Understand performance monitoring. ▶ This objective may include but is not limited to: methodology, procedures, effects of network, CPU, memory and disk, creating a baseline, perfmon, resmon, Task Manager, and performance counters.	Chapter 14: Performance Tuning and Tools
Understand logs and alerts. ▶ This objective may include but is not limited to the purpose of performance logs and alerts.	Chapter 15: Automating with Logs and Alerts
Understanding Server Maintenance	**Chapters 13 and 15**
Identify steps in the startup process. ▶ This objective may include but is not limited to: BIOS, boot-sector, bootloader, MBR, boot.ini, bcdedit, POST, and Safe mode,	Chapter 15: Planning for Server Downtime
Understand business continuity. ▶ This objective may include but is not limited to: backup and restore, disaster recovery, clustering, AD restore, folder redirection, data redundancy, and uninterruptible power supply (UPS).	Chapter 15: Planning for Continuity

(Continues)

TABLE A.1 *(Continued)*

Objectives	Chapter and section
Understand updates. ▶ This objective may include but is not limited to: software, drivers, operating systems, applications, Windows Update, and Windows Server Update Service (WSUS).	Chapter 15: Understanding Windows Update
Understand troubleshooting methodology. ▶ This objective may include but is not limited to: processes; procedures, best practices, systematic vs. specific approach, perfmon, Event Viewer, Resource Monitor, Information Technology Infrastructure Library, central logging, event filtering, and default logs.	Chapter 13

INDEX

Note to the reader: Throughout this index boldfaced page numbers indicate primary discussions of a topic. *Italicized* page numbers indicate illustrations.

Command Prompt *v.*, 19–20, 22
commands in, 20
features, 19–20
Group Policy cmdlets in, 171–172
restarting services, 89
Server Core installation and, 43–44
starting/stopping services, 86, 88
PPTP (Point-to-Point Tunneling
Protocol), 253, 254
Preboot Execution Environment. *See* PXE
Presentation Layer, OSI model, *270*, 271
Pre-Windows 2000 Compatible Access
group, 160
Primary Domain Controller server. *See*
PDC server
principle of least privilege, 92
Print and Document Services role, 12, 21,
42, 242, 246, 247
print jobs, 243
Print Operators group, 160
print servers, 231, 242–246
Print Spooler service, 79
printer pools, 244–245
private top-level domains, 118
private virtual networks, 317. *See
also* VPNs
privileges
least privilege principle, 92
service, 84–85
problem management, incidents and, 278
processors
maintenance, 322
performance counters, 304–305
Profile tab, user account Properties
dialog, 153–154
properties, event log entry, 285–286
protocols, 194–195. *See also
specific protocols*
protocol analyzer, 217
protocol listeners, 213
Public Key Infrastructures (PKIs), 227,
228, 229
Publishing Service, WWW, 211, 213, 214
PUT method, 211
PXE (Preboot Execution Environment),
37, *38*

Q

Qemu, 27

R

RA. *See* Remote Assistance
rack mount form factor, 8
RADIUS (Remote Authentication Dial-In
User Service), 13
RAID (redundant array of independent
disks), 64–67
disaster recovery and, 340–341
dynamic disks and, 69–70

EDB files on, 199
fault tolerance, 64–67, 72
hardware-based, 64, 67
levels, 64–67, *65*
software-based, 64, 67
RAM, 58, 324. *See also* memory
random crashes, 275
randomization, Group Policy settings
refresh and, 177
RAS and IAS Servers group, 158
RDBMS (relational database management
system), 192
RDC (Remote Differential Compression),
238, 240
RDP (Remote Desktop Protocol), 250,
255, 260
RDS. *See* Remote Desktop Services
REACT methodology, 264–269, *265*, 276
Read and Execute permission, 235
Read permission, 232, 235
read-only DCs, 121
Read-only Domain Controllers group, 158
recoverability, 317–318
recovery, disaster, 340–343
recovery options, service, 84
recursion, 106–107, *107*
redundancy, disaster recovery and, 341
redundant array of independent disks.
See RAID
Registry, 168–169
Registry Editor, 79–80
regulatory compliance, 99
relational database management system
(RDBMS), 192
relationships, trust, *109*, 109–110
Relative ID Master role. *See* RID
Master role
Reliability and Performance Monitor,
281, 283, 302. *See also*
Performance Monitor
reliability report, 284
remote access technologies, 249–262.
See also Remote Desktop
Services; VPNs
Remote Assistance (RA), 250–252
Remote Authentication Dial-In User
Service (RADIUS), 13
Remote Control tab, user account
Properties dialog, 155
Remote Desktop, 255–258
Remote Desktop Protocol (RDP), 250,
255, 260
Remote Desktop Services (RDS), 255–260
application virtualization, 260
defined, 14, 79
licensing, 258
RA *v.*, 250
Remote Desktop *v.*, 255–258
Terminal Services as, 154, 255
user account Properties dialog
Profile tab, 154
Sessions tab, 155
Remote Desktop Users group, 160
Remote Desktop Web Access, 259, 260

Remote Differential Compression (RDC),
238, 240
Remote Installation Services (RIS), 37.
See also Windows Deployment
Services
remote interface control, 250
Remote Management, Windows, 81, 287
Remote Registry service, 79–80
Remote Server Administration Tools
(RSAT), 174, *175*, 183
RemoteApp, 260
removable storage, 60, 322
Remove-ADComputer, 148
Remove-ADGroup, 148
Remove-ADGroupMember, 149
Remove-ADObject, 149
Remove-ADUser, 148
Repair Your Computer option, 29
replication, 111–112. *See also* Distributed
File System
DCs and, 102
defined, 100, 110
DFS, 238–239, *239*
intersite, 111–112
intrasite, 111
multi-master replication model, 102,
112, 241
single-master replication model, 112
WAN-friendly, 238
Replicator group, 160
Request for Comments. *See* RFCs
request/response process, HTTP,
209–210, *210*
Research stage, REACT, 266–267
resmon, 283, 300
resource access processing, DCs and, 102
resource forests, 117
Resource Monitor, 282–284, 300–301
resources, hardware, 51–53
restart-service command, 89, 92
restore and backup plan, 341–343
Resultant Set of Policy, 148, 179, 181
reverse lookup zone, 131
review questions, answers to, 349–360
revolutions per minute. *See* RPM
RFCs (Request for Comments), 211
959, 218
1090, 68
1813, 68
2606, 126
2616, 211
2617, 225
2831, 225
3010, 68
RID (Relative ID) Master role, 103,
122, 145
rights, user, 236
RIS (Remote Installation Services), 37.
See also Windows Deployment
Services
roaming profiles, 150
role services
Remote Desktop, 259
roles and, 9